Journeys through Hell

Stories of Burn Survivors'Reconstruction of Self and Identity

DENNIS J. STOUFFER

ROWMAN & LITTLEFIELD PUBLISHERS, INC.

ROWMAN & LITTLEFIELD PUBLISHERS, INC.

Published in the United States of America
by Rowman & Littlefield Publishers, Inc.
4720 Boston Way, Lanham, Maryland 20706

3 Henrietta Street
London WC2E 8LU, England

British Cataloging in Publication Information Available

Library of Congress Cataloging-in-Publication Data

Stouffer, Dennis J.
Journeys through hell : stories of burn survivors' reconstruction
of self and identity / Dennis J. Stouffer.
p.   cm.
Includes bibliographical references and index.
1. Burns and scalds--Psychological aspects. I. Title.
RD96.4. S76 1994 362.1'9711--dc20 93-8826 CIP

ISBN 0–8476–7891-1 (cloth : alk. paper)
ISBN 0–8476–7892-X (pbk. : alk. paper)

Printed in the United States of America

$\bigodot$ ™ The paper used in this publication meets the minimum requirements of
American National Standard for Information Sciences—Permanence of
Paper for Printed Library Materials, ANSI Z39.48–1964.

Dedicated to the Memory of

Bill and Madeline Stouffer, my parents
Nick Massaro, my teacher
Ted McFarland, my friend

"Get ready to weep tears of sorrow
as bright as the brightest beads,
and like the bright beads you string
to wear round your throat at the burial
gather your tears and string them
on a thread of your memory to wear around
your heart or its shattered fragments
will never come whole again."

From *Flamingo Feather*, by
    Laurens van der Post, quoted
    by Clark E. Moustakas in
    Loneliness

"From the living comes death, and from the dead, life;
from the young, old age; and from old age, youth; from
waking, sleep; and from sleep, waking; the stream of
creation and decay never stand still—construction and
destruction, destruction and construction—this is the
norm which rules in every circle of natural life from
the smallest to the greatest. Just as the cosmos
itself emerged from the primal, so must it return once
more into the same, a double process running its
measured course through vast periods, a drama eternally
reenacted"

From *Psychological Types* by Carl Jung

Contents

Foreword

Dennis Stouffer's *Journey's Through Hell* is a remarkable book. It is remarkable first of all that he was able to do it. It was very difficult to find people able to talk so insightfully about their terrifying experiences. It was far more difficult to create the situations and human partnerships so vital to encouraging their soul searching and communing. Dennis had to convince them, with his quiet reassurance and caring, to relive their terrors and to share them with him. It is not something that many of us would dare to try and very few of us would be able to complete. He worked on this for many years, often against great discouragement from academics who had no understanding of why he was making this "journey through hell." Now that I see what he was discovering from his communings with these brave people, I feel sure that he preserved with such equanimity and optimism because he was drawing strength from them.

This book is also remarkable because it attempts to present some of the most basic aspects of human experience in the language of the social sciences. Social scientists rarely attempt to probe the depths of the human heart and soul. Most social scientists do not even allude to the human heart and soul and the few who do commonly assert that human beings are nothing but appearances—"self presentations." If the people Dennis presents to us in this book believed that they are nothing but their surface appearances, they would have presumably departed and died away. They did not believe that. They knew that as human beings they are much more, that they are not the mere shadows of everyday appearances flirting across the stages of everyday life. Dennis has descended into the inner depths of human experience, through the portals of terrifying experience that rip away everyday appearances, and revealed the depths of human courage, strength, and hope. This journey through hell shows us how these people experienced a death of their old social selves and found the inner strength to go through rebirth. The journey through hell brings us to a pinnacle of hope, a transcendence of both everyday illusions, and of despair.

This book is most remarkable because it does not merely "study" the trappings of these experiences. We do not know, or need to know, what "soico-economic statuses" these people may have been burdened with in their previous lives. Rich or poor, tall or short, they went through a common struggle and found a common triumph. Dennis has plumbed the inner depths of human experience and shown us how to transcend the trivia of appearances that trap most social scientists. Indices of social status and of gross national product come and go, and will be little remembered, but the brave struggles of these people are things for all time. This book is a study of human beings, but it is also a testament to human nature and the human soul. It is a transcendent work. Reading from the terrors of these people gives us some slight sense of their journeys through hell, but is also gives us some sense of how we human beings all struggle and sometimes reach that pinnacle of hope and transcendence.

Jack D. Douglas
La Jolla, California
September 1994

Acknowledgments

I wish to thank all the survivors and their family members who allowed me to interview them for this study. Some appear here, others do not, but they were all generous. For many, sharing their experiences was traumatizing, and I deeply appreciate their kindness and assistance. I also thank Dr. Jack D. Douglas for his friendship, and his many years of good counsel. He was among the few academics, along with Melvin Pollner and Harold Garfinkel at U.C.L.A., who could understand why a graduate student would be warrantably concerned with fire prevention and protection issues as legitimate concerns of sociology. I also thank Dr. Carol Barrett for her advise and considerable wisdom, and Drs. Stephanie Mines, Joseph Kotarba, and Thomas Vendentti for their input in this project. Darryl Gaslan, Michael McEachern, and Peter P. Lyster have unknowingly influenced this project, and I thank them for their years of friendship and many long discussions into the late night, enjoying good cigars and speaking of the themes that are common to this book, and to all human journeys. Bill Horn and Larry Petersen are acknowledeged for their recommendations. I recognize Bruce Zawacki, M.D. and Alan Jeffry Breslau for their early support of this project, and I am especially indebted to the late Norman Bernstein, M.D., and his kind words of encouragement shortly before he became critically ill. Over many years, Dr. Bernstein has helped many survivors of disfiguring injury, and his unique works have influenced my interest in the human results of burn injury. I also thank Mary Ellen Ton for generously allowing me to quote from her very moving account of her journey through hell, *The Flames Shall Not Consume You*. I also acknowledge the assistance of the Alisa Ann Ruch Burn Foundation. The staff and the directors offered considerable encouragement, and I especially thank Shirley Turner and Stephanie Knizek. Finally, and very importantly, I thank my family. Judy, my wife and friend for many years, has always been inspirational and supportive. Her love and kindness indelibly mark whatever I've accomplished here, and I am grateful. My children, Elan and Erik, have been very understanding of my need for time spent alone to complete this journey, and I realize that it was hard for them to let me have some of their time. More than any books, or others, Judy, Elan, and Erik have taught me about the depth of human caring and love. I will always be in their debt.

Introduction

During the Vietnam period, David A. Christian was the most decorated member of the U.S. armed services. A graduate of West Point at the age of nineteen, David was a captain at the age of twenty. Over a period of less than three years he received forty decorations, including three Purple Hearts and the Congressional Medal of Valor. At twenty-one his military career ended when he was discharged because of burns he had suffered in a field operation. He was not unfamiliar with injury; he had been wounded by gunfire on three occasions and injured by shrapnel when tank ordnance exploded near him, but these experiences were not his worst.

In what he described as a moment of sheer terror, the most terrifying moment of his life, he was accidentally burned with napalm, with "friendly fire" as the military like to call it. Napalm is gelled gasoline. It burns like gasoline, cruelly and agonizingly adhering to the body, which it destroys.

David considers himself fortunate. Only 40 percent of his body was burned, only 40 percent of his skin was destroyed, but the experience ended his military career and radically altered his life. In a keynote address to the First World Congress on Burns, hosted by Alan Jeffry Breslau and the Phoenix Society, David talked of the stigma related to his injury. For David, being burned changed his identity. Being seriously burned forever changed who he was and who he could be. Yet, over time, through determined will and action, and with the support of those who loved him and maintained faith in him, David rebuilt his life and himself. It has been a painful and difficult process and it still continues.

David was not facially burned and, from a distance at least, his hands do not appear badly scarred. But the stigma didn't result from his physical appearance alone. It was also do to his status as a living example of what the innocuous sounding "friendly fire" could do.

This is a study about catastrophic burn injury. Burns serve as a prototypical example of catastrophic injury and the experience of profound personal loss. It is an exploration concerning the personal catastrophe that results from sudden injury. In a number of ways, what happens to burn survivors is similar to the problems faced by survivors of other catastrophic injuries and diseases. The focus is on understanding the personal meaning of severe injury from the survivor's standpoint. This leads to a deeper understanding of the nature of exceptional personal loss and the process of recovery. We will look at how survivors cope with the implications and effects of severe injury, disfigurement, and, frequently, disability in their everyday lives. The present work is about terror, significant loss, pain, and stigmatization, which result from major burns. However, this is also a study about hope, growth, fulfillment and the forward-looking emergence of the self which, in encountering terror, severe injury, and the threat of annihilation, transcends its finite condition and moves toward growth, individuation, and fulfillment. Rather than having lives that are overwhelmed, truncated or destroyed, most of the survivors presented here have, in spite of significant loss and irreparable physical change, created lives of value for themselves. Some have not, but even those who are overwhelmed by their injuries continue to seek normality as a daily project. None of the survivors interviewed here have withdrawn from everyday living, though a few remain tormented in significant and varied ways.

Catastrophic burn injury suggests more than injury. What is suggested cuts to the core of the person's very existence. Psychologically, burn injury, particularly when the person was enveloped in fire, threatens annihilation and the total destruction of self. The image of Dante's *Inferno* comes to mind, with souls languishing in interminable pain and incision-like agony from which there is no escape. The metaphor of being instantaneously cast into hell is especially profound and evocative. Many survivors will say that being burned, and the medical care that followed, was like being cast into hell.

There is another, less overwhelming, less dramatic image sometimes associated with a survivor's experience of burn injury, that being burned, as terrifying and as painful as it was, was viewed by some as a purification and transformation, resulting in both a rebirth of themselves, and a rebirth of meaning in their lives. The dualistic image of destruction and punishment[1] in contrast with the image of purification, transformation, and rebirth, are common themes in mythology, cultural rites, such as the horrifying Hindu practice of immolating the wife of one who has died,[2] and in Judeo-Christian beliefs. Personalized, these beliefs can be found in the accounts of several burn survivors who appear in this study. The experience of being critically burned, for all the survivors who were interviewed in this study, resulted in significant personal change. For many, not all the changes thus realized were defined as negative and, for a few, the resulting changes were defined as predominantly positive.

This study examines the coherence, deformation and reconstruction of both self and social reality. The self, together with personal identity, and the normal world of everyday reality, are inherently threatened by burn injury. How the survivor reconstructs self, identity and social reality are important themes in this study. A central interest is understanding how the survivor discovers and constructs personal and social meanings following his or her injury. It is through the construction of meaning that the survivor is able to understand what the burn means to his or her life. Through this process, the survivor reconstructs self as well as his or her world.

The search for and discovery of "meaning," (that is, significance or sense) is not the concern of only philosophers, theorists, or a Don Quixote who confuses the world of the seen with the unseen, the ordinary with the extraordinary. Instead, meaning is a central issue in each of our lives. Meaning becomes especially problematic when we face significant dilemmas, problems, or crises. Nowhere is this fact more clear than when we examine the personal experiences of those who have been suddenly and irrevocably rendered "victims" by whatever significant and overwhelming process.

The search for meaning is often seen by theorists as a problem endemic to contemporary, technological societies. The theme is familiar: through machine production, through removal of the person from intimate ties to nature, God, family, and group and through the occupancy of multiple and often contradictory roles, one faces a meaningless and chaotic cosmos. Membership and participation in odd religions and strange cults, the proliferation of the New Age movement and a host of holistic therapies can be seen as attempts by people to find significance and meaning in lives that are, in some fundamental sense, destitute. The search for meaning is a continuing theme in material as diverse as the writings of Herbert Marcuse and Rollo May.

As a theme, meaning as a problem has been especially prominent in existential thought. Viktor Frankel, a survivor of a Nazi concentration camp, developed Logotherapy to help people find meaning in habitually unhappy, often neurotic lives. For the burn survivor, the problem is less esoteric. In being horrendously injured, the person finds that much of what was stable in life has been destroyed, damaged, or seriously threatened. In a deep sense, the problem of meaning confronting the burn survivor is not unlike that faced by the concentration camp survivor (Frankel 1963; Kogon 1958; Cohen 1953; Steiner 1966).

In his preface to Frankel's book, May states a central theme of existentialism:

> To live is to suffer, to survive is to find meaning in the suffering. If there is a purpose in life at all, there must be a purpose in suffering and in dying. But no man can tell another what this purpose is. Each must find out this for himself and must accept the responsibility that his answer prescribes. (Frankel 1963, xiii)

To a considerable extent, this statement applies to the challenges faced by the burn survivor and to the survivors of other forms of overwhelming personal loss.

Provided our most basic bodily needs are met, most of us seek significance of some kind in our lives. Yet doing so, we do not typically think about our search for significance and meaning. Each of us is continuously interpreting the world about us, both the world within our grasp, our close-in personal worlds, and the more distant world we know only indirectly. That search is, however, generally taken-for-granted[3] and routine. And while we don't think about it, it is through the ongoing, always present, everyday work of interpretation that we are constructing meanings, for ourselves and those close to us with whom we interact. We continuously seek understanding and our place among others, day in and day out, for this is one of the fundamental and unavoidable facts of being human.

While meaning remains invariably problematic, even about the most ordinary and mundane events for some of us, we typically pay no attention to the fact that throughout our day, as throughout our lives, we are actively engaged in seeking meaning and in searching for underlying patterns of significance in the tapestries of life that we each weave. It is in times of crisis, or in times when our judgement is seriously questioned by ourselves or others, that we most clearly recognize this quest for understanding. A major problem for the burn survivor involves coming to terms with the injury and, for better or worse, this will be done, often provisionally, with the process of discovering what the injury has meant continuing for many years, if not for a lifetime.

"Provisionally" refers to the fact that the survivor's understanding of him or herself, and what he or she has gone through, is an open horizon, subject to continuing review and reinterpretation as his or her life changes and evolves. Over time, what the burn means to the survivor will change, in greater or lesser degree relative to the specific survivor and the events and people in his or her life. Indeed, those survivors who have serious, long-term coping problems attributed to their injury may have undergone the least change, over time, concerning the meaning of their injury. That is, they have, in a sense, fixated on the negatives of the burn and remain unable, over time, to come to any positive understanding of what the burn means. They remain stuck in a morass of unresolved anger, self-pity and frustration about what has happened to them and what others have done to them because of their scars. They are unable to find any way to transcend what has happened but they continue to search for acceptance, however elusive it may be. This is in contrast to other survivors who eventually find positive significance in their experience and who, thereby, are able to go on with their lives. What is of consequence is the quality of the meanings that the injury comes to have for the survivor, whether they assist the survivor in growing and moving past his or her injuries, or whether they truncate the survivor's life.[4] Through understanding how meanings are constructed, it is possible to better understand how selves and identities are constructed, maintained, altered and reconstructed not only by burn survivors but by all of us in the face of momentous personal challenge and threat.

For the burn survivor, many of the routine typifications made, and the meanings normally held about the world, about him or herself, and about objects in the world are radically changed by his or her emergent condition as a burn victim.* Reality is not he same and the survivor's orientation to everyday life, which had previously been assumed, is radicalized and inverted in the most inimical and terrifying manner. For the survivor, meanings, objects and self become frightfully problematic. Actions which were previously routine, in the most ordinary manner, become impossible or difficult. Familiar objects, such as mirrors and eating utensils, become threatening, painful, difficult or impossible to use.

The world of the survivor becomes like that of Don Quixote. Nothing is as it seems or as it should be. The ground has given way in a manner which is both terrifying and nauseating. The feeling of being at home in the world, of being familiar with one's surroundings, is lost. The allusion to Quixote provides a reference to both the theoretical import of this study, as well as a significant insight into the process of meaning construction in the lives of burn survivors. For Don Quixote, the ordinary objects of everyday life took on extraordinary meaning and significance. Those things seen but unnoticed by others, as routine aspects of the Spanish landscape, became pregnant with wonder for Quixote. A windmill wasn't a windmill, it was a dragon; Dulcinea wasn't merely a country girl, she was a princess.

While the Quixote tale can be seen as a journey into the private world of madness, which was carried out against the backdrop of everyday life, it can also be seen as something else (Schutz 1964, 135-158). What this tale suggests is not the mere confounding of reality with fantasy or delusion, but instead, the construction of a separate province of reality, a subuniverse of meaning, the interpretation and significance of which was available only from a very specific stance that places in doubt the routine meanings of objects in the world. Indeed, the global meaning(s) of the world itself may be radicalized. The Quixote problem was much like that of Don Juan's teachings as depicted in the works of Carlos Castaneda.[5] Both represent the immersion of the subject into multiple realities which are profoundly and mystifyingly discrepant from the predominant reality of everyday life. In the case of Quixote and Castaneda, the esoteric subuniverse of meaning which both come to occupy is radically juxtaposed with the ordinary, paramount reality of everyday life. The "discrepant" subuniverse of meaning is, according to Alfred Schutz, "characterized by

---

* Burn "victim" refers to the survivor during the early, acute phase of care. Usage during that phase frequently parallels usage by survivors themselves who may initially see themselves as victims, and only later see themselves as survivors.

peculiar modifications of the basic categories of thought, namely time, space, and causality." (Schutz 1964, 139)

This suggestion by Schutz diverges somewhat from what I am suggesting, particularly in reference to causality; however, it suggests another parallel to the situation of the burn victim This is especially so during the acute phase of hospitalization when the world has been shattered for the survivor and he or she is thrown into terrifying realities from which the only escape is the world of memory, imagination, and fantasy. That world might consist of recalling one's friends and family, thinking about the future, or using mental imagery techniques in order to cope with pain. Spiritual themes are also of frequent importance as the survivor copes during this time with severe pain and social isolation.

The theoretical parallel with Quixote is this: from an existential or phenomenological standpoint, interest here is vested in understanding how people construct meaning and in doing so how they construct themselves and their worlds. The self is understood, inexorably, as an achievement rather than an object or fixed structure of traits that somehow directs the person. Further, the self is seen as an ever-emerging product of social interaction and communication, grounded and dialectically co-emergent in the process of reality/self construction. Hidden behind the most ordinary facade of daily life are significant social, cognitive and emotional processes which are necessary for the ordinary to achieve the status of "ordinary" or routine. The obvious and ordinary of daily life turns out to be, upon investigation, anything but ordinary. The most routine social settings, where any normal person can clearly see what is taking place, are not pregiven to participants but do, instead, represent an occasioned achievement, a production by participants within the situation or setting (Garfinkel 1967; Douglas 1967; Pollner and Zimmerman 1970). The world as given to consciousness is recalcitrant and massive; it is taken-for-granted within common-sense as being so obvious that it is not, in general, problematic. Yet, experiential parts of that world, especially those sectors defined by the subject as his or her own, are frequently problematic, questioned, and difficult. The occasion of problems, disruptions, and dilemmas can result in questions about what is ordinarily treated as routine, stable and sure in the person's life. In true situations of crisis, the person's fundamental, taken-for-granted beliefs about reality may be thrown into question and doubt. This is especially true for beliefs held about one's personal world, one's worth, and one's existence. Following injury the burn victim may experience his or her world as shattered. He or she may have, from previous experience, no way to comprehend what has happened.

Even after the person is recovering, the ordinary, routine, and seen-but-unnoticed activities of daily living often take on the presence of extraordinary significance. Ordinary objects can become especially enabling or disabling as the survivor attempts to reconstruct his or her shattered life. Such simple tasks as brushing one's teeth or holding a cup can become challenges that are not only exceptionally difficult to carry out but that cause intense pain as badly burned hands gingerly attempt to hold a toothbrush or cup.

How is it that Quixote can be compared to burn survivors? For the person recovering from severe burns, the most simple autonomous acts such as toileting can become insurmountably difficult. Not only may severe pain and difficulty be involved but the person may require considerable nursing assistance as well. In the case of several males, for whom nurses had to hold their penises while they urinated, this basic, normally very private act took on extraordinary meaning. It became for them a degrading experience, which, in part, destroyed any feelings of autonomy they had thus far been able to maintain. There can be fewer things more basic and ordinary than toileting yet under special conditions, one's inability to take care of such matters can pose a significant challenge and threat to identity and to self. Another example taken from many survivors involves eating. The severely burned person often has trouble eating, for he or she is critically ill and food holds no pleasure at all. The idea of eating can be sickening and once the person can eat, burned hands and arms may prevent or severely limit the person's ability to use a fork or spoon. Eating and the utensils required take on special importance. They may mean acute pain and the person may dread the next time he or she has to eat for it will be a tiring, arduous process. If the nurses are doing their job, by forcing the person to care for him or herself, the patient may have little or no assistance as he or she struggles to be independent. Ordinary objects take on extraordinary significance in the life of the survivor. With continuing effort, when the survivor can finally raise an arm without spilling the food, this simple act can mark a monumental achievement.

In being able to perform ordinary, routine actions such as feeding oneself, buttoning a shirt, or preparing a meal, the survivor can find evidence that he or she is returning to normal. Indeed, "normalization" is, in part, contingent on just such accomplishments, which are slowly and incrementally achieved and frequently noted as rites of passage toward recovery.

When the survivor returns home, perhaps after several months, and is finally able to tie shoes and bake cookies, these simple events are tremendous achievements that allow him or her to finally *feel* that he or she is indeed getting better and returning to normal. A survivor used to strenuous daily exercise, who finds that he can just barely, and with great difficulty and pain, move his hands outward on the bed, may discover special meaning in this simple act: it becomes defined as exercise, it is his or her initial attempt to exert control over a terrifying condition and situation.

Undergirding this study therefore, is an interest in self, identity, and social reality viewed from a standpoint within sociological social psychology. Specifically, the theoretical orientation of this study is taken from symbolic interactionism in sociology and from constructionism in psychology. This work is significantly informed by existential and phenomenological themes which have emerged within sociology and psychology over the past twenty or so years. Of particular importance are the works of George Herbert Mead and those who have followed in his tradition. Following the work of such sociologists as Jack D. Douglas, Joseph Kotarba, Norman Denzin, John Johnson, and Andrea Fontanna, the present study is descriptive, qualitative, and interpretive. Burn survivors are treated as resource experts. Their accounts and personal stories are treated not as ancillary data but are seen instead, as the preeminent vehicle through which their lives can be understood. Indeed, it is maintained that in order to understand the lives of survivors, central importance must be granted to their stories, accounts, and reports for it is only in this manner that we can gain some understanding, as distant as it may be, of survivors' subjective experience of catastrophic injury. In saying this it must also be stated that, as outsiders, we can never fully understand, in any deep sense, what burn survivors have experienced, regardless of how vivid or detailed their accounts. Their lives, though recounted, can never be fully articulated and, even if complete articulation were possible, we could not walk in their shoes. Their lives and experiences, their pain, suffering, and anguish remain, in a most primary sense, private and ineffable. At best, this study merely suggests what it is like to be catastrophically burned and to survive.

There will be little attention to existing studies on the psychosocial effects of burn injury. While some studies are clinical and qualitative, most are not (Steiner and Clark 1977; Davidson, Bowden, and Feller 1981; Young 1974; Bernstein 1982). The majority of existing research represents instrument-based, quantitative studies (Pruzinsky and Rice 1992; Larson et al. 1992; Malt 1980). Such research utilizes everything from questionnaires created for a specific study to the MMPI or Coopersmith Inventory. A number of the studies use personality trait assessments in the attempt to isolate what are presumed by the investigator to be objective, stable "personality" features about persons who were burned. Personality, as theoretically conceptualized within mainstream psychology, offers little of heuristic value to this study. Indeed, psychologists are themselves increasingly critical of "personality" theories; the fortress of personality assessment and traditional theory is under attack, no longer only by anthropologists, philosophers, and sociologists but by psychologists as well. Among psychologists, this is especially noted in the works of Rom Harré, Kenneth Gergen, Paul Secord, John Shotter, Theodore Sarbin, and Karl Scheibe who have collectively done much to move psychology out of its mechanistic world view. Luckmann's critique of positivism is instructive. Here, he describes the basic precept of a positivistic viewpoint:

The Copernican postulate of the mathematical structure of reality, the Galilean doctrine of primary and secondary qualities and the notions of causality generally associated with Newtonian mechanics combined to produce a new view of reality whose persuasiveness was probably based as much on its extraordinary aesthetic appeal as on its continuous popular verification in the applied successes of applied science and technology. [By this reasoning] man is part of nature; nature consists of primary qualities; man is reducible to primary qualities; there is no world of human affairs for which scientific understanding is not possible, in principle, through a reduction to the mathematical manifold of space and time. (Luckmann 1973, 155)

Elsewhere, Luckmann notes that

In all social sciences disciplines the theory of measurement carries the imprint of the Galilean cosmology. The researcher unwittingly adopts individual or official bureaucratic data whose comparability is unwarranted. No Galilean primary qualities having been discovered in human conduct, assortments of secondary qualities are measured as if they directly represented primary ones. The consequence of social science naïveté concerning its epistemological reflexivity is, on the most prudishly hidden level of "operationalized" research procedure, measurement by fiat. The data of the social science are pre-interpreted.

We do not have [in the social sciences] "raw" data to which are added common-sense interpretations which are to be discarded by some "purifying instrument." Interpretations are made in, and bound to, ordinary historical language. The data of the social science are therefore from the outset irrevocably part of historical worlds of everyday life. (Luckmann 1973, 176-180)

Sociologists, such as Douglas, and ethnomethodologists, such as Garfinkel and Cicourel, have written rather extensively on the problems that beset positivistic social science, whose practitioners attempt to objectify social reality and persons through the application of quantitative methods: in doing so the researcher attempts to emulate the natural sciences (Douglas 1971; Garfinkel 1967; Cicourel 1972; Andreski 1972; Sorokin 1956).[6] The typical interest of both sociology and psychology involves a search for the cause of behavior. Cause reflects the mechanistic perspective of the early natural sciences. The traditional practitioners of sociology and psychology frequently remain oblivious to the fact that the natural and physical sciences, as exemplified especially by quantum physics, have long ago abandoned the notion of simple, unitary cause-effect sequences and the physicist, who often appears as the model of the detached scientific observer, at least since Heisenberg, has recognized that he is part of the equation he or she formulates, for the physicist is part of the observed process. Common-sense reasoning pervades even the most "scientific" studies and no remedial action formulated by the investigator can eliminate the pervasive influence of prescientific reasoning from the work of formulating theories, discoveries, rules, or equations. Garfinkel, in studying the work of radio astronomers who were engaged in discovering pulsars, has cogently demonstrated that their "scientifically detached" work is anything but detached from the common-sense world that is necessarily presumed as a background against which scientists pragmatically produce discoveries (Garfinkel 1981). Garfinkel has clearly demonstrated that the most abstruse practice of science inherently involves practical reasoning carried out in the language of everyday life. In contrasting the traditional social science perspective with one that seeks a more comprehensive understanding, Douglas states that

> Any scientific understanding of human action, at whatever level of ordering or generality must begin with and be built upon an understanding of the everyday life of the members performing those actions. The only valid and reliable evidence concerning socially meaningful phenomena we can possibly have is that based ultimately on systematic observations and analyses of everyday life. (Douglas 1970b, 11-12)

Perhaps the most caustic critic of positivism in the social sciences has been Stanislav Andreski. He has argued that quantification, which is the hallmark of positivism in the social sciences, is sheer mysticism and camouflage:

> If we look at the types of data used by the protagonists of the quantitative methods outside economics, we can easily see that the overwhelming majority consist of accumulations of responses to questionnaires–about the most superficial kind of information one can think of. It is as if somebody had tried to build a science of meteorology solely by making elaborate computations of the fluttering of flags. (Andreski 1972)

He also states that the "devotion to quantification may be due not only to purism but also the desire to have an excuse for sweeping dangerous or unpleasant issues under the carpet." Unfortunately, besides being highly contradictory, which is not necessarily an issue, most of the studies on burns are quantitative and therefore tell us very little if anything about the post-injury lives of survivors. The exception to this statement would be the pioneering clinical studies by Dr. Norman Bernstein and a few others who have focused on post-injury quality of life issues.

Almost all of the existing studies on burns use various tests or instruments. These are supposed to reveal personality traits or stable personality characteristics which are attributed to the burn victim/survivor.[7] From the standpoint of the present study, instrument-based studies are flawed in that they reveal nothing concrete about the survivor's life. Quantitative studies are highly abstract, while the interest here is centered on examining the survivor's concrete, lived existence. Existentially oriented sociologists historically have been critical of personality theories, seeing them as overly static and mechanistic. More recently, psychologists have become increasingly disenchanted with personality theories as heuristic and explanatory devices, and they have begun placing greater emphasis on constructionist and cognitive models, which bear striking parallels with those developed by symbolic interactionists and existentially/phenomenologically oriented sociologists.

A very clear and substantial rejection of traditional psychological notions of personality (traits and dispositions) can be found in the works of existentially oriented psychologists and psychiatrists such as Rollo May, Clark Moustakas, Ludwig Binswanger, and Irwin Yalom. This rejection extends as well to psychologists who do not identify themselves specifically with an existential orientation, such as Kenneth Gergen, Mary Gergen, Theodore Mischel, Rom Harré, and Carl Rogers. The theoretical orientation taken by these writers has not as yet penetrated any recent research on burns, except for that conducted by psychiatrist Norman Bernstein, who was interested in such issues as understanding the meanings of burn injury for survivors. Dr. Bernstein has done much to help us understand the lives of burn survivors and those who are disfigured, but his work remains unique.

In considering traditional research on personality and self-conception, the words of psychologists Kenneth Gergen and Mary Gergen, who have been influenced by the works of both William James and George Herbert Mead, are instructive:

> Traditional research on self-conception is earmarked by two widely prevailing characteristics: such research tends to be both mechanistic and synchronic. It is mechanistic in its assumption of an internal structure governed in mechanical fashion by external inputs, and it is synchronic in its concern with the causes and effects of the individual's characterization of him or herself at a given moment....The traditional views fail to appreciate the individual's understanding of him or herself as a historically emerging being." (Gergen and Gergen 1983, 255)

In discussing personality traits, Mischel notes that the search for stable traits has generally been of little use in gaining insight into the concrete lives of people. He states that

> Empirical studies of self-control point up the idiosyncratic organization of persons, the lack of coherent linkages between trait-characterizations, which attempt to specify what people are like in terms of some reasonably small number of dimensions, and people's behavior. Attempts to predict what people will do, or what the same person will do in different situations, on the basis of trait characterizations have had very little success. (Mischel 1977, 9)

With similar concerns, Barry Schlenker comments, in discussing personality studies, that

> Projective tests are notoriously unreliable. Response sets are vexing. Predictive indices are weak and do not replicate...the argument about whether personality has predictive utility is tantamount to an argument about whether personality exists, or whether there exists a stable self. The answer is, of course not. (Schlenker 1985, 54)

Schlenker goes on to argue that personality assessment studies have limited, if any, predictive utility and that an observer, looking at seventy years of studies that have used assessment measures, would have to conclude that there is strong evidence that enduring psychological dispositions, as contents of self, are not unequivocally describable (Schlenker 1985, 54).

While attention to quantitative studies will not be made, such studies do suggest lines of inquiry to be followed. In this sense, previous research is seen as sensitizing, by informing us about specific survivor sub-populations whose members report depression, anxiety, difficulty with intimate relationships, problems in returning to work, and more. What such studies do not show is how the survivor reconstructs his or her life, and thereby, himself or herself. If we are to understand the long-term effects of catastrophic trauma, it is necessary to get into the lives, so to speak, of the survivors. We need also to better understand how their injuries effect those who are closest to them. I set my task as inquiring into the lives of those who live behind the numbers presented in other studies.

Survivor Selection

The specific methodological perspective used in this study follows the biographical or "life history" approach as suggested by such researchers as Douglas, Denzin, Kotarba, and Bertaux. This perspective places special emphasis on understanding the lives of the informants as articulated within their biographical accounts or stories. Understanding who and what people are becomes contingent on understanding how they got to where they are, how they conceptualize themselves, and how they construct their lives as an ongoing accomplishment carried out against the backdrop of the social worlds in which they live. Further, to understand the survivor, it is necessary to understand how the survivor constructs his or her experience, and how they fabricate, on a routine basis and through interaction with others, their personal worlds. In discussing the biographical method, Ferrarotti states that:

> The specificity of the biographical method implies going beyond the logical-formal framework and of the mechanistic model which characterizes the established scientific epistemology. If we wish to make sociological use of the heuristic potential of biography without betraying its *essential characteristics* (subjectivity, historicity), we must project ourselves straight off beyond the framework of classical epistemology. (Ferrarotti 1981, 20)

Daniel Bertaux, who began his career as a mathematician and physicist working in the area of artificial intelligence before becoming a sociologist, states that "the scientificity of sociology is a *myth*. If there is such a thing as *sociological knowledge*, the way to reach it is not with quantitative methodology. And the main obstacle towards it is precisely the belief in sociology as a *science*. In a word: *positivism*"(Bertaux 1981). Bertaux goes on to explore the methods of life history research and his words could easily have come directly from many of the researchers who are referenced above. I have used this type of methodology in working with the interview materials I gathered from survivors. All interviews were open-ended without a specific question protocol being used. Questions focused around the following:

1. Personal/Family background
2. Nature and circumstances of being burned
3. Experiences in the hospital (pain, autonomy, control, and related themes)
4. Support from family/friends
5. First seeing oneself in a mirror (facial burns).
6. Going out in public
7. Going home
8. Intimate relationships
9. Meaning of the injury

There was no attempt made to randomly select subjects from any survivor population. Persons attending burns recovery groups at two burn centers were contacted either directly or in writing and asked if they could be interviewed for this study. Thirty-four consented and twenty-eight were interviewed. Six persons were unavailable because of time constraints. The potential population of survivors who could have been interviewed was approximately three hundred. That is, three hundred persons were contacted for this research on two occasions but only thirty-four agreed to be interviewed and most of them came to the burns recovery meetings that I attended. In addition to the initial group, three interviews were conducted with survivors whom I met while I was at the First World Congress on Burns in 1988.

Burn Injury in the United States

From the standpoint of the social sciences, burn injury remains an unrecognized social problem in America. The same can be said of virtually all issues that pertain to destructive fire. Social science practitioners in sociology, psychology, and anthropology have demonstrated little interest in fire or its results. The one notable exception is arson, where there has been some attention by psychologists and, less so, by sociologists. Even in psychology, most interest has been devoted to juvenile arson and its prevention, but little research has been directed to the broader issues of destructive fire.

It is estimated that there are well over two million reported burn injuries in the United States annually (Brody and Johnson 1979; Brodzak and Thornhill 1980; Hall 1987). There are approximately six thousand fire deaths and, if other burn deaths are counted (from scalds, chemicals, contact with hot objects or substances, electrical, and radiation sources) there may be nine thousand or more burn deaths every year in the United States (Hall 1987). As there is no centralized or mandatory collection of such data, there is no firm estimate of actual deaths. Many deaths, which are actually caused by burning, are attributed to other causes or complications, (i.e., major organ failure which follows from burn injury and is, in fact, a direct result of burn injury) (Feller and Flanders 1979; Hall 1987).[8]

Further, it is estimated that nine million lost workdays are attributable to burn injury (Praiss and Feller 1980). Of the reported injuries, approximately seventy-five thousand to one hundred thousand represent critical, life-threatening injuries for which protracted hospital care is required (Deitch and Staats 1982). Approximately twelve thousand to fifteen thousand burn patients are treated annually at specialized burn facilities while the remaining injured are treated at general, acute care facilities. Fires and conflagrations represent the third leading cause of accidental death in the United States (Metropolitan Life 1979), and fires are ranked second and third as the leading cause of accidental death to preschool-aged boys and girls, respectively (Metropolitan Life 1982).

The very young and the elderly are at special risk for burn injury, preeminently due to restricted mobility and motility, and the poor and non-whites are also significantly overrepresented relative to burn injury and death (Brodzak and Thornhill 1985). According to Lynch, in his excellent study of the consequences of social isolation, single persons are also at heightened risk of dying in fires and explosions by a factor of approximately eight times that of couples (Lynch 1977, 88). Of all industrialized nations, the United States is the clear leader in fires, fire and burn injuries, and fire and burn deaths (Schaenman 1982; Schaenman and Seits 1985; Hall 1990a, 1990b, 1991a, 1991b).

It should be clear from these data that burn injury and death represent a significant if not catastrophic social problem. Burns are a truly overwhelming personal catastrophe. They cause extreme and prolonged pain, and too frequently result in pronounced disfigurement. The lives of those injured and the lives of their families are disrupted, often for months, or even years. Serious burns are the most severe survivable injury that a person can sustain (Bunch 1981, 61; Dimick 1982, 16), and they are one of the most costly and medically intensive injuries that can occur to a person. Burns potentially, and very gravely, compromise every organ system. Infections often occur and death is a serious risk even in moderate injuries, especially for the very young, the elderly, and those who are already ill.

Over the past few years, there has been a moderate decline in fire deaths according to data gathered by the National Fire Protection Association. Whether this decline is stable remains to be seen.[9] At the same time, the incidence of burn injury appears to be climbing. When one considers those who are injured or killed, the direct as well as indirect costs, the disruption and dislocation of individuals, families, and communities, one then begins to appreciate how wanting our prevention efforts have been. Serious burns can occur anywhere to anyone. One is potentially at risk from the most mundane activities to the most unusual, from residential fires, vehicular and industrial accidents, brush fires, or fires during surgical procedures (Stouffer 1992). The costs are indeed high. What follows—the accounts by survivors who have journeyed through hell—will clearly depict many of the human costs of burn injury.

1

The Shattering of Everyday Life

All is in flames. The eye and all the senses
stand in flames, kindled by the fire of love,
the fire of hate, by the fire of delusion;
through birth, ageing and death, through pain
and lamentation, through sorrow, suffering
and despair is the fire kindled. The whole world
is wrapped in shadowe and smoke; the whole
world is devored by fire; the whole world quaketh.
 Buddha, "Fire Sermon" in C. G. Jung
 Psychological Types

Being seriously burned causes a rupture or breach in the person's routine experience of normal, everyday reality. Another way of describing this is to say that being burned shatters the person's experience of the everyday world in which he or she lives. Being suddenly and severely burned radicalizes the person's normal world of activities and the self's orientation to the world. Normal, routine activities are irrevocably and instantly halted and the world into which the person is thrown is fundamentally different from normal, everyday reality. Suddenly uprooted from normal experience, the burn victim is hurled into a world of pain, terror and anguish, a radically and horrifyingly altered world from which there is no escape. Routine projects in which the person was recently engaged, such as going home from work or eating dinner with friends in a favorite restaurant, are suddenly and irrevocably transformed into experiences of terror, sweeping the person into a vortex of chaos where absolute and immediate survival issues are the only things that matter.

In being burned, the person may instantly find himself enveloped in fire, facing death as he is pinned under a burning vehicle or she may find herself in a momentary place of safety, though to escape the surrounding fire, there may be *no choice* other than running through gasoline-fed flames. These situations suggest annihilation, and they are taken directly from experiences of survivors in this study. It is difficult to imagine a more terrifying experience than finding oneself on fire. The primordial image is that of corporal destruction and excruciating, unimaginable pain. For most survivors, intense, unrelenting pain is recalled not from the moment of their burning but from their experiences in the burn center. Every survivor who recalled his or her hospitalization, in one way or another defined the experience of hospitalization as being terrifyingly hell-like. Even those survivors who had previously experienced other serious injuries or illnesses for which they had been hospitalized, could not initially comprehend the agony or terror through which they would live in the days, weeks and months following their burning.

While most survivors were fully conscious of being burned, three had little or no awareness of being burned (Maria, Ralph, and Trisha). This is especially noted for Trisha who recalled almost nothing concrete about her initial experience until several weeks later, and much of what was recalled then centered on unending pain.

In virtually all the cases, regardless of how catastrophic the injury, the person had little understanding of how badly he or she was injured. In most cases, even where the survivor saw charred skin, there was no immediate comprehension of the enormity of the injury. Survivors reported thinking that after a few days in the hospital, they could leave the burn center and return to home, work, and their normal lives. Virtually no survivors, even those who knew that they were seriously injured, had any substantial understanding of what they faced in the near as well as the distant future. Survivors only learned just how marginal their existence was much later, perhaps many weeks later, as loved ones, friends, or medical staff informed them of the gravity of their injuries. This chapter will provide a rare glimpse into one most marginal situation. Of central concern will be how the survivor defines and conceptualizes his or her burn experience and the experiences immediately thereafter.

The World of Everyday Life

The world of everyday life, or the *life-world* following Husserl (Gurwitsch 1970, 48), is the world of all our activities; it is the world of our animate being in which we carry forth our daily lives within the wide-awake attitude or stance (Schutz 1973; Luckmann 1970). The life-world provides the grounds of conscious existence: "we are subjects for this world, namely as ego-subjects experiencing it, contemplating it, valuing it, related to it purposefully" (Rogers 1985, 49). Our existence with the life-world is naive and mundane. The life-world serves as the paramount reality of our lives (Berger and Luckmann 1966; Gurwitsch 1970, 3). Yet the life-world is a sociocultural aretfact, experienced by the person in culturally specific ways (Rogers 1985, 51). While the life-world is taken-for-granted and naively experienced, it is forever and without remedy, incompletely intelligible (Rogers 1985, 51) and it can be experienced directly only in a most limited manner by the any subject, as a *finite province of meaning*. All human praxis, that is, "the full range of human conscious activities in the intersubjective and historical world of everyday life" (Luckmann 1973, 147) presumes the life world. It is from everyday life, or paramount reality, that we take leave, through daydream, fantasy, and sleep. Barring death or coma, it is to everyday life that we return, again and again. It appears to us as being massive, already-there, objective, obdurate, and inevitable (Berger and Luckmann 1966, 147). The reality of everyday life is socially organized through human activities, that is, through sociocultural practices and institutions. It is also, on a personal level, organized through our actions, and around the locus of our bodies within the present of our experience (Berger and Luckmann 1966, 22). We are fully aware of that reality but we treat the reality of everyday life in a taken-for-granted and unquestioned manner. We treat the reality of everyday life as a given, and it appears to us to be separate from our activities; yet it remains, invariantly, a human product:

> It is important to keep in mind that the objectivity of the institutional world, however massive it may appear to the individual, is a humanly produced objectivity. The process by which the externalized products of human activity attain the character of objectivity is obectivation. The world is objectivated human activity. The paradox [is] that man is capable of producing a world that he then experiences as something other than a human product. The product acts back upon the producer. (Berger and Luckmann 1966, 60-61)

In a similar manner, Schutz states that

> We, however, who live naively in this life-world, encounter it as already constituted. We are, so to speak, born into it. We live in and endure it, and the living intentionality of our stream of consciousness supports our thinking, by which we orient ourselves practically in this life-world, and our actions, by which we intervene in it. Our everyday world is, from the outset, an intersubjective world of culture. It is intersubjective because we live in it as men among other men, bound to them through common influence and work, understanding others, and being an object of understanding for others. It is a world of culture because, from the outset, the life-world is a uinverse of signification to us, i.e., a framework of meaning. (Schutz 1967, 133)

While it is taken-for-granted and massive in its existence-as-such, the world of everyday life is surrounded by uncertainty and indeterminateness (Schutz and Luckmann 1973, 9). Problems, dilemmas, and crises occur that can threaten sectors of everyday life which the person treats as his or her personal, privatized world. Such problems may be highly localized, specific, and transitory or they may be more global, generalized, and extensive through time, radically altering virtually everything the person has treated as stable and certain in life.

Further, each of us lives in numerous worlds or multiple realities, which are defined by work, play, activities with others, so on, and so on. We may hardly notice when we shift from one realm of reality to another, so ordinary are such changes. Alternately, we may notice a sudden shift and the discrepancy between our "worlds." As I write the words that you now read, I am directed to and absorbed in a project to which all attention is drawn. As my attention shifts to my five-year-old son, who is now asking me to read him a story, I enter into a different world of interest and attention. We continuously shift back and forth from one realm to another, and then another, and normally pay no attention to the fact that we do so. As we live out each day, our lives are filled with numerous unnoticed and sometimes-noticed, movements such as these. That we live in the world of others, that we feel ourselves to be within "reality," and that we assume our consociates, our loved ones, friends, neighbors, and our enemies, those we do know and those we have never met, also relatively exist within this reality, is taken-for-granted:

> The everyday life-world is to be understood as that province of reality which the wide-awake and normal adult simply takes for granted in the attitude of common sense. It is the unexamined ground of everything given in my experience, as it were, the taken-for-granted frame in which all the problems which I must overcome are placed. (Schutz and Luckmann 1973, 3-4)

The world of everyday life, or the life-world, is pretheoretically given to consciousness and it preexists any scientific or lay theories about its existence (Gurwitsch 1970, 48). Following Husserl, this pretheoretical attitude toward the reality of everyday life was called, by Schutz, the *general thesis of the natural standpoint*, or *the natural attitude* (Schutz 1964). Within the natural attitude, the subject is oriented toward the world through an incorrigible belief in the absolute factualness of the world and reality. To question the fundamental reality of the world is to necessarily assume a radicalized frame of reference, which is itself posited within the person's world of reality. Extrication becomes impossible. From the standpoint of the natural attitude, "ego-subjects are apprehended as fellow-men who have consciousness of the objective world as I do in spite of differences in perspectives and in degrees of clarity. It is also taken for granted that we can communicate with one another " (Schutz 1966, 51).

At its roots, the world of everyday life is fundamentally social in origin and it is open to further explication and elaboration. Our understanding of the world and our orientation to it are intersubjective (Schutz and

Luckmann 1973; Luckmann 1970; Berger and Luckmann 1966; Schutz 1963, 1966), meaning that our understanding of the world is shared with others through discourse or language. Perception itself presumes the pretheoretical existence of the life-world; that which is constituted in consciousness, as objects of experience or objects within the world, are apprehended against the background of the life-world.

The world of the person's everyday life is local, practical, particular and personal. This world is not experienced globally, randomly, or in total. On one hand, the world is structured by its relevancy for the person, through his or her intentions, concerns, and activities. On the other hand, the world is structured through social practices, institutions, and the activities of others. Knowledge of ourselves, and the world and its objects is historical, intersubjective, and relational. We are grounded within the world through the locus of our bodies and, as persons, our identities and biographies are invariantly historical or temporal. We have identities that are symbolically constructed and expressed through language and feeling. Reflexively, feelings and moods are objectified, that is to say, they are articulated, through language. Further, the self becomes an object of its own temporal experience preeminently through language. Through thought and "self-talk," alone and in interaction with others, we constitute or produce ourselves, our identities and the identities of others, as objects of our experience in the world of daily life. Language, through conversation, is the medium through which we constitute and interpret the world and ourselves (Sarbin and Kitsuse 1994; Shotter 1993; Psathas 1973, 66; Worf 1956; Lee 1959; Langer 1951). As such, the world is already objectified through intentionality, that is, the world inevitably and massively appears to us as being *already there*, prior to our perception of its constituted elements, realms, and dimensions.[1] As such, the taken-for-granted world provides a continuously available resource as well as a continuously present background against which and within which our activities and projects are carried forth.

We discover the meanings of our lives temporally—through time—and temporality is the fundamental condition of human life that makes us historical (Mead 1959, 1962; Heidegger 1962). Indeed, following Heidegger, temporality is a basic structural condition of human existence. Human existence, which Heidegger has described as Dasein (Da=Being, sein=there), not only is itself historical but, also, human existence is invariably *historizing* (Heidegger 1962, 427). Sadler, in referring to Heidegger states that,

> As a temporal being, I am always in my future, and my future is always coming toward me into my present, enabling me to interpret the whole of my concern....The future grants me my freedom and provides the perspective which enables me to understand the

meaning of my past. My existence is toward the future. It is also constituted by my past; yet my past, my history, is always moving ahead of itself into my future. (Sadler 1969, 85)

Temporality is the condition within which the self emerges, reflexively, as an object to itself. Our direct and immediate engagement in the world is inevitably in the present. We are, so to speak, condemned to be locked into the present. But the present is continuously and invariantly becoming and disappearing, *at the same moment*, and what marks the present as distinct is its simultaneous becoming and disappearing (Mead 1959, 1). The moment of immediate experience represents the confluence of past and future. When we look at ourselves, our actions, our relationships with others, all of these are embedded in a temporal/historical context: we think of our past and we project our anticipated futures from a standpoint within the emergent present. Yet the present may be subjectively construed as extended in time, the present may spread into the future, which is ever becoming. Past, present and future merge in the unfolding situation or event within which self is engaged and reflexively aware:

> Past, present, and future belong to a passage which attains temporal structure through the event, and they may be considered long or short as they are compared with other such passages....The past and the future are the boundaries of what we term the present, and are determined by the conditioning relationships of the event to its situation. Pasts and futures extend beyond these contiguous relations in passage. *We extend them in memory and history, in anticipation and forecast* [my emphasis]. They are preeminently the field of ideation, and find their locus in what is called mind. While they are in the present, they refer to that which is not in the present, as is indicated by their relation to past and future. (Mead 1959, 24)

Through a specific construal of the present, the present may be experienced as never ending, as enduring. Such a construal of the present arises, for the burn survivor and for others, through bodily sensations, feelings, and moods. Boredom, anxiety, and depression may create the subjective impression that the present doesn't end, and that the person cannot extricate himself or herself from its obdurate endurance. This is especially in evidence when the survivor is overwhelmed by unrelentless pain which seems to go on forever with little or no relief.

The subject's awareness of time is radically affected by moods, feelings, and one's reference to the past, to projects at hand or to projects which are anticipated. The burn victim, feeling isolated and experiencing acute and interminable pain, may feel absolutely trapped; he or she may subjectively experience minutes as if they were hours or days, each moment seeming like an eternity as he or she is tormented by cutting, knife like pain while awaiting the next injection of pain medication. The experience of personal or subjective time can therefore be said to be contextual, situated, and directly related to the concrete situation within which the person is reflexively engaged, socially, psychologically, and bodily.

The self, as an object to itself, is historical or temporal in the basic sense that what we think about, such as ourselves as having just performed some action, is referenced to an action that is past. In looking at ourselves, in reflecting, we essentially stand forth or out of the ongoing flow of experience or, following Schutz, out of the flow of duration. Within that flow, the person is immersed in temporal experience but does not attend to his or her immersion as such.

> [The] flow of duration goes forward in a uni-directional, irreversible movement, proceeding from manifold to manifold in a constant running-off process. Each phase of experience melts into the next without any sharp boundaries as it is being lived through; but each phase is distinct in its thusness, or quality, from the next insofar as it is held in the gaze of attention....When, by my act of reflection, I turn my attention to my living experience, I am no longer simply living within that flow. The experiences are apprehended, distinguished, brought into relief, marked out from one another; the experiences which were constituted as phases within the flow of duration now become objects of attention as constituted experience. (Schutz 1967, 51)

In the present now of experience, through a reflexive act, the self looks back upon itself as an object of its own experience. Consciousness, directed from the immediate present to a past action of the self, is directed toward the self-as-object within an open temporal horizon. Onflowing experience becomes differentiated and discrete. Such experiences are "apprehended not by living through them but by an act of attention" (Schutz 1967, 52). In order to be meaningful and interpreted, experience must be past and it is through a reflexive act of attention that experience becomes meaningful. The horizon like groundwork of experience is invariantly open to interpretation, as are the objects within the horizon. The burn survivor, in determining the meanings of his or her injury, will look back upon life prior to being burned. Assessing the meaning of the injury in the present will be contingent upon assessing his or her history. The past meanings of self will be referenced in the process of constructing and reconstructing his or her postburn identities. Furthermore, the construction of identity and self represents an ongoing, unfolding evolutionary process.

The grasping of objects by consciousness, the turning of self ("mind") toward objects by consciousness, is, following Husserl, termed *intentionality.* Perception is never of raw data, for there is no raw data; "data" is, upon perception, already interpreted. Perception is already cognitively organized pretheoretically by consciousness through intentionality. Immediately upon seeing or perceiving, objects are seen within a context, within a *horizonal background,* and the objects themselves, as they appear to come into being or as they emerge from their background horizon, are already pretheoretically imbued with meaning. Objects within the world take on meaning not simply through the attachment of our subjective values to the objects within our awareness but, more fundamentally, our concern acts to define and structure the meanings of objects, events and, whatnot. In the primordial world of actual lived experience, our concern structures or prefigures that which is apprehended or perceived (Shrader 1967, 35). Reality as such cannot be directly apprehended. Reality can be apprehended only through our use of interpretive categories, types, and concepts. This is to say that we may apprehend, elucidate, and understand our worlds only through our subjective constructions of those worlds (Shrader 1967, 33). Also, perception implies a context or situation and a self. Perception is never, therefore, of raw data, and perception is invariantly context and self-sensitive. The meanings attributed to the self inherently color the objects of perception by imbuing them with meaning. The process is circular. At the moment of looking at ourselves and our actions, what we attend to, sense, perceive, or see has already passed us by. We can but capture it, whatever it may be, as a reflection, as a memory of what just was. Recoverability to memory is crucial to rational construction; what is unrecoverable remains ineffable and, thereby, it cannot be verbalized and it does not, for all practical purposes, exist (Schutz 1967, 53). As beings-in-the-world, we are also essentially and inevitably grounded spatially (Sadler 1969, 80-87). We are here, in a particular place and time, in a particular situation (Grabau 1976, 115) in which we are engaged in the world cognitively, bodily and emotionally.

The concrete situation we are in now, which transcends us, shades the meaning of our existence in the present, and bears upon our future. The burn survivor who is confined to a bed, in agonizing pain and with arms outstretched and fingers pinned with surgical steel, discovers him or herself to be in a radically different world than he or she could have ever anticipated. The concrete situation and how it is defined will, in large measure, determine the meanings and feelings that are ascribed to self. The self emerges in lived situations and all lived situations "incorporate elements derived from biographical events that exclusively belong to the individual as individual" (Yalom 1980, 36). While events are personalized relative to direct experience, events are also generalized or typified relative to the presumed state or condition of others, such that the survivor could say of another, "Were he in my situation, suffering this pain, he would not have said that about me." Past and future meet in the emergence of the lived moment in which we are engaged, and that moment is historically informed, thereby portending the future. As beings-in-the-world, we are characterized by process rather than by fixed essence. We are characterized also by openness to the world and to others. We are essentially *possibility* and *relation-in-process* (Sadler 1969, 80; Harries 1967, 171).

The world of everyday reality is socially constructed and it is constituted through language. Thus constituted, it is continuously subject to transformation, deformation, and destruction. That people create reality, as a human artefact, both actively through our projects, actions, thoughts, and feelings, and passively through intentionality, is unseen or ignored by consciousness. People "forget" that they are the authors of the meanings that they discover in their world. The observer forgets that the meanings and patterns he or she finds in nature are meanings and patterns that are imposed and construed upon that which is defined as being "nature." The subjects's "forgetfulness" constitutes the naive nature of the subject's relationship to the life-world, or to everyday life. Rogers, in citing Husserl, is very clear:

> The core naiveté is the continuous, full-fledged unawareness of intentional achievements, both prereflexive and reflexive. Naiveté means, first of all, that individuals fail to see that they themselves constitute the objects of their experience. In the natural attitude [our normal experience of the world], consciousness not only forgets its constitutive functioning but also provides no status for epistemology and metaphysics; they are unrecognized and unadmitted. (Rogers 1985, 58)

Human consciousness, through language, constitutes the meanings of both the background and the objects which are seen as emerging from the background and that thus serve as objects of immediate attention. Background and foreground merge together; what is background at this instant may serve as an object of direct attention in the next moment. The person's construal of the world as objective or object-like is directly provided by language usage. Following Berger and Luckmann's work, Rogers is instructive:

> Language is so central to common-sense knowledge, meaning, and understanding that human beings must talk about themselves until they know themselves. Everyday language offers a veritable treasure house of ready made pre-constituted types and characteristics, all socially derived and carrying along an open horizon of unexplored content. Through language, subjective knowledge becomes objective and to that extent idealized and anonymous. Objectivation thus involves an essential, though inadvertent, forgetfulness that consigns the subjective to a fugitive status. Language provides the roots of

intersubjective, anonymous knowledge that we take for granted in common, as we transcend biological limitations. (Rogers 1985, 57)

The world of the survivor finds him or herself is a symbolic, meaning-imbued and meaning-structured world, just as is the world of normal, daily life. Each world thus created preeminently consists of meanings made available through language. Feelings, moods, and bodily sensations comprise the world of the self and they serve to structure the survivor's experience and world. Moods and feelings arise from the ways in which "the self discovers itself in the world and defines its way of being there." (Natanson 1970, 23). These emotional states arise from the situation within which the person is engaged, and they are contingent upon how the person construes his or her situation. The person's interpretation of the situation, how his or her condition is understood, in part gives rise to emotion. Emotional states also refer back to the situation, potentially altering how the person construes his or her concrete situation. There is a dialectical and reciprocal relationship between emotion and situation. Each modifies, and potentiates or mitigates, the other. Feelings, moods and bodily sensations are therefore situationally emergent, interpreted, and transformational. But in the case of injury bodily sensations and moods take on wider and more obtrusive proportions. Pain is more than sensation and feeling. The person interprets or attaches particular significance or meaning to what is experienced. Such definitions and interpretations constitute, in part, the available range of self definitions that can be made by the person.

All symbolic universes thus constructed, such as the normal reality of everyday life, regardless of their particular form, are incipiently problematic and *all social reality is precarious* (Berger and Luckmann 1966, 103-106). Societies are themselves, "constructions in the face of chaos" (Berger and Luckmann 1966, 103). The apparent stability or permanence of reality, society, or the world is an artful accomplishment, an interpretation by consciousness made possible by language and the normal repetition of everyday life. The order that is found in the world, in the microcosm or macrocosm, is constituted, produced, and imposed by human consciousness. The patterns thus discovered may indeed replicate patterns in nature, physics, or mathematics, but it remains that the pattern or meaning discovered "out there" (that to which I can point as objective features of reality) is invariantly founded within the cognitive constructions and practical activities carried forth by the observer within the framework of everyday life. Consciousness, as William James noted, is onflowing, ever emerging as process, metaphorically like a stream. Language is the tool of consciousness through which we construct the world of human experience. Tiryakian notes that

Consciousness is not simply a given, nor is it an irrelevant factor in the true scientific description of emperical reality; it is a cardinal aspect of that reality, so that we cannot adequately describe what we perceive there in front of us without describing our perception and consciousness of what is external. Consciousness is not something passive, a receptor of stimuli, like a fixed prism of a camera; it is the self in its subjectivity intending toward the external, that is, projecting itself to the outside in activities. In consciousness things outside the self are transformed into *objects* to and for the self, an object being a meaningful entity in a perceptual field. That is, the self in its active subjectivity constitutes reality by means of an intentional reaching for things outside itself, to which (and to whom) it bestows meanings and expectations and in terms of which the self orients itself in its activities. (Tiryakian 1973, 195)

The reality that people create through their everyday engagement in the world is not strictly an individual achievement: it is contingent, social, and intersubjective in the invariant sense that it is created through language, which is itself a social process and product rooted in, and emerging from, human communicative interaction. The reality of the world, and how that reality is constructed and construed, is invariantly related to the definitions made, not only by self, but by others as well, broadly available to the person through generalized knowlege and cultural recipes of "what every normal person knows" within a given culture, society, and subpopulation.

For the survivor, an understanding of what has happened will relate back to the assessments made by others—family, medical staff, and friends. In part, what the survivor understands about the injuries will be contingent on what others understand about his or her injuries and what they have communicated to the survivor. Just as important as direct communication to the survivor, what is unstated may come to hold special importance for the survivor as he or she attempts to make sense out of what has happened and what is continuing to happen. Indeed, the survivor may harbor significant fears and terrors, never seeking from others to confirm or disconfirm what is feared, based not only on terrifying imaginings but based also on what others haven't mentioned.

The fact that the survivor relies on information, directly given or merely suggested, is also seen in those who have been unconscious for some time. The survivor will discover what happened during this time not only through memories of the event, through hallucinations and dark, frightening images, but finding out "what was happening to me" will be contingent on information supplied by others who were witnesses. In this situation, it can be seen that the survivor's biographical creation of self therefore relies on definitions, opinions, and judgments that are suggested by others who serve as resources. That others are critically involved in the construction of meaning for the survivor indicates the intersubjective, shared nature of both meaning as well as self-construction. Interwoven into the very fabric of the person's activities and projects are other people, whose projects and selves interpenetrate his or her projects. "What was happening," at any moment (and to which the survivor can point as *objective facts* in the accident, in his or her care, pain, fears, and so on) involves meanings which are not emotionally detached from the survivor, but instead, are meanings for self; they directly relate to how the survivor assesses and construes him or herself as the central object of his or her experience.

We perceive, apprehend, and understand the world through typifications, through reference to *types* or *schemata* that are constructed and utilized to interpret and understand the world to which we attend. Typification is a process of abstraction "through which the specific here and now of an object or event is abstracted from its specificity and seen with regards to its character or quality" (Psathas 1980, 9). Typification is a process of generalization. Through typification, objects and events, people and occasions are seen as generic types, as existing within definitional and meaning-imbued categories. Psathas indicates that typification must occur prior to perception since that which is perceived is perceived as an exemplification of a type (Psathas 1980, 9). Typification provides the grounds of perception. In part, typifications are provided as cultural scripts, as standardized social knowledge used for interpretation. As such, they are routinized and broad; they are subject to modification, change and "filling in" to fit present exigencies. Suddenly thrown into an overwhelming situation, the burned person will try to understand what has happened through reference to actual previous experience and typified sociocultural knowlede.

Typification also suggests the routinization of everyday life. Activities within everyday life are typically routine; they are repetitious with variation, and this fact provides the bedrock of everyday reality (Weigert 1983, 76). Variation itself is routinized as typical or normal divergence or digression from normal activities or from business as usual, provided divergence is not extreme. The integration of the problematic, such as difficulties with a fellow worker, arguments with one's children, or the breakdown of one's car while going to work, lends credence, often obtrusively, to the reality of daily life. While temporarily difficult, such problems do not threaten, in a global manner, the world that is taken for granted nor do such problems seriously threaten self. Much of the work of Erving Goffman has been concerned with the "repair work" that is undertaken to rectify normal problems, normal breaches in interaction, and other minor situational threats to self. The routinization of daily activities, which is contingent on the activities of others as well, such as family members, fellow workers, store clerks, and others provides for the person's sense of stability about both self and world and this routinization provides the basis for institutionalization (Berger and Luckmann 1966, 149). In crisis situations, the routines of daily life are disrupted or destroyed. The problems which confront the burned person are no longer subsumable under the person's categorical understanding of ordinary problems or routine disruptions of everyday life. Not only is the crisis not routine, but also in this very fact, the routine structures of the world and the self are threatened. Burn injury ruptures the very routiness and the taken-for-granted quality of the person's world. Stability is destroyed and the person's reference to standardized ways of understanding the world and self, from the person's stock-of-knowledge (Gurwitsch 1970, 12) may drastically fail. Typifications about one's world and self no longer make sense, and they are not relevant. Indeed, in such dramatically changed circumstances, what was typical, ordinary and taken-for-granted may appear absurd. Typical and routine solutions to problems no longer fit the situation and one may feel irrevocably and absolutely threatened to the core of one's existence. Death is the ultimate threat to identity and self:

Subjective identity is a precarious entity. It is dependent upon the individual's relations with significant others, who may change or disappear. The precariousness is further increased by self-experience in marginal situations. The *sane* apprehension of oneself as possessor of a definite, stable and socially recognized identity is continually threatened by the surrealistic metamorphoses of dreams and fantasies, even if it remains consistent in everyday social interaction. The experience of the death of others and, subsequently, the anticipation of one's own death posit the marginal situation par excellence for the individual. Needless to elaborate, death also posits the most terrifying threat to the taken-for-granted realities of everyday life. (Berger and Luckmann 1967, 100-101)

The special situation in which the person is confronted with his or her possible extinction, was termed by Jaspers, a *limit situation* or *boundary situation* (Jaspers 1956, 178-180). This extreme situation, where one is pushed or thrown to the finite limits of existence, is essentially experienced as engulfing and overwhelming the person. Berger and Luckmann have termed this situation *marginal*. In the marginal situation, one finds one's own existence and one's being marginal, questionable, and in profound doubt but it is important to understand that the person may not be fully aware that he or she is in such a situation until after it has passed, at the "final" (provisional) understanding of the profound enormity of what has happened.

Boundary situations are like walls into which the person runs, without warning, a wall upon which he or she flounders, according to Jaspers. It is a limit; it is an unbending and confounding entrapment. The boundary situation is unique in that it potentially displays or reveals the dubious character of human existence and of the self's engagement in the world. Furthermore, it reveals to the subject the possibility of his or her extinction and it graphically shows the finite character of human life. All that is treated as being stable and meaningful is shown to be precarious and subject to deformation and dissolution. The essential precariousness of our human lives is beyond remedy or control. The recognition of the precarious nature of human life, of one's own life in particular, results in a feeling of loss, the loss of a sense of security that had been afforded by one's life and by one's world, a security falsely conveyed by the routines of daily living. The subjective feeling of being at home in the world, of being comfortable and in familiar surroundings, may also be radically altered or lost (Yalom 1980, 45).

In the confrontation between self and limit situation, there is the profound sense of personal alienation or estrangement. Under conditions of extreme threat to our existence, the discovery of our fundamental precariousness confronts us with terror and dread, which cuts to the pit of the stomach. Terror grips us like a demonic, external force over which we are impotent. It permeates our being and we feel helpless, lost and excruciatingly alone. This recognition of crisis may be experienced as a sinking feeling, as intense nausea, a pounding of the heart, or as cold sweating, which momentarily grips us. The threat imposed by boundary situations is the threat of annihilation. We feel isolated, alone, alien, and lost.

The experience of extreme crisis, which is the situation in which terror emerges, is apprehended as encompassing or enveloping the self. Not all crises represent the occasion of terror. Terror emerges only when our existence is fully recognized as being threatened and when the possibility for escape appears limited or nonexistent. Crisis ruptures that sector of the world that is taken as being categorically and inextricably "mine." What is "mine" is a special, personal subuniverse of the outer life-world (Luckmann 1970, 580). The injury or death of a loved one, the sudden and unexpected loss of a job, divorce, physical assault, or sudden catastrophic illness, all of these represent crises that potentially threaten the self and the person's deepest sense of identity. Burn injury is an extreme form of crisis, one that is deeper and more globally threatening to the being and integrity of the person.

It is within crisis situations or, to use a term coined by Maslow, within peak experiences,[2] that one most clearly stands outside normal reality, in *ek-stasis* (Berger 1969, 43). This can be understood as standing outside the self, where the person feels a distance between the here and now of the self and that which the person has previously taken him or herself to be. In such extreme, extraordinary situations, the self is seen in a radically different light. Significant issues and questions may be raised which never were asked before, which the person never had to face before, as the threat of exceptional loss and dramatic change are confronted. The burn survivor may feel forced to take up issues, of both his or her past or present, which are emotionally painful and feared. He or she, in being confined for a long period of time, may feel forced to evaluate his or her life, a task that, under ordinary circumstances, may not have been undertaken.

Everyday life is shattered by the experience of being burned. In an instant, the routine world of familiarity is no longer. The seriously injured person is thrown into a situation of pain, anguish and suffering over which he or she can exert little if any control. All routine projects are halted and the person is swept into a vortex from which it seems no extrication is possible. Without remedy, the person's temporal/spatial orientation within the world is radically altered. The ground gives way under the burn victim and he or she may feel swallowed as if by an abyss. Routinized typifications about who and what he or she is, no longer serve to orient the person to the previously known world. The burn victim is dramatically and suddenly no longer at home within his or her world. He or she is cast adrift in a frightening, hostile world for which there has been no preparation, a world beyond anything which could have been imagined or anticipated from the standpoint of normal life. Not even the survivor's worst nightmare could have suggested the confounding world into which he or she has been cast adrift.

The situation in which the self discovers itself as a social object is never complete; the person's interpretation of that situation will transcend the immediate situation, and interpretation will suggest both the past and the future within an open horizon. Finding him or herself critically burned, the person will attempt to understand his or her situation both through reference to the past and through anticipation or projection of the future.

The body localizes our being within a concrete physical location, in a finite spatial/temporal horizon from which our view of the world emanates. My body not only grounds me to the world but it also localizes me within the social world. The situation I am in is circumscribed by the spatial/temporal horizon in which I am embedded; and the situation includes not only the space where I am and the time within which I am located, but it includes also the experience of emergent meaning and feeling. The dimensions of time, space, and meaning are each found to extend beyond the immediate present of my attention with each portending the future and pointing back to the past. In being traumatized, the experience of both temporality and spaciality are radically altered for the patient. The experienced world becomes narrow, confined and restrictive. The person may be quite disoriented and lost. Confinement, social isolation, normal sensory deprivation, acute pain, and the use of drugs can further distort normal experience of time, space, and self. These are problems not only for burn victims, but also for many persons who have experienced serious traumatic injury. (Lilliston 1985)

For example, in actually living through agonized confinement in an ICU bed, where arms and legs are splinted and immobilized one is in acute pain, thoughts will be directed to or drawn toward the anticipated future; when the next injection is coming for pain, when splints will be removed, or when debridement will take place. The person anticipates the future, and suggests to him or herself the meaning of self in a future state. Space is projected, or anticipated, in the apprehension and hope that soon, one will not be confined, that soon one will be out of the bed, and out of the hospital. The pull of such anticipation, which presumes the importance of projects and activities in the normal world and ignores the subject's actual condition, is so great, that some patients such as Peter (expanded later) may physically attempt to escape. In Peter's case, his desire to flee was later attributed to his overwhelming need to return to work, to a job he had just started. His attempt to escape was also ascribed to his inability, due to drugs and acute illness, to comprehend his medical condition. The condition of being heavily medicated severely limited Peter's ability to understand his condition. Were he not sedated, so that he could better appreciate his condition, his desire to return to work may have been just as salient though he would most probably not have tried to escape from the burn center.

The importance of Peter's explanation is not that it is necessarily objective (upon questioning, Peter could potentially find other unstated and plausible reasons for escape) but that his explanation constitutes for Peter a reasonable account of his conduct. He creates knowledge about himself, and, in so doing, he literally constructs himself through the creation of his biography. He is also construing himself as a particular type of person, and he is making sense out of behavior that he might otherwise feel is odd, atypical, or nutty. In a deeper sense, his account suggests the construction of and reference to covert norms or rules concerning expected, appropriate conduct for being a sick patient in the hospital. In this case, such rules are tacit background assumptions that serve to anchor his account. The survivor's reference to and use of rules, can be read throughout their accounts. For Peter, the reference to tacit rules about sensible patient conduct, which are contrasted to his actual conduct, provide the requirement for constructing a rational explanation about himself, thereby making sensible behavior that otherwise appears strange.

The movement of the body through localized space defines that space. The space within reach is limited by the body. The space surrounding the body is not merely physical space but it is space incorporated into the subject's body image; a radicalization of that space, potentially radicalizes the body image (Schilder 1950, 212-213). The *here* of my body is not merely a place in space but it is the place of my corporal existence in the world. My body image is a way of stating how I am in the world

(Merleau-Ponty 1962, 100-101), and further, body image is social in origin (Merleau-Ponty 1962, 217). Body image is not just the private experience of the subject. Like the self, it is created out of our interpretations of how we think others see us as well as it being a reflection of how we see ourselves

When seriously burned, the body is radically and immediately altered; parts of the body may be horrifyingly damaged or destroyed. Fingers, hands, arms, feet, and legs may be so injured that amputation is required, and such deeply extensive loss obviously transforms the way in which the person is within his or her world, altering the most personal feelings and beliefs about self.

Not only is appearance radicalized, but such severe injury or loss drastically changes the way in which the person-as-body can be mobile within the world. The body-as-instrument, for negotiating the physical environment and for interpreting the environment through senses such as touch, may be irrevocably damaged so that previously routine abilities, such as feeding oneself, or touching another person, are temporarily or permanently lost. The most basic elements of self-care, previously taken-for-granted, may be impossibe, especially during the acute phase of hospitalization.

Even with recovery, the person may, like a young child, have to relearn very basic tasks, such as tying shoes, buttoning shirts, or a thousand others, which the person previously performed and never thought about. It is frequently the achievement of such ordinary tasks that make our lives seem normal, especially after a period of time when we are unable to do them. John, who is briefly mentioned at the beginning of Chapter 5, had both hands amputated after a serious electrical burn. John noted that he could no longer caress and feel his wife's breasts. He and she had to learn to be intimate without his hands. Losing his hands, whatever other profound meanings and feelings were involved, was a threat to his sexual identity with his wife. Without hands, tactile communication that was previously available was lost and the loss was for both partners. For Sara, an older woman who was badly burned in a brush fire, being able to again feed herself and button her blouse without assistance was of immense significance in allowing her to feel that she was recovering. Being able to do these routine tasks provided a basis for Sara to see that she was becoming normal again.

What is being discussed here is *normalization*, the process through which the survivors and others can find objective clues to the return to normal life. Normalization is incremental; it involves the survivor's assessment that he or she is moving away from the injury and it frequently involves assessments made by others. The discovery that life is returning to normal is founded upon pragmatic acts accomplished by the survivor. For one survivor, such simple tasks as preparing a meal, driving a car again, or being able to tie shoes provided hope and reassurance that she was no longer as damaged as she had been. The accomplishment of simple tasks, like feeding herself, fastening her own buttons and baking cookies grounded her to a life which was becoming normal. John's return to work and his ability to maintain intimacy with his wife and find ways around the loss of his hands during intimate moments were all demonstrable facts for John and his wife that his life, and their life together, was returning to normal.

The immediate and radical changes wrought by burn injury significantly alter the meanings attached to routine objects in the burn survivor's world. The body itself is radically transformed, in a most frightening manner, and the meanings of objects, relative to their use by the person, may also be significantly altered. To return to the example of eating, a fork may no longer be a simple or benign instrument. With hands badly burned and nurses demanding that the patient feed him or herself, or not eat, survivors can be brought to tears of agony. Grasping a fork may be excruciatingly difficult and painful; special forks with long, padded handles may be fashioned by the Occupational Therapy Department* to assist the person in complying with the treatment and rehabilitation program. The staff's insistence on the use of such devices may be required in spite of the patient's objections and ultimately, the patient will usually come to understand that such demands, though creating pain and frustration, were necessary.

The experience of the self cannot be detached from the body, nor can what we bodily experience be detached from the self, yet traditional psychological studies often split the process. What the body experiences in its world-embedded corporeality, the self will structure or pattern into meaning, provided such experiences stand out from what is typically taken for granted as routine. That is, most of the time we are only dimly aware of our bodies, we disattend to our bodies except under special circumstances of consideration or under special sensory conditions, such as when we feel discomfort, hunger, thirst, pain, or bodily pleasure. Even then, our bodies will not be attended to as being problematic, but instead, we will turn to the perceived condition creating the sensation to rectify it or, in the case of pleasure, perhaps to increase or prolong the sensation or to merely give ourselves up fully to the sensation, as in orgasm.

In considering accounts or narratives about being burned, the experience of the body as being on fire remarkably did not include, for many survivors, reports about extreme pain, which an outsider would imagine. There was pain, for those who can recall the experience, and the pain may have been perceived as overwhelming, but pain was not the issue to which the survivor reportedly attended. Survival and escaping from the fire or the situation of burning was the central issue. A number of

---

* It is in occupational therapy, and also in physical therapy, that much of the rehabilitation work is done with the patient.

the survivors do not recall, in any detail, the experience of being burned. It, like the initial hospitalization, is but a foggy, dimly remembered experience, like a nightmare. It is one that is remembered only in a shadowy manner though the memories, for some survivors, still evoke feelings of pain and dread.

The following section contains exerpts from eight survivor inter-views. They provide firsthand descriptions of how the burns occurred.

Eric Mathews: Vehicle Accident

Eric vividly recalled his accident when he was critically burned in a Volkswagen microbus that rolled over.

I was driving a '64 VW van, which are known for rolling over and catching on fire. I was attempting a U turn, at which time I hit the center divider, rolled over. I woke up inside the van with it on fire. At that time I looked around for anybody else, because I just woke up; I was knocked unconscious.

When I woke up it was just fire and panic, and first things first—get everybody out first before I get out. At that time there was an explosion which blew off the back door, which gave me an avenue of escape, so I [crawled] from the fire and from the explosion. I was pretty much beat up from there.

D: Do you recall any specific things, do you recall pain?

There was a panic, and so I'm sure it was the shock of so much happening, like an overwhelm of sensations, so it was just sort of switched into automatic. I wasn't really thinking about it, just searching for anybody else and then I remember the explosion, at which time it was just too much to take. Then there was pain, and the screaming. I remember searching, then the explosion and then just trying to get out.

The "overwhelm of sensations" is a typification for explaining how he "automatically" acted to get out without being aware of specifically thinking about what he had to do. There appeared to be no time to think or to ponder, he was enveloped in the immediacy of the situation and only later does he find ways of interpreting what he did.

I collapsed halfway out. And then there was someone on the side who came and pulled me the rest of the way out, and put me in the center divider. I was rolling around frantically, trying to...as if I was trying to put out the fire, but it was already out. The pain was still there.

D: Did you have any idea how badly you were injured?

No. The funny thing is, my dad was a fire fighter for twenty-three years. But there was ignorance on my part and on his part about the seriousness of burns. I saw my finger, the one I lost, and I was just in shock,...looking at my body in disbelief, and the pain...there was a lot going on.

His father's occupation constitutes a reference for the burn. His father, who had seen burns many times and who had, perhaps, talked to Eric about these experiences, did not truly understand the consequence of the injury, nor did Eric. Eric is saying that neither he nor his family could appreciate the journey they would make even though his father was more familiar with burns than are most people.

D: What did you see when you looked at your body?

I don't know if it was selective memory, or what, but I remember being black and charred and stuff like that. Just like a nightmare, like "No, this can't be." That's the shock of it, it's like pain, trying not to believe it just happened. My finger, and I said, "I just lost my finger" [it was so badly burned, to bone, that it was amputated].

He had an experience that he defined as a "near death" experience:

When I went over and hit my head, I think, is when I went through this tremendous sensation of speed in the light. And then certain events took place there, which I believe was the decision of my life, my choice of whether to go through the pain or not.

D: What kinds of things do you recall reliving at that moment?

It was a tremendous speed into light. The tunnel was there, I'm sure but it wasn't so much a tunnel. It was just going toward the light and being in the light. For me, it was more that a choice was given. There was an awareness of what happened. The choice of life was *there*. For me to pass over would have been an easy thing to do at that point because when there's so much pain, your spirit has to leave. So there was an awareness of my life to that point and also what would happen if I chose to go back and so I chose to come back. Life is so good and I had such a good time and I make things that I want, happen to come about, that the choice was easy. My ignorance of how bad it was might have helped me survive it. My attitude was, I've had a broken collarbone from playing sports or from motorcycle riding. So to me it was just another form of injury that I had to recover from.

For Eric, it was his choice to live or die. Death would have been easy; it was there. He also sees the situation as providing some awareness of what survival might entail. To die was to give up a good life, and not realizing what he would endure if he lived helped him make the choice to live. Being previously injured was compared to what he anticipated the choice to live might mean or entail, and for him this was just another injury from which he could recover. What is seen within his narrative is a statement about how he decided to survive, since he, in fact, believes and says that the choice was his. He suggests not only that he actively made this decision, but also how he made it. The decision was made in reference to his past life. From his perspective, this decision was significant in interpreting what was to result from the decision. The meaning of pain and loss would be at least partially interpreted by way of reference to this decision. It matters little that, from a medical or "objective" stance, such a decision could be doubted, disqualified, or ignored as having any effect on the fact that he survived. His previous life provides the rationale for surviving. What he said about himself is embedded in a temporal horizon: realizing what he would endure if he chose to live anticipates the future, it suggests the projection of the self into what is assumed will be. Furthermore, the reality in which he made his decision was other than that of being engaged in the accident. Having made the decision to live, his awareness returns him to the immediate situation. He goes on to say:

I would say that I saw the van roll, but I don't know if that's just some re-creation or if I really saw it. I would be, like standing off to the side watching it take place and on fire and then once I made my decision to live, I was back in. That's when I woke up. In fact, I did ask the police and paramedics about this little girl in a white dress.

D: Okay, what was that? Was this someone you saw?

That, to me, represented a spirit that was present to me and what was heard by me at the time was "It's all right. This is meant to be." It means nothing to anybody else; but to me, at the time, I understood... and the best thing I can think of is...and again, the rose [?]. It seemed like a small image so I said "little," and "girl" because it was long haired and wore a white dress.

I was sure I saw it. In fact, I feel that's why I turned it into her because I saw it there and then it rolled. So it might have been that I hit [the divider] and then it [the accident] was instantaneous.

D: So are you saying that you had the accident because you saw the image of the girl ?

No. I would say that the entity was there because of the pain I was going to have and the entity was there to reassure and comfort me. It was to help me through and that was when I was out watching this take place, where I had no choice to go through this, the "valley of the shadow." There was no doubt pain was going to happen. At the time it was clear. It was like, "Well, you got yourself hurt. You've got to get better." In that other state [where he was unconscious and saw the entity] it would definitely have been an intentional decision [to live].

Not all of what Eric recounted as his interpretation of what occurred in the accident was available to him as direct experience at the time of the accident even though this might be suggested in the narrative. The meaning of the "entity" became clear after the accident as he reconstructed, while in the burn center, what had happened to him. Eric was the only survivor who reported an experience that was self-defined as a near death experience.

Susan Bayer: Vehicle Fire

Susan was burned in a vehicle fire in 1973 in Boston. A few years after recovering from her burn injury she developed breast cancer, requiring a radical surgery. Her husband, an oral surgeon, still blamed himself for not correctly interpreting her symptoms as suggesting cancer. In describing the fire she said:

There was a Porsche parked in one of those narrow garages, and my sister-in-law and I were going for a ride in the car because it was brand new. When she turned on the ignition the first time, it didn't start, and the second time she tried to start it, the car exploded. I had a choice of staying in the car and getting asphyxiated or getting out of the car which meant stepping right into the fire, because gasoline was flowing down the side next to the car. So I took the option of getting out and I fell into the fire. I slipped, it was grease and gas and slippery, and my brother-in-law pulled me out of the fire and my pants had soaked up all the gas so they couldn't put the fire out right away,...my husband beat it out a couple of times and they put the hose on me then I went to the hospital.

D: What do you recall thinking about when you were in the car?

I gave careful consideration to just sitting there and dying. I knew I had to make the decision and I made it in a fraction of a second but I knew if I sat there in the car I was going to die. There was no other way because the smoke and fumes were so intense. I opened the door and looked out and saw that the fire was right there. I would have to step right out of the car and into it. So I closed the door a little bit and sat there and thought, "Well, you can sit here and die for sure or you can step out into the fire and try," and before I knew it I was out.

D: Do you recall what you were thinking or feeling as you sat in the car wondering what to do?

I just knew I couldn't stay there,... I had no choice but to get out. I was terrified about getting burned. I thought if I could just run through the fire fast I might be okay. It just was the only choice I had. I was very scared.

D: So you stepped out and your brother-in-law grabbed you?

Well, it was going so fast then, it all happened in such a short fraction of time that I wasn't even aware that I slipped. I do remember that there was a sloped driveway and I remember crawling up to it. If I had been there two seconds longer, I would have panicked. I was crawling and couldn't make any headway.

D: What do you recall after you were first burned?

I never lost consciousness. *I refused to* [my emphasis]. I was the one who told my husband that my leg was still burning. So, he got it out the second time and that's when they hosed me down. I was able to get up and move away because I didn't want to be near the fire. I then noticed that my leg didn't work. It really hadn't occurred to me that I was burned that badly. The thing that I associate with burns is being cold. I was wet and I was evidently going into shock. I was just unbelievably cold.

D: You were not in pain?

No, no pain at all. That's why I couldn't really figure out what was wrong with my leg because I didn't hurt anywhere. I had decided to let them take me to the hospital just to check me out, and thought that I would go home immediately thereafter. I was very optimistic. I really didn't have any idea what was really happening to me. I was very concerned about my husband because *I could see his burns and I couldn't see mine* [my emphasis]. He was just hysterical about me.

Throughout the narratives of survivors, it will be noted that many of them were unaware of how badly they were burned. In the case of Susan, her definition was constituted in reference to two physiological factors: (1) she didn't experience severe pain. The background expectation for her was that if she wasn't in pain, she must not be badly injured; and (2), she could not see her own injuries. While the subject's body is available to her or him as it is to no other person, the body is not fully available visually. In not being able to see her burns, and in not feeling her burns, she had no objective signs or symptoms that would suggest a critical injury. Her body masked the actual meaning of the injury and her situation by not providing the signs or symptoms that would allow her to experience herself as seriously injured. If she had been in acute pain, or if she could have seen her burns, her assessment might have been very different. And her experience of cold instead of pain, which might have been expected, may have also served to hide from her an understanding of the seriousness of her injuries.

Since the car as well as the garage were burning, Susan was forced to make a decision. She could stay where she was and not be burned for the moment, or she could get out. But getting out meant she would have to go through the fire. She knew she must do something. When she opened the door, she found the fire to be "right there," and, in getting out, she would be stepping into the flames. This is a situation imbued with terror of death and annihilation, and it is a situation where she sees herself as having virtually no control. Her possible actions were limited to remaining where she was, and being killed, or running through fire. In either case, she was confronted with an overwhelming situation that presented her with the immediate threat of injury or death. Her normal world, in which she anticipated going for a drive in the new Porsche, was instantly shattered and she was faced with a crisis that breached her normal, everyday reality. She was thrown into a situation from which there was no possible escape. Any decision had a high price of injury or death.

Time is constituted in a radicalized manner from that which is typically experienced in everyday life. Her inner sense of time is contingent, it is judged in relation to the presence of spreading fire and the fact that the car was filling with smoke. Time is speeded up so much so that she doesn't have time to think much about what was going on. Thought as well as action is severely constrained by the critical nature of the situation. This will be the case for other survivors as well.

Paul Guiterez: Training Fire

I was being hired as a fireman and I was undergoing an eight-week training period and I was in my last couple of weeks. Six weeks prior to that I had been a furniture salesman, so I didn't have any experience at all with fire fighters or fires except for the training and practice I got in the academy with a few live fire drills. I wasn't afraid of any of them, none were very hot or intimidating and I wasn't afraid of the one I got burned in either, but the point I'm trying to make is that I am new up the street and didn't have a lot of experience.

What they had done was set up in a concrete drill tower. They set up some palates to burn and some hay, and threw jet fuel in there to really get it going good. And once the fire got going really good and really hot and really rolling, they went ahead and let us put it out. Both captains of the fire department told me to go ahead and put on an air pack. I was the first one to report to him at the front door. He gave me an inch and a half [hose] line and told me to put the fire out. He said it was burning at the back corner.

So I got on my stomach and laid down and started crawling in with some hose and there was people behind me I could feel at my heels. It was dark and smoky and it was very warm so I had to lay down on the ground because the heat was very intense. I got fifteen to twenty feet into the building and I couldn't see anything. I'd been there two or three minutes. At that time my ears started to burn and I tried to get down as low as I could but I couldn't get away from my ears burning so I figured it was time to get out. So I turned around and tried to get out on my hands and knees. I couldn't find the door and all of a sudden my arms, my back, my legs, my neck, everything started burning. I felt as if my skin was peeling off. I felt a sharp stinging all over my body.

D: You had full fire turnouts on?

Yeah. The turnouts were real old that they just used for training. But I felt my skin peeling off and I knew I was getting burned, because I felt so much of my skin peeling off. I continued to try to find the door and I couldn't and I couldn't find my hose either. I found this wall that was still burning and it was burning low to the ground and I knew that this was the wrong way so I turned to the right for a ways and I was thinking I was in a different area of the room so I thought the way to go was to the right and then left and then I found an opening and went left and then I passed out. The next thing I remember they were looking for me. The room had cleared of smoke some so I noticed a silhouette coming towards me but he passed me as I was sitting up against the wall. I saw the silhouette of the door through the smoke. And I walked to the door and stood up and I didn't want anybody to carry me out, too proud to be carried out and I didn't want anybody to know that I couldn't handle myself. But I knew I was hurt severely. I guess I must have passed out, or fainted and I fell into the arms of two people who were standing there and caught me.

They cut my clothes off down to my underwear and doused me with water. They covered me with a sheet and they poured water on my body which relieved some pain. They just put me in the back of a fire department station wagon and rushed me to the burn center.

For Paul, the fact that he was burned is referenced back to his past job of being a furniture salesman. This fact is seen by him, and is provided as an explanation to me, as a way of maintaining his sense of competency. He was not burned because he was foolish or incompetnt, he was burned because he was the new kid on the street, one who was unfamiliar with fire. He defines himself not as incompetent but as inexperienced. By referring to his inexperience, he is distancing himself from the cause of his injury. Cause becomes linked to inexperience, a fact over which he had no control. His feeling of integrity, as a competent person, is maintained by disassociating himself from the errors that led to the burn.

This interpretation is especially important for self-esteem, but for other reasons as well. One of the facts that he and his lawyer subsequently had to demonstrate in court, when he sued the fire department for his injuries, was that his injury could not be attributed to his error or incompeternce but was, instead, a direct result of being ill prepared by his training to enter fire conditions he was told to enter by the training officer. Being seriously injured was attributed to the erroneous decision of training captains. Error was attributed to others and was defined by the inadequate preparation he was given, by the ineffective protective clothing he was issued, and by the fire conditions he was sent in to extinguish.

Jeff Asmore: House Fire

We had just bought a stone house and one of the gifts for the family and my mom was to have the carpet in the kitchen removed and put tile down. And so my stepdad put gasoline on the carpet to eat away the glue. And while we were removing the carpet it just ignited.

D: Where were you in the house?

In the kitchen. My mother and my younger brother Tim died three days later. My other brother Roger, he got burns on his legs, his feet were burned severe. He had a large cut from the chandelier that fell from the explosion, it was cut real bad, but as far as the burns, the burns weren't that severe. I went through the window. And my brother Tim, he was thrown through the door. And he got up and ran out the door. My mom and my younger brother,...A neighbor came to the back door and opened up the door and saw my brother lying on the floor behind the bed. He picked him up and after carrying him out he carried us out.

D: Were you aware of what was going on?

Yes, I knew everything that was going on. I didn't lose my mind. I just didn't know exactly what had happened. I was inside the back of their car [neighbors] and they also put Roger next to me and I was crying at the time. And when I saw Roger I stopped crying and started looking at him. And somebody came up with a large pair of underwear and told him to put it on so I started laughing, it was something that was funny. And an old lady came up to the window and was looking in at me and my brother. And I spoke up and said, "What's wrong with you bitch?" It was just something I said and I don't know why I said it. It was just something that came out. I saw my mom, she was lying outside the front door. It didn't look like her. She was just lying out there and she was all black. Her whole body was black.

D: Do you know how she got out?

She crawled part of the way out and then my stepdad, he said that he pulled her out. I saw him and I saw some other people around my mom but I don't think my stepdad did because he was a little...he had problems, serious problems and numerous times he threatened to kill us all. *It just didn't go together with him saying that he pulled her out of the fire* [my emphasis].

D: When you were in the car did you know you were burned?

Yeah, when I was in the fire. When the explosion took place...when I became conscious, I opened my eyes for just a split second. I could see everything, everything was just there. I saw my mom, she was under the table. And I saw my brother running out...getting up because his clothes were on fire [Tim]. It was cold after getting out.

D: Do you recall pain?

The only pain that was really felt was hot and cold flashes. Like I would get cold where I wanted to be covered up and then I'll get too hot and then I wanted everything off. That was right outside at the car. That was the most painful part, right at first.

Among all the survivors interviewed for this study, Jeff seems to me to have the life that is the most tragic. He stands out as the survivor who was least able to cope with the changes wrought by the accident and as the person who was most embittered by what occurred. His adjustment to his injury seems precarious and tenuous. He has been institutionalized and placed in protective custody at least twice because of fears that he would commit suicide. He has been thrown off buses and evicted from apartments, reportedly because of his appearance. He reports repeatedly asking doctors to put him to sleep because he cannot endure the pain of living. He disdains his remaining family, and hopes "to see them in hell."

Other survivors were also physically and emotionally damaged, but only Jeff, who was burned as a twelve-year-old, lost family members. While it cannot be discerned in the above interview material, what emerges for me, throughout his interview, is the feeling that in losing his mother he lost the only person he loved and, in so doing, he lost most of what was valued in his world. He intimates that his stepfather may have deliberately caused the fire, an image that continues to haunt him.

He sees the fire as possibly being deliberately caused because his stepfather established the circumstances which led to the fire. His stepfather bought new carpeting to put in the house and he had the family remove the old flooring using gasoline while he was outside. Very importantly for Jeff, and more than once, his stepather had threatened to kill the whole family. Jeff's understanding of the possible cause of the fire includes, therefore, physical features of the event (using gasoline to remove the old floor covering), as well as behavioral factors connected with his stepfather's conduct. Also important were Jeff's assessment and interpretation of his father's intention to do harm to the family. The latter interpretation transcends the present situation of the fire, but it informs his interpretation about the present situation.

In this particular instance, it can be seen how an interpretation of the cause of the event is transituational, referring to Jeff's construction of his stepfather's imputed mental state. The properties or specific elements that Jeff constructs as causally defining the situation in which he was burned are also in evidence. This is important because it suggests not only how he interprets and defines the situation, but it also suggests the interpretative process through which he has gone in order to arrive at such an understanding. Like several other survivors, Jeff refers to his mental status at the time he was injured or immediately thereafter. He didn't "lose his mind," and while not knowing immediately what had happened, he knew something extraordinary had occurred. It was categorically beyond normal experience and it was that which threw his mother under the table and sent his brother Tim running out of the house, on fire. His initial interpretation displays the provisional nature of the actual meaning of the situation. His knowledge was initially indeterminate. The immediacy of the event, as it was happening, was not understood fully; it was only some moments later, after direct engagement in the fire had terminated, that Jeff could realize what had occurred.

This is similar to descriptions made by survivors of the Cerritos (CA) Aero Mexico plane crash disaster who, while on the ground in their homes, initially experienced a tremendous roar, a deafening crash, and then fire. While running from their houses, and finding surrounding homes on fire, they knew "something" terrible had happened, but comprehending exactly what had occurred, through their immediate engagement in the situation, required time. Understanding a situation frequently requires distance between self and experience. With "distance," which may be spatial as well as temporal, more specific definitions of the situation can be made as the context as well as the particulars of the occurrence come into view. Direct, overwhelming engagement in the experience can limit the person's understanding of the situation. For Jeff, his knowledge of what happened followed the immediacy of the occurrence, much like his understanding of how his stepfather may have intentionally caused the fire was retrospectively defined.

That Jeff and several others specifically refer to not "losing" their minds or not being unconscious when burned suggests to me that people commonly construe such a calamitous event as causing one to lose one's mind or to become unconscious. Further, to lose one's mind is to lose control. Recall that Susan never lost consciousness because, as she believed, she refused to do so. Jim Gonzales, one of the next cases, felt that if he closed his eyes he would lose consciousness. Of interest here are the ways in which consciousness is defined, construed, and understood in relation to being severely burned.

Mike Lawson: Motorcycle Accident

My burn happened when I was on a motorcycle. I was going around the block to see if my brother had done some brake work on it. Brakes worked. Made it two blocks and a car turned left in front of me, hit me head on, and the gas tank exploded. I had just filled it up, there was five gallons in it and the truck came in from the left and hit me head on because he was turning left. So he pinned me underneath the truck. There was a pool of fire about ten feet in diameter; there was gas everywhere. Gas had soaked into my clothes. I whipped the bike off me, crawled out from underneath the fire, crawled out from underneath the car, and crawled from the fire and some bystanders were kind of yelling at me, they couldn't come any closer. They were yelling at me to get up and move out 'cause I was in a state of shock. I was just instinctively trying to get out, and they were yelling "Come on get up and get out of there." I got up and ran out, after I crawled about ten feet, I got up and ran another ten feet before I collapsed. And they wrapped me in blankets and tried to put the fire out.

They put my chest out with a blanket, [they'd] go down and try to put my legs out, and my chest would start on fire again; then they'd start working on my chest again and my legs would start burning. I was just saturated with gasoline. It's a Friday night and everybody heard the explosion and all these fire engines came from the volunteer station and they had backup fire department from Desert View and the central dispatch sent the paramedics from Desert View. Then seven CHP [California Highway Patrol] units came and four sheriff's units and, God, everybody...I didn't screw around, might as well do it right.

D: So you were aware of what was going on, were you conscious?

Yeah, I was conscious. I was lying on the grass. All I can remember is lying on the grass and repeating my name over and over again to the paramedics. I was in a state of shock. I don't remember much at all, just bits and pieces here and there. They were asking me my name and address over and over again to see if I had a concussion.

D: Were you in much pain?

I remember very little from the accident. My leg was broken. And that was the only thing that hurt at first. In the first week or so, I didn't have much pain, but of course, the third-degree burns didn't hurt at all. But my back, it was just agony. My back was second degree. That just put me through hell. My back was excruciatingly painful.

D: Did you ever think about how badly you were injured?

I don't really remember, I just pieced it together. I knew how bad I
was. When they were bringing me out of the emergency room in
Cahuenga, the CHP officer who was doing the report was walking
next to me and was taking the report. He said, "I'll see you later"
and I said, "No, you're not going to see me later." I knew how bad I
was, I mean, I was cooked, I was fried. That was it for me. When I
was down here [Valley Burn Center] my dad came into see me at
three in the morning or so. He walked in the door, and this has all
been related to me, and said, "Well, how are you doing Mike" and I
said, "Well dad, I really fucked up this time." So I knew how bad it
was, I knew I was a basket case. There was no doubt at all that I was
very bad off. I didn't think I was going to make it at first.

D: Were you afraid of dying?

You know, it never crossed my mind, I never thought I was going to
die.

Mike recognized that he was seriously injured. It is not clear,
however, to what extent he thought he might be facing death. At one
moment he says that he knew he was a basket case and he thought he
would not see the highway patrol officer again. Here, he appears to
recognize how critically injured he was and that he might die. In the next
part of the interview, however, he states that he never thought about
dying. I think that he could have recognized how tenuous his life was,
that he was terribly injured, and that he might not again see the CHP
officer, yet, at the same time, he may not have considered death to be
probable or even possible. No one I interviewed, regardless of how critically they were burned, thought that they would die. The idea was
entertained by a few, but it was then dismissed. Some may have hoped
they would die, but none seemed to really think it would happen. We
seem to have a unique ability, under truly devastating conditions, to ward
off thoughts of our own deaths. We anticipate a reprieve, we hold out
hope in the face of interminable challenge, and we believe that somehow
we will survive. Thoughts of death are pushed aside and out of consciousness as the subject's attention is turned toward ancillary but related
themes.
    From a psychological position, this fact, if it indeed is typical of
persons who have been severely traumatized and whose death is a very
real physiological possibility, might be attributed to defense mechanisms
such as denial. Alternately, it can be suggested that the subject finds it
exceptionally difficult, if not impossible, to concretely anticipate his or her
own death except in rather broad, general terms or in very specific limit
situations as discussed previously. We lack experience that would provide
the perspective and understanding necessary to grasp our own death as a

concrete, ultimate possibility. We can think about what death may be like, we can imagine what form death may take; but it is impossible, under conditions of everyday life, to grasp the meaning of death for either ourselves or for others.

Further, it seems impossible to see myself as dying in any definitive sense because I am experientially not there. This, I believe, is so with those who are suddenly traumatized and who instantly face the possibility of death. The situation may be very different when one endures a longer trajectory of dying, when one sees his or her own progressive weakening and debilitation over time, but even here, the Heideggerian dictum that to live authentically requires that I embrace fully the recognition of my own finitude frequently falls on deaf.

Elisabeth Kubler-Ross and Edwin Schneidman's comments are instructive. Kubler-Ross states that

> In listening to our terminally ill patients we were always impressed that even the most accepting, the most realistic patients left the possibility open for some cure, for the discovery of a new drug or the last minute success in a research project. It is this glimpse of hope which maintains them for days, weeks or months of suffering. (Kubler-Ross 1969, 139)

and

> The initial denial was as true for those patients who were told outright at the beginning of their illness as it was true for those not told explicitly and who came to this conclusion on their own a bit later on. (Kubler-Ross 1969, 38)

Kubler-Ross depicts five stages as being common to the process through which the dying person journeys. These stages are seen as coping mechanisms or as the death work of the terminally ill person (Schneidman 1974, 4-5) and they have also been analytically applied to "grief work" resulting from other forms of significant loss. Kubler-Ross was dealing with terminally ill patients as opposed to very recently traumatized patients. This is of consequence, for her patients had a longer time to be aware of and adjust to their declining conditions than did those who were suddenly burned. While several writers have disagreed with Kubler-Ross on the sequential existence of all five stages in dying patients, her work must be considered pioneering. Schneidman specifically finds, in patients he has worked with, that the five stages can be in different orderings relative to the specific patient, and that some stages may be entirely absent or exceptionally fleeting, and he questions entirely the existence of definitive stages:

While I have seen in dying persons isolation, envy, bargaining, depression, and acceptance, I do not believe that these are necessarily stages of the dying process, and I am not at all convinced that they are lived through in that order or, for that matter, in any universal order. What I do see is a complicated clustering of intellectual and affective states, some fleeting, lasting for a moment or a day or a week, set, not unexpectedly, against the backdrop of that person's total personality, his *philosophy of life*. (Schneidman 1974, 6)

Schneidman, like Kubler-Ross, uses the concept of denial, traditionally understood as a defense mechanism, to explicate the orientation of some people to their respective impending deaths. Schneidman discovers an alternation between accepting death, and understanding that one is dying, and denial.

Jim Gonzales: Motorcycle Accident

I don't know if we were coming from the gym or going to it. And we're coming down Miranda and this guy made a left-hand turn right in front of us. I saw him coming and I locked eyes with him and right at the time, I said to myself, "If I close my eyes I don't think I'm gonna make it." I didn't want to lose consciousness. And the next thing I knew I was sitting on the pavement in flames. Got up, and I never saw my left leg. I got up and fell back down because this leg was so badly broken. And this girl came up to me and took off her blouse and started putting the fire out and then some woman with a fire extinguisher put me out. And I kind of blacked out at that time.

D: And what about your friend who was driving?

When the accident happened, I kind of knew he wouldn't make it. Cause he was like maybe from here to the Honda car outside (50 feet). And I remember yelling at him, "Fred, Fred" [he is crying as he tells this]. I was yelling at him and I could see he was just a big ball of fire, you know? And right at that point, I was blacking-out, not remembering everything. But back in the back of my mind, I didn't think he was going to make it and I couldn't do anything...

What stands out for me in Jim's narrative here is his relationship with his friend who died. It was difficult for Jim to speak about his friend. This was the man who got Jim a job as an apprentice electrician some years before. They were best friends. Jim recalls little about the accident. He vividly remembers locking eyes with the driver of the car that hit them and he remembers thinking that, if he closed his eyes, he would die. In recounting his most painful memory, when he saw his friend engulfed in fire, he broke down and cried. Not only must this have been terribly horr-ifying, but he could do nothing to help his friend and he was sure that his friend would die. It will be a long time before this image fades.

Peter Shrader: Vehicle Accident
(Interviewed with his wife, Lynn)

D: Did you see the fire blowing back toward you?

Yeah, I saw the engine was on fire, the front of the car caught on fire and when I noticed it, I pulled off the freeway. And when I pulled off the freeway, by then both my arms were on fire. By the time I got off the off ramp, my whole shirt was on fire, both arms, my face, my hair. I lost half my hair. I just knew I had to get off the freeway; that's all I was thinking, get off the freeway and out of the car. I was afraid to stop on the freeway because I thought someone else would hit me and I didn't want anyone else in it. I saw the engine on fire and I had a choice. My concern was, I didn't want anybody else involved at the time. So I pulled off the freeway and there was a ditch. And the car rolled two or three times. But when I pulled off, I was going fifty or forty-five miles an hour. And the car rolled a couple of times and I pulled into a field, and the field I pulled into caught on fire.

And when I pulled off, all of a sudden the whole car was engulfed in smoke and everything. The door was shut and I couldn't open it. So I had to kick it with my foot and I broke the door in and I just dived out the car [it was actually a truck]. Two seconds after I got out of the car, the car blew up, it just went up in smoke.

D: What were you thinking when you were trapped in the car?

I had to get out;..just trying to get out of there. I knew I'd get killed if I didn't get out and the car was on fire. I was on fire;... I was scared, real scared.

D: Do you recall pain during that time?

Oh, yeah. What's really weird is I'm able to remember precisely what happened, exactly what happened. And it doesn't bother me. I've never had any nightmares about it, you know, when you're in the hospital they have you see a psychiatrist. And he kept asking me all these weird questions, and to me they were weird because I was very fortunate, I guess. *It's just something that happened that I just have to live with* [showing how he construes and interprets what happened]. But, when I was burned, I kept saying, I kept yelling to stop the burning...When my arms were on fire, it really scared me 'cause I never had anything like that happen to me before. And it really hurt, but I was just trying to get it put out.

D: When you got out you didn't try to run?

No, I couldn't. My legs, I guess they were froze. I just couldn't move. I dragged myself, but I just couldn't get up and run. I don't know if it was the shock, or the pain, or whatever, I just couldn't run. I got out of the car and I just more or less dove, just to get away. And then I remember, I was in a sandy field. I just started putting sand on me and then this gentleman helped me. And he kept throwing sand on me and he helped me back to the freeway. By that time the paramedics and fire department got there. They put me in the ambulance. And I told them. I said, "Please call my wife." Like I said, I was very alert.

Like several other survivors, such as Susan, Mike, Paul, and Burk (below), Peter was burned in a place of possible entrapment. Unlike Susan, who was momentarily safe in the vehicle, Peter was burning in the vehicle, yet his initial action was to continue driving as he attempted to get off the freeway in order to avoid a further accident with other vehicles. Unlike Paul, whose knowledge of his burning was defined in terms of feeling his ears burning and his skin peeling off, and Burk who felt his hands burning, Peter saw fire and saw himself in flames. Neither Paul nor Burk could see themselves burning. Knowledge of their respective conditions, that each was burned, was provided by the feeling of pain for both Burk and Paul. For Peter, visual recognition with pain was of consequence.

Peter thought that if he didn't get out of the car, he would be killed. Getting out initially provided the basis with which he could know that he was going to live. He was alive, he was outside the car, and that meant that he was safe. Except for pain, which may not be severe if the burn is deep, the burned person may feel reasonably intact. The awareness of the immediacy of death is contingent on knowledge that one is critically injured and near death on one hand, and on subjective feelings which are seen as suggesting death, such as from intense pain or being overwhelmingly ill, on the other hand. Burn victims may feel neither severe pain, due to deep destruction of skin and nerve tissue, nor may they feel critically weak or ill immediately after they are burned. Even in seeing his or her burned skin hanging loose, there may be no recognition of the seriousness of the injury: the person has no background knowledge, and no physical symptoms, against which to estimate or assess his or her injury. For this reason, it is easy to understand how Peter, and Mike above, while realizing that they were seriously hurt, did not understand how seriously injured they indeed were and that death was a very, very real possibility.

Sharon West: Flaming Drink Injury
(Interviewed with her husband Paul)

D: Do you recall what happened, do you recall pain initially?

I can remember, like the whole accident happening. Five of us were at a round table, we were all just talking. And then a friend of mine said, "Shar"... and I turned, and thank goodness, you know you wonder why things happened [her being called, and the fact that she turned her face away just as the flammable vapors ignited] because otherwise that would have come right at me, face forward. She called and it hit me to the right, which my right ear was burned very bad, which I mean, it looks a heck of a lot better now. If it was burned anymore, Dr. Fredricks said they would have to do reconstruction. So I turned and it hit me in the side of the face. I got it in a lot of spots, like I got burned here on the right wrist and just a lot of strange areas that I don't quite understand.

D: What did you do then?

Initially I got up and I ran which I guess was the worst thing to do, but at the moment, you're not thinking logically. My whole blouse was on fire and I'm running and trying to get away from it. Someone knocked me down. I remember "roll, roll," people were just constantly rolling me. I remember the paramedics were there very fast. I was taken right to Methodist Hospital which is just three blocks away. I know they gave me some morphine right away, I'm sure to calm me down.

D: Were you in much pain?

Oh, you are. But they had a lot of morphine, then they had me all doped up in the hospital for I don't know how long it was. They had a lot of morphine and so I didn't feel anything, or remember those first days.

A night out with friends was instantly transformed into moments of terror and months of pain for Sharon. She is grateful that she turned, thereby avoiding the full impact of the fire and she attributes the fact that she ran to not thinking logically. She recalled pain, but more than pain she recalled feeling cold at the restaurant as well as later in the ambulance.

Burk Lassering: Tunnel Fire

Burk was a stunt man. He was burned while performing a stunt in which he was to run through a burning tunnel. The stunt was being performed for a popular network television show. The tunnel consisted of a frame with meshed wire over it. Covering the wire was burlap which had been drenched with a flammable liquid. The burlap was ignited and he ran through the tunnel. He was dressed in fire resistant clothing which was supposed to ensure his protection, but something went terribly wrong. At some point into the tunnel his hands and feet started burning. He could not turn around and he was surrounded by fire, facing entrapment.

D: Can you describe what it was like for you when you were being burned in this tunnel you were running through?

When I was burning in that tunnel, the pain was unbelievable. There is a tape that you can hear me screaming and moaning on. You hear the sound of some creature, in unbelievable pain and it is obvious from the guttural sounds and the shrieks and the screams, sounds of me falling and hitting the ground and you hear me gasping for breath. But those pains that I was feeling at that time was disorienting and shocking to the body and I had no idea of what was going on, I was just trying to get out of that god damned tunnel. That is all I was trying to do.

When I left the tunnel and saw my hands, I knew I was badly injured. I told them to get me to a hospital right now and *I think if I had known then what I was asking for when I said "Get me to a hospital now" I would have asked to put a gun to my head. Because I don't know right now that if I was burned again whether I could withstand that amount of pain again* [my emphasis]. But, if I am burned again, I will bet I will go right back because I'm not a quitter. It is just so unbelievable how much pain you go through. I've had a broken back, I had my appendix taken out, had both my legs broke, my arms broke. I have never in my life experienced the amount of pain that I experienced on the day of the burn or in the weeks that followed. I am amazed not only in myself, but in human beings as a species. And my God, it amazes me just how much pain we can take and not go totally insane. I think burn patients take more pain that they receive from an injury like this than anybody can ever imagine.

D: Did you think you might not get out?

I don't think I was thinking about anything inside of that tunnel except getting to the other end and getting somebody who was going to help me get out. People have asked, "Why didn't you turn around?" and it is virtually impossible to turn around in that tunnel and go back the other way. But they are not thinking about the unbelievable pain that I was suffering and the total disorientation you get when you are like that. Because when you are hurt like that, I don't believe anybody stays oriented because I was realizing that I was burning up and that I had to get out of there. I thought my whole body was going to burn up, so I can't really remember, think honestly, *but I think what I have done, in my mind is take excerpts from things inside the tunnel and rebuilt this whole situation in my mind. I have gone through this one time in the tunnel , but made the trip again and again in my mind and organized it in such a fashion to say that this is what happened* [my emphasis]. So I'm better than forty or fifty feet into the tunnel. And to turn around and to get out by twisting around, if I had lost the handle [a guide handle that ran on a cable along the tunnel], I couldn't see.

I had just thought about, for several weeks, just running through that tunnel of fire. And so I closed my eyes and started to run 150 feet and I was in so much pain that all I could think about was getting to the end. And if I had dropped down and tried to roll out and somehow got tangled up in that wire, what would have happened? What if one of those holes had caught me under the arm, I can't see, and what if, in all that confusion, I couldn't see and instead of crawling out underneath the wire, all I could feel was pain and heat, what if I crawled back into the fire? You know, thinking I had made the exit and crawled back in the tunnel, hit a solid wall and get trapped back inside and then I wouldn't have ever known what was going on or what to do. And the only way I could possibly think of is to run.

But I think that when you have that much pain you just go where your mind is telling you to go. And I had been thinking for two or three weeks, run 150 feet and get out of the fire and if you keep telling this to yourself, it is a form of brainwashing. Everyday, just run, run, run, don't stop just run. And I believe that is what happened when I got inside there.

Over a period of sixteen years, I've met eight people who have been seriously burned in fires where they intentionally placed themselves in danger. Seven of these were fire fighters, the other was Burk. The occupational role of the fire fighter requires that he or she be exposed to danger. Burk's case was very different. He was risking his life, not to protect others, but to promote himself as a stunt man, and to entertain others. This is not my criticism of what Burk did. Instead, it reflects statements that he made in the interview about himself, and it reflected statements he had heard from other stunt men who were subsequently critical of his stunt. Being burned represented a failure where he had sought success on national television.

It was not that Burk was not careful in preparing for the stunt. The whole stunt seemed, from his perspective, to be carefully designed and executed. Others may have done it differently, and I could easily think of design changes, both of the tunnel and how he was equipped, which could have allowed his rescue were he to get into trouble. His burns were directly related to the failure of his gloves and boots which were, he was told by the seller, supposed to withstand the temperatures to which he would be exposed. A court case is pending against the equipment manufacturer and vendor.

Burk's account is especially instructive because he is very descriptive and some of the themes that are discussed in this study are depicted in his narrative. He metaphorically describes himself as some creature encountering acute terror and pain; the sounds he emits are so dramatic that they do not sound human. He was gasping for breath and disoriented; he had no idea what was happening except that he knew he was burning, and he had to escape. In escaping from the tunnel, he knew he was badly injured and he knew he needed medical care. Had he understood what medical care *really* entailed, in terms of pain, he would have wanted to die. Retrospectively, the meaning of the present, in finding himself burned, was contingent on discovering the meaning of the future. His understanding was also provisional and subject to further change or elaboration as events unfold in his medical care. In order to understand the pain he went through, and to suggest how horrendous that pain was, he refers to past injuries and the pain he previously suffered. He constructs a biographical history which assists him in making sense out of the present.

Yet for Burk, there is no comparison. Being burned was nothing like what he previously experienced in all his injuries. Even so, the fact that there was no comparison, and that the pain of being burned was far greater than his previous injuries, provides Burk with a way of shaping and defining the pain of his burn experience. In part, he grasps his experience in the present, and understands it, through biographical reconstruction.

Simultaneous with suggesting that he may have wanted to commit suicide had he known what pain he was going to go through, and saying that were he burned again he could perhaps not endure the pain, he also stated that he wasn't a quitter. In enduring several other injuries, and the terrible pain of his burns, he construes himself as a specific type of person, one who is a survivor, one who can take punishment and survive, that is, he is different from many others. In part, this is how he believes he survived.

In discussing what happened in the tunnel, and why he couldn't turn around, he illustrates the process through which he construes meaning and knowledge of both himself and the incident. Pain and disorientation, along with his belief that if he turned around he might be entrapped, became focal points, or anchors, for accounting for what happened as well as why it happened. He also stated that he "rebuilt" what happened in the tunnel by reliving the experience many times. Reliving what happened suggests reinterpretation and coming to terms with what occurred, but more than this, it depicts how he constructs himself. What happened in the tunnel is not "business as usual," it is not an ordinary event. Up to this point, this is the most monumental event in Burk's life. In accounting for his mental disorientation and disorganization, and in making it sensible and rational, he also makes his actions sensible, thereby suggesting how he defines himself. Burk is like an expert detective who must reconstruct a crime scene. That which is reconstructed serves as a interpretive model for his understanding. In doing so, he constructed a version of what happened. Ultimately, and until further notice, that version becomes what happened. His account, provisionally to be sure, serves his understanding as objectively factual and real.

Throughout the above recollections, survivors are not simply telling us how they were burned. Being burned is not just another ordinary event in the world of everyday life, and it is not just a dramatic event which is recounted by a detached, or neutral observer. They tell us what is was like when they were burned, but their stories do more than this. They also elegantly tell us how self, identity, and reality are fabricated through the vehicle of stories. The survivor's stories suggest the manner through which everyday life, whether it is mundane or extraordinary, is constructed, interpreted, and reconstructed. At the same time, and through the same medium, that of conversation, the evolving, changing and emerging construction of self and identity occur. This is true for the ordinary events of life, and it is also true for the most unusual or dramatic events. Self, identity, and social reality are interwoven. Physical events occur which are separate from the person's interpretation of those events, but it is through interpretation and definition that the physical event is integrated into the psychological reality of the subject. Further, such interpretation frequently involves the collaboration of others who assist the survivor in his or her understanding. The stories also clearly depict the historical nature of self and identity; as the survivor recounts what happened, he or she is actively producing their biography. Thus it is, that through their biographies, they come to understand themselves. For several, recounting what happened was difficult; it was still too close and too painful. Yet they were willing to talk, and it was clear that some felt that the process was cleansing in nature. Talking about a trauma is often said to be cathartic. Talking is a central principle of crisis intervention, regardless of the specific trauma. It seemed, for several survivors, that this was the case during their interviews. A number of survivors, for several reasons, said that they had really never spoken much about what had happened. For some, it was a feeling that others didn't want to hear about it because it was too horrible. For a few, it was because others, family members, really didn't want to hear about what happened, or how their injuries caused problems. There was for these survivors, perceived indifference to their plight. And indifference was especially cruel because it was expressed by parents. Over time, for most of the survivors, it can be expected that their understanding will change as they attribute unfolding events back to their injury. For some, such attributions are positive: for others, they are not. This process will be further seen in the following chapters.

2

Burn Center Experiences

For many of the survivors in this study, their experiences in the hospital seemed to be at least as traumatic, if not more so, than were their initial burn experiences. For most, their initial experience of being burned lasted only a few moments. During that time, they were absorbed in surviving, in getting away from the fire or the situation in which they were burned. For a few, such as those burned as children or those who were unconscious when they were burned, there is no recall of actually being burned. But for others, there are shard-like memories, pieces of images that are recalled from the initial acute period when they were heavily sedated and critically ill. Some of what is recalled is vivid; these are memories of anguish and unrelenting, interminable pain. These are memories of oneself no longer in control of one's situation, condition, or life.

Sectors of personal experience in the first days or weeks in the burn center are, for many survivors, difficult to recall in any full detail. What can be remembered is available to them, in significant measure, only through accounts by relatives who visited them and from reports by nurses who cared for them. They do not directly recall what happened to them except in bits, pieces, and fragments of dimly recalled, hazy experience, which has a dream-like quality. The accounts and reports by others served to fill in missing sectors of experience for many survivors. Information supplied by others was used by survivors to make sense out of what they experienced during the acute phase of their hospitalization. Reports by others served to define, objectify, and make real experiences that were felt to be distant, remote, and only partially accessible to their own consciousness.

Part of the survivor's own biographical history and identity is therefore available only secondhand, through accounts, reports and information supplied by others. Self-history here becomes inherently intersubjective, meaning that the survivor becomes aware of the fact that without such information supplied by others, they would not know or understand what happened during specific periods of time. Unrecognized periods of time, literally experienced as the absence of the self's consciousness in the world, are stated by several survivors as being "periods of lost time," denoting the subjective feeling that *to lose consciousness of the self, or identity,* suggests losing time because the reflexively objectified self is defined, perceived and experienced as being absent from the world and absent from the passage of events and time. To be absent is to lose any perspective on time. Absence is not experienced as uniform or consistent through a broad, retrospective block of time; rather, it is punctuated and contrasted by remembered fragments, often vividly recalled, others only dimly sensed, of things that occurred during this period of acute illness. Following Berger and Luckmann, the acute phase of injury, during those periods when the survivor is little aware of what is occurring, is conceptualized as subuniverses of meaning that are distinct from the typical wide-awake consciousness which characterizes everyday reality. The meaning of the symbolic subuniverse is uniquely contingent, as noted above, on information supplied by others. The reality of the hospital, as a unique subuniverse of meaning, is starkly and frighteningly different from the person's everyday life. Time and routine become dictated not by the person's self-imposed projects, but by the institutional regimen of care that is mandated by burn center staff and by attending physicians. One's life becomes centered around the "program" (Mannon 1985) of care and recovery, often to the frustration, protestation, and anger of the critically injured patient.

Those elements of the subuniverse that stand out for the survivor as directly experienced and as reportable, serve to anchor the information supplied by others. Those experiences will be treated as concrete, objective, and real in fact and until further notice, that is, they are provisional and subject to subsequent articulation. That the survivor had such experiences will not necessarily be problematic in itself, but the meaning of the experience, the how and why of occurrence, may be inherently problematic for the survivor. In turn, information supplied by others will provide the sense or rationale for the concretely perceived experiences. For example, the survivor may report having nightmares about people chasing him with sharp objects; he may recall screaming about pain and vividly remember being immersed in stinging hot water while nurses pulled skin off his body. He may recall dreams about being skinned alive or she may recall dreams of being chased by "death." He or she may recognize that some of these experiences were dreams and nightmares while others were not, but the survivor may be unable to differentiate clearly between the two. These are experiences that stand out; they are recalled with differential clarity, but they are recalled as subjectively available lived experiences. In "waking up" and reporting such experiences, or in asking family members or nurses about what has been happening, the patient may learn that he or she had been having hallucinations, often softly crying or yelling rather incoherently about pain; and that he or she had been taken to whirlpool baths where dead skin was removed. This explanation can then be "attached" to the subject's own experiences, thereby establishing the coherent meaning of the experiences that were originally perceived as disconnected, nightmarish, and incomprehensible. Both the remembered experiences and those reported by others will potentially be integrated with the elements woven together as if they were a tapestry, into a relatively coherent biographical history for the survivor. As such, the person is constructing a situated definition of identity and self that can be displayed and reported in reference to the question "what happened to you in the hospital?" Questions about what happened in the hospital are not only of importance to others; they are critical to the survivor as he or she attempts to uncover what happened, thereby recovering missing experiences of self. Questions about self and identity are contingent on discovering what happened.

The subjective experience of lost time, the loss of feelings of autonomy and self-control, the experience of pain and suffering, fears of death for some, or wanting to die for others, and the slow recognition that one is going to be forever transformed by being burned are all emergent themes, stated by survivors as concrete, objective experiences during the period of hospitalization. These themes and others will be examined below in specific survivor cases.

Trisha Carson: Vehicle Accident

Trisha did not recall the accident, nor did she know she was burned until she woke up in the burn center at Grove County Hospital, a teaching hospital affiliated with a university. Trisha was burned when the car in which she was a passenger was rear-ended while stopped for a traffic signal. She did not recall any of the initial care she received at the accident site, or in the emergency room. Trisha's last recollection was being in her boyfriend's car. Her next recollection was finding herself badly injured in a burn center. She did not know that she had been burned, and being told that she was burned was not comprehensible in reference to the routine possibilities of her world. Routine understanding pertaining to her being burned, except as a victim of a thermonuclear war, did not seem to exist for her. Being burned suggested to Trisha that she must have been burned in a war:

D: So you were conscious when you were brought to the hospital?

No. I was unconscious the whole time, I never regained consciousness all through the emergency room. And I don't remember a thing until I woke up in the hospital. And I was up in the hospital in bed and I said, "Where am I and why am I here?"and they said, "Well you're in the hospital, at Grove Medical Center Burn Center and you have been burned." In my mind, the only way I could have been burned was by a nuclear war, and I said, "Oh, there was a war?" Well, they thought I didn't have all my senses about me.

One of the first things she recalls after she first woke up in the burn center occurred, she believed, after about two or three weeks had passed. This involved the amputation of part of her right hand. She recalls this, but recognizes that she was unaware of most that took place in the first weeks of her care at the burn center.

> I think it was in the first two or three weeks when I had to make a choice of whether I had any fingers on my right hand. I think for the first several weeks I remember only very vaguely. I remember the first day and the thing that I kept asking them was to get June, who is my best friend. But I couldn't see, my eyes were swollen shut. And they finally got her and June was besides me and talking to me and I said, "Bobby is here isn't he?" and she said, "Yeah, how did you know?" I just knew. I remember little things like that. I knew that the top of my head was burned and this man who is a good friend of mine came in and he's very bald and he said, "Oh, we are going to have to go out and look for hair pieces together." I remember that. And people like my friends say that I will never remember things like they tell me one day, and something else the next day, but I think that that was not because of me but it was because of the drugs. It was gone...it was just gone.

> I don't remember so much the first few days, and after the nerve endings started to mend and that's when I start remembering how painful it was, especially when they took the bandages off. In the morning I knew, I'd always remember crying, I'd have breakfast and I couldn't do anything with my hands so she [her nurse] had to feed me. She would brush my teeth and then give me an injection. It was morphine. And then I would have twenty minutes for that to take effect and then they would start taking off the bandages.

For Trisha, the fact that she was given drugs serves as a basis for her to understand how it was that she was unaware of what occurred to her. That "it was gone," "it" being conscious awareness of experience, is interpreted in reference to information supplied to her after the fact by others, most commonly the others would be medical or nursing staff, as well as family members and friends. In this manner, that which is missing, her awareness of herself for a block of time, comes to make sense to her and that which is missing can be comprehended and integrated into her biography, or her history, even though she has, in fact, no direct awareness of that history.

D: So with the morphine, was there still pain?

Oh, yes.   In the morning we would take the bandages off and then
they would put sheets around me and then wheel me down the hall
into the hydro room.   But I couldn't have the sheets touching my
head because it was too painful! My shoulders were covered. It was
just like somebody took a knife,...I never want to remember the pain I
went through again. It was terrible to take the bandages off, I had so
much pain. Get to the bath, get out, get into bed. What was the
worst thing was getting them off, getting into the chair.

D: So they also took the bandages off at your bed?

By the time I got out of the tub and back to the burn unit and then
they would put bandages back on and then I would ask for another
pill. The one thing I remember is being so cold. You would just
shake and sometimes they would bring those [heat] lamps.

Trisha contrasted how she reacted to the pain of being burned with
how another patient reacted. The other patient was the man in whose car
she was burned. He was also burned, but much less extensively than was
Trisha. She was speaking about differences between the ways in which
women and men cope with pain and the contrast was offered between
herself and her boyfriend who sustained relatively minor burns in the
accident.

A case in point is the man that I was in the accident with. He would
just moan and groan and my friends would come out of the room and
they just couldn't believe it, I mean they didn't know whether I was
going to live or die and he was just burned on the back of his head
and on the back of his hands and they were covered up.

Trisha had little support from this man after he recovered. He rarely
visited her and their relationship did not continue. I also believe that she
felt he was responsible for her injuries being so severe since he did nothing
to get her out of the burning car, even though he was not unconscious
after the accident, and he was able to extricate himself from the 300 Z. Her
friends could not understand why he was complaining so much since his
burns were not severe. She embeds her friend's interpretation of his
reactions within her conception of her own reactions to the burn. His
reactions to his burns, moaning and groaning, as reported to her by her
friends, became a basis for comparing herself to him. In turn, this definition
provided her interpretation for the presumed differences between the
reactions of men and women to pain.
      In addition to the issues presented by the loss of direct experience
and by pain, Trisha spoke of other problems that confronted her, such as

the loss of contact with others. Fortunately, she was able to have visitors and they provided critical support during her hospitalization.

D: You were able to have visitors in the burn center?

> Yes, they had surgical gowns on. I would have died without them. One day when I was in terrible pain, it hurt so bad, it must have been a day after debridement, my friend came by and I said, "Please rub my forehead." Everyone would hold my feet, because they couldn't do much with my hands.

When Trisha speaks of dying in the absence of visits by friends, she is, I believe, speaking of emotionally withering in the presence of unrelenting physical as well as psychological challenges that confronted her on a daily, hourly, and moment-to-moment basis. She is speaking of the self; she is reflexively defining the self in reference to the situation she faced, and she finds that it was through the presence of others that she could go on. What she says here, does not differ remarkably from what many others reported. Many survivors attributed their survival, in part, to the support they received from family and friends.

D: Your friends were important in supporting you?

> If they hadn't been there to help me, I wouldn't have had anybody. My family was all gone, they were in the Midwest. But they [burn center staff] would let me have anybody I wanted to have, any hour of the day as long as I wanted to see them. And as I said, I never had too many people in the room. But they came a long way to see me...I could have never done it without them before, during or after the fire.

Peter Shrader
(Interviewed with his wife, Lynn)

Peter was initially transported to a small hospital that serves a developing area west of Los Angeles. He was stabilized in the emergency room and some of his burned clothing was removed before he was transferred to Valley Burn Center, which was approximately twenty-five miles from where he was injured. He recalls parts of the initial experience of being transported to the emergency room (ER) and he remembers some of what took place in the ER, but his direct knowledge of what transpired in the burn center, during the first two or three weeks, is almost nonexistent. He has vague memories and images, and he can recall bits and pieces of what happened, but it isn't clear. For the most part, his experience of what happend is available through information supplied by other, especially by his wife.

D: Were you in much pain?

Oh, yeah, I was. It was burning, a real tremendous burning sensation. I was,...what was really weird was I was more concerned with them getting hold of my wife. And gave them my home address and everything saying, "Please call my wife." There was nothing really else on my mind at that time, it seemed like, well 'cause I wasn't all there anyway, I was in shock, and I couldn't really say whether they were ignoring me, or you know. It seemed like it took a long time for her to get there.

Lynn was the one who decided what burn facility Peter would be taken to, Valley or County, and part of the decision was based on insurance coverage. Valley would only take patients if they had insurance, and both Lynn and Peter felt fortunate that they still had insurance from the job he had just left. A factor in Lynn's decision to have Peter taken to Valley Burn Center was her belief that at County, he would be the subject for experimentation since she knew it was a teaching facility. Another element in her interpretation was the fact that she had once been in school with someone who had been burned and she was afraid of the care he might receive at County. She was concerned with what Peter might look like if he did not receive the best available care. The "best care" was defined by Lynn as being available at a private hospital:

And I know they'd be experimenting, I know they experiment and stuff down there...I just wanted him someplace where I knew he was gonna get the best treatment that he could get. I was all freaked out anyway. I...once I found out about the burn, when I saw him, and he was completely black, it scared me. Because I've seen people with burns before [someone with scars she defined as being from a burn], and I'm wondering what's gonna happen, you know. What's he gonna look like when this is all over with. Not that...now it wouldn't matter. At that time, that's what was going through my head.

D: Did you know, before you saw him, that he was burned?

Yes. Then they told me what happened. They didn't want to scare me on the phone, they wanted me to be able to drive up there safely. All they would tell me on the phone is that he had been in an accident and that he was asking for his wife.

D: What happened when you saw him?

I was crying, he just told me "Hi," and "I love you." I thought he was going to die. I knew that he was real bad when I looked at him. They told me he was burnt. They didn't have to tell me the extent, I don't think they even knew, because they were just keeping him there, to transfer him somewhere else till I got there. And when they told me what happened, well..., I passed the accident site on the way down there. And I thought, and I told my daughter, I says, "Oh, my God, I wonder if." You know, "that was terrible, I wonder who was in that?" And then I realized afterwards that that was probably where he had the accident [his vehicle was already gone so she didn't see it]. And when they told me...all I could do..., all I remember is sitting down in the hallway right on the ground and just crying before I could even walk in to see him. It really scared me. I didn't know what to expect. And then I saw him, and I saw his face was black, that scared me even worse. It was terrible to see him,...the skin was burned off his face and arms, and the smell made me sick. I'll never forget how he looked, and the terrible smell.

D: Before you saw him did they tell you what his condition was?

No. I never found that out until later. Dr. Berris came out and talked to me and told me he didn't have a chance, that he would die in three days, that the burns were too extensive. I mean, he gave me a lot of hope there! The whole time he was in the hospital, they gave him no hope. But he pulled through anyway. I mean, the man was just, there was no hope at all. But they're amazed how he did heal. And how good he's doing now.

In passing the accident site, Lynn suggests the suspicion that it was where Peter's accident may have occurred. This thought was dropped until after she learned what had actually happened. The scene she had witnessed previously, the meaning of which was problematic and only tacitly suggested to her by its very appearance, and which was then manifested in terms of her knowledge that Peter had been in some type of accident, is now understood in a new light, in a new configuration, which is significant to her as depicting what happened to Peter. Her understanding was constructed over time. The full meaning of what she saw as she originally drove past the accident had a "wait and see" quality to it, the actual meaning requiring prospective information which was not yet available. This suggests how experience, meaning, and knowledge are time-embedded accomplishments, contingent upon, in this case, information supplied by others. Here "others" refers to nurses who told Lynn what had happened. More broadly, this suggests how reality is situationally fabricated as a humanly achieved artefact. That Lynn went through this constructive process is, for her, neither an issue nor is it problematic. It is taken-for-granted. How Peter is doing now, as Lynn's assessment in the present, is informed and contrasted with Peter's previous condition as she understood it. Her understanding of his previous condition, which was especially grave, provides, in part, for a definition of how well he is now doing, in spite of other unstated problems he might now have. The surgeon's conservative assessment is referenced in understanding how critical Peter was, as well as in understanding how well he is now.[1] Her account displays the historical, interpretive features which she utilizes, but which she takes for granted, as she constructs an assessment in the present.

In reference to several accounts by survivors, the surgeon's conservative approach to informing the family about the patient's prognosis appears routine. The rationale for this is that it is a way of managing the bad news that can be anticipated by medical staff. The family then, at least in terms of the medical information they have been given, has a basis for preparing for the worst.

While it seems clear, from the survivor accounts gathered in this research, that the surgeon is often very cautious in informing the family about the medical trajectory anticipated for the patient, it is equally clear that surgeons typically ignore their own judgments; at least they ignore what they tell the family by aggressively fighting to save the life of the patient. This is another way in which clinical judgments about the patient's condition and assumed outcome are provisional. Many survivors interviewed in this study are here in spite of initial assessments that suggested that they could not survive. Though the family may be told that their loved one has little, if any, chance for surviving, the surgeon and medical staff will fight, often against incredibly poor odds, to prove themselves wrong. This attitude, in part, accounts for pushing the limits of burn survival well past boundaries that were thought to be invariant just a few years ago.

D: You apparently had some serious complications. What do you recall?

> **Peter:** I do remember that when Dr. Berris finally talked to me. They were scared. The first three or four weeks they couldn't touch me 'cause my lungs were so bad. They had to cut my throat open.

> **Lynn:** It wasn't that long, hon.

> **Peter:** Well, that's what it felt like.

> **Lynn:** They started that debrasing [debriding] and everything right away, about a week afterwards.

Peter: Yeah, he was talking to me, at that time, I guess my lungs
were filled with smoke and he said that if they had done surgery, the
wrong thing would have killed me. And they were really scared to
do anything at all. And I guess at that time also, my ear, see, I don't
remember a lot of this, because I had trouble with my ear.

D: I can see that your ear was badly burned. Was it just on one side?

Peter: Yes, just on the right side.

Lynn: Well, the other one was burned but not off. It's got just a
little skin grafting on the left ear but the right one was real bad.

Peter: See, at that time I was out of it, so I didn't know what was
going on. He [ear, nose and throat specialist] told my wife that he
was worried about my hearing, whether I'd be able to hear the same
when I got out of this.

D: Do you remember any of this time in the hospital?

Peter: The first three or four weeks I don't remember any of it. They
tell me I was going through a whirlpool and all this other stuff. And
the chamber [high pressure oxygen therapy in a sealed, hyperbaric
chamber]...being put in the chamber. I don't remember any of that
part.

    As with other survivors, Peter's recollection of the first days and
weeks of his care in the burn center is not remembered. In order to
understand what happened to him, he must reference information supplied
by others. Elsewhere in the interview, Peter does recall some events or
images, such as his attempts to get out of bed and go home, but these are
tenuous and shadowy remembrances.
    Lynn continued to work through most of this time; she took off only
the first week when she virtually lived at the hospital. She felt that
working kept her mind off what she and Peter were facing. The burn
injury radically altered not only Peter's life but Lynn's life as well.
Routine activities, such as going to work, eating lunch, and picking up
their daughter from school were altered to fit new demands that were
perceived as imposed on her situation. Working was seen as an asset
which kept her busy, as was the support of their daughter whom Lynn
mentioned several times.

    It kept me busy through it, which helped a lot. I don't think I would
    have been able to handle it as well if I'd been sitting down there all
    the time like a few other women did, with their husbands. I couldn't

have done that I don't think. I did start smoking again, through all this. But the drive was just exhausting. I'd go to work at 7:00, leave at 2:00 without a lunch, come back here and pick up my daughter, which is about a half-hour drive, and then drive back out there which is about forty-five minutes and sometimes it was a hour and a half depending on the traffic.

Lynn could never anticipate how Peter would be when she reached the burn center since his condition fluctuated on a daily basis. This fact was especially difficult for her. One day he would be doing well, and the next day he would be in a crisis:

One day he'd be fine, the next thing, one day, I walked in and there's machines flying all over the place into his room. The nurse turned me around and said, "Go in the waiting room, his lungs collapsed." And then I sat back out there. That time I was alone, I didn't have my daughter with me. You never know what to expect. He'd be fine for three or four days and then his lungs would collapse again or something else would go wrong.

Several other spouses described similar experiences where they were never certain of what was going on or what might happen to their loved one. The situation was one of prolonged anxiety and fear. Often such experiences would go on for many weeks in cases involving persons who were more critically injured. Walt, in speaking about Sara,[1] describes the situation as one of waiting, in a heightened sense of awareness, or concern:

Most I could say is that you have this feeling that you're sitting on the edge, that you're sitting on a keg of dynamite all the time. Not depressed, but on edge, ready for anything.

The above statements suggest that the subjective experience of the world is routine, that our trust in the world is stable, at least provisionally, and until further notice, that we can take-the-world-for-granted,[2] and feel that we are at home in it.[3] The sense of stability in the world, the person's sense of security in the routine "giveness" of the world is lost. Stability is lost to the condition of not knowing what is going to happen next. Stability, for a spouse like Lynn or Walt, as a feeling about one's world, is inextricably linked to the changing condition of the loved other. Personal feelings of security, and trust in the presumption that tomorrow will be like today, may be lost. It can be seen here that this experience extends not just to the burn victim, but to family members as well. Fortunately, for most, the sense and feeling of stability, which is lost, can be rediscovered as

* Walt and Sara, not discussed elsewhere, were burned in a brush fire.

things settle down, as the crises become less frequent, and as the survival of the patient becomes more assured. Sitting "on the edge," waiting for something untoward to happen, aptly describes the feelings of many survivors and family members.

D: Peter, what is the first thing you remember at Valley?

> About the fourth week I was there, the first three weeks I lost. And I didn't really wake up until, or realize what was happening, it was the start of the fourth week. All I remember is I woke up.

D: And what do you remember?

> I remember bandages around my face, and that kinda scared me a little bit, when I woke up. My face was surrounded with bandages and I could just look out.

D: Do any particular things stand out?

> Not really. I wanted to get up and go home. I remember that 'cause I was very strong willed. And my wife says, couple of times, I got out of the bed. And I had IVs in both arms, and I was hooked up to oxygen. I'd take everything out. I remember the nurses yelling at me.

> **Lynn:** And walk down the hall because he [thought] he was coming home.

> **Peter:** I remember them yelling at me,... things were bothering me. I had trouble breathing at that time. They kept having something in my mouth and it hurt me, so I kept taking it out and then somebody would come in and yell at me. Because I was taking things off I shouldn't have been.

> **Lynn:** When his lungs collapsed the first time, they did a trach, real quick. They had it in his mouth at first, plus they had a feeder tube, they had a tube going over in here, into his lungs, draining it, which was just gross. He was hooked up to all the life support systems. He had IV's..., God, I felt sorry for those nurses though, because I'm sure that eighty times a day they were hooking him all back up. They'd hook him up, he'd pull it back out. They finally had to tie him to the bed, feet and hands to where he couldn't [get up].

> **Peter:** I didn't realize. I do remember them telling me they had to tie me down to the bed 'cause I would take things out. And they finally

wound up tying my hands down. And now I do remember Dr. Berris and somebody else coming in and yelling at me, telling me to leave things alone, that I was taking things out and I shouldn't be doing it.

What is seen here is not only Peter's reported experience as he recalls nurses yelling at him, but also how he constructs part of that experience *in the present* for himself and for me, basing the construction, at least in part, on information supplied by Lynn. Accounting for what happened became an intersubjective task where, in effect, a script was created. He directly recalls distant things that occurred, based on what Lynn recalls, about the events in the hospital. These experiences seem to emerge out of a fog of consciousness, with Lynn supplying the opening through the haze by reporting events to which Peter can anchor his account. His biography is intersubjectively constituted between himself and Lynn, relative to their attempt to produce an answer to my question. In somewhat different terms, we also see how the self is situationally constructed as a self-reflexive object* and how an identity is created, each intersubjectively, through the interactive dialectic of language.

D: In any way, do you think you understood how seriously you were burned?

Not really. At that time, I just started a new job and I was concerned about that job and I wanted to get back to that job. I had to go to work. And I didn't care what I looked like. But see, at that time, when I woke up after three weeks, I was in pain, but it didn't bother me that much. I guess some people can tolerate more pain. It's something that happened that I just have to live with. I wanted to get up and just walk out, which I guess I tried a couple times. I remember going over the bed. They had the bed all the way up and I jumped over the railing, and my wife said it took a several nurses to get me back in bed. That's all I remember. I was afraid of losing my job. That was more important to me than anything.

D: Was there some point when you decided you weren't going anywhere?

Yeah, basically when I got to the other side [the subacute unit]. And I could start doing things for myself. At that time I was quite upset with the nurses. I guess I gave them a real bad time and all I wanted to do was lay in bed. And they wanted me to do this and do that and I didn't want to do that.

---

* This is discussed in the next chapter.

I wouldn't eat. The doctor came up, one of the young doctors came in there and jumped all over my case. I know that because I lost forty pounds. I wasn't hungry and I didn't want to eat. I drank, I was into fluids. And then they finally got to the point that they put a big sign on my window, I remember that, "This patient is not to drink anything until he starts eating." No fluids until I started eating. He came in there and a nurse was gonna give me something to drink and he took it away from me. I remember that. I went a day without eating or drinking anything and it just got to the point where I had to have something to drink, and the only way I could get anything to drink is if I ate. So I just gave in and started eating. Everything they put in front of me, I ate. Then they let me have anything I wanted.

D: Did the doctors tell you what was going on most of the time?

Lynn: No, they didn't, to me they didn't care about the spouse, they only cared about the patient. The doctor would catch me once in a while. I did talk to the nurses several times, they would tell me, "Oh, he's doing so good today." or "He's not doing so good today." And that was about the extent of it. Just that there was no hope, no hope at all. He wasn't going to make it through, he was gonna die, and all this stuff. I thought a doctor was at least supposed to be a little optimistic. And after he lasted a week, the doctor said, "Well, he still won't last another week."

D: Did you try calling him or getting in touch with him?

He was just never around. I know I called his office more than a couple of times but, you know, after you call several times. I said, forget it. I knew they were taking good care of him, 'cause I was looking at the results.

D: What were you thinking when you kept being told that he wasn't going to live, that he was just hanging on. What did this do to you?

By looking at him in there, how stubborn he was, if he didn't die within the first three days like they said, there was a good possibility that he would live. I'd get scared once in a while when his lungs collapsed, and all those machines would be flying...scare you half to death. But, you know, then you just go and sit and wait and wonder, did he make it through, or did he die. You've always, I always was thinking, well, maybe he's gonna die or...,but then, your thinking, maybe he's not! It keeps you confused, the whole two months I was there with him, they kept me confused. And I knew God was there with him, and that's what helped me through all this too.

There are several interesting statements here that suggest how Lynn defined Peter's condition and how she decided, provisionally, that Peter was going to survive. "How stubborn he was" refers to her definition of Peter's character. "Stubborn" is part of her schema for understanding what and who Peter is, and in this case she relates her assessment of a characterological trait to surviving. That he is stubborn implies that he does not give in, he does not give up and that he is a fighter. Both Lynn and Peter, during other parts of the interview, made references to Peter's stubbornness as providing an explanation for his survival. This character trait, which both she and Peter locate as an objective feature of his personality, is then tied to, or becomes an index of, his medical status.[4] As such, stubbornness is embedded in a temporal horizon within which Lynn finds, has found, or could find instances of stubbornness that she could then display by providing categorical instances of such behavior. The horizon is tacit, it is not articulated, it is not specifically defined, but it is necessarily present in her emergent definition (McHugh 1968). Were she questioned about how Peter is stubborn, her answers would constitute a biographical history for Peter. The whole point here is that her definition, or her assessment, is temporal, situated, and problematic, and that it is used to constitute a definition or explanation of how he survived a devastating injury that might have otherwise killed him.

Secondly, her statement that if Peter didn't die after the first three days, he probably had a good chance of surviving, is directly linked to the initial assessment made by the surgeon, but it is obviously connected to only part of what the surgeon said. The surgeon's assessment was exceptionally bleak, but here Lynn, in implicitly referring to the fact that the assessment was in error, finds in the failure of the negative assessment a basis for hope. She mistrusts the surgeon's assessment, or she would have given up hope that Peter would survive. This definition also is temporally constituted as she necessarily refers to the passing of three days, that is, she refers to his history over this period of time, she refers to what happened to him during this time in actuality, in contrast to what the surgeon said would happen. This retrospective construction suggests a future course of events for Peter that she projects or anticipates, namely, her feeling that he will therefore survive. This depicts the open, future-anticipating and horizonal character of reality and world construction.

Lynn probably went through ruminations, iterations, and reiterations of all that the doctor said; she probably agonized over what he said, but in the end, she finds hope in what was a negative judgment and she then suspends trust, or comes to place in doubt, assessments made by the same physician who furnished her the grounds to find hope. What is of consequence here is that this displays the process through which Lynn actively produces her interpretation. Her interpretation was a gestalt, this was one of its constituent features as was her reference to Peter's stubbornness.

The other part of her assessment was based on her reference to God protecting or healing Peter. Further on in the interview, this theme was elaborated.

D: At any time did you feel you might not live, did that ever occur to you?

No. I knew when I was sitting on the ground, and I got out of the car and saw the car explode. I knew that I was gonna live. There wasn't any doubt in my mind. And I didn't think it was as bad as they said it was until I saw the pictures, and 'till the doctors told me. When I got to the hospital, and they finally put me on the good side, the doctors would come in there, even doctor Gersing would come in there, and look at me. He looked me right in the eye one day, I remember, and said, "I don't even know how you made it through this." He says, "By all rights, you should be dead. No way you should be alive." I knew I was gonna live. And I knew everything was gonna be okay eventually.

When Peter was in the burning car, he knew if he didn't get out he would be killed. As noted above and in the last chapter, it was in getting out and in seeing the car burning that Peter knew he would survive. It was not until he saw pictures of himself, and until his surgeon frankly spoke to him, that he realized how extensively he was injured. This has been similarly reported by other survivors and I wonder if their initial ignorance affords some physiological protection. Had they understood early their initial condition, one wonders if some of them might not have survived.

Eric Mathews: Vehicle Accident

Eric was transported to a large burn center following his accident. His burns covered approximately 95 percent of his body. Much of the burn was deep, in some places down to bone. Some fingers were so badly burned that they had to be amputated. His nose was destroyed and was subsequently reconstructed, as was one eyelid. Here, Eric is discussing his hospitalization.

I remember the ambulance drive there, but that was in and out. I was talking to them, and they thought that was bizarre knowing how much I was burned. And then, at the hospital, one of the nurses just happened to come up and grab me. There was so much pain that the instinct was just to get away. Because of the adrenalin that was being pumping from being in shock, I just tossed her across the room. Some woman grabbed me and it was just automatic. She thought I was on PCP, and stuff like that but it was just natural. They grabbed me to put me down on the table and stuff like that. It was just instinct on my part just to get away from the pain.

D: And what do you recall about the hospitalization?

From that point they put you on morphine. The morphine has a disorienting effect. So I was already in a situation where my senses were in overwhelm, in pain and a disoriented sense to begin with. And then the morphine added to it and so it was like the bottom falling out of the floor.

D: And you were on a circle bed?*

Yeah. So the disorienting effect of the burn and trauma of that plus the disorientation of the drugs, then you're in a bed that, at times, I was almost upside down. And so, it was complete bewilderment. There's no firm ground to put your foot on. There's even no awareness of what's right side up. For the first two months, I think also because of the severity of the burn, I was floating in and out of awareness. I'd be talking, making sense, when all of a sudden I'd slip into something else. The family and friends at that point were, well, "He's not all there." And worried about those things.

For Eric, his violent behavior toward the nurse is understood as a consequence of an automatic, unavoidable response to pain and being touched. In this way, untoward action, which would otherwise not be like his normal conduct, is stated as not implicating him as a conscious, moral agent in his conduct. The nurse's belief, if what Eric depicts is correct, that he was using PCP, is a moral assessment made by her, and it is based upon his situational behavior. For the nurse, that assessment explicates Eric's behavior in reference to presumed conduct outside the fact that Eric was burned. Eric's reference to an automatic response, which is an interpretation of the cause of his behavior, serves to distance him as culpable for his action while his explanation for how he could throw a nurse across the room is referred back to his previous physical condition.

The statements by Eric elegantly depict the devastating effects of the burn. He cogently describes the experience of one who is thrown into a bizarre world like those depicted by the artist Isher, a world which is radically alien and strange; he is estranged from the world of everyday experience which he had previously taken-for-granted. His experience

---

* A Stryker bed, consisting of a narrow bed suspended between two large steel circles or rings, allows the patient's position to be rotated and changed. Stryker beds are commonly used for spinal cord injuries, and very large burns.

illustrates what was theoretically described previously as the collapse or shattering of the everyday world of reality. There is no firm ground for Eric, the world as he has known it has literally been destroyed. He is disoriented and there is no firm ground upon which the self can be oriented. There is no firm ground to put his feet on. His description suggests that he is cast adrift in a world of radically altered spaciality and temporality.

> The fact that I was burned, the fact that the doctors and nurses had been preparing the family that I wasn't going to make it,..they were preparing for me to die. They saw those effects of seemingly nonsensical talking. And through that, there were certain points that I would agree that I had hallucinations. I would agree that I was disoriented but I would also say that there were experiences again of the light, as you would say, "out of body," that I knew was going on. I watched them taking care of me and I watched myself in the debridement and different experiences like that. Also, there was an awareness of hearing them, but not being able to express it because of the respirator and all that.

> The body itself was so damaged that it could not be used for what it normally would have, anyway. And so the awareness, the spirit, this entity which houses this body could depart from the body. And God. I give credit to God. The reason I'm still here is because of God.

His "near death" experience extended to the hospital and to part of his initial care. It is not important here to wonder if he did in fact have a near death experience. What is important here is that he defines his experience in that way, and it is through his definition that he forms a retrospective understanding of what happened to him. Furthermore, through this definition he is able to provisionally understand how he could experience himself as detached from his body, a most extraordinary experience. Regardless of any challenge raised by others to the authenticity of his experience, for Eric his experiences were real and, as such, they constitute his reality. It is also noted that he attributes his survival, in part, to God and to guidance from an entity, a young girl, who appeared to him during his accident.

D: What was the hospitalization like?

> Well, at first there wasn't any energy, so I was cooperative because I had no choice. They did everything for me: eating, going to the bathroom, bathing...hour after hour. I was fortunate to have Dr. Gresslings working on me and one of the nurses, hour after hour,

doing above the normal bit of debridement, just clipping off all of my dead skin.

D: Were you sedated when this occurred?

Well, the first two months, it was disorientation. Then I finally snapped to. One day that I remember really coming back was, I was asking about who won the Super Bowl and she goes, "That was two months ago!" "Two months ago? Wow, who won?" Because I was so far shaken up, on my way back, it was all so slow, time, coming back into it. For the rest of the time, it was just a new experience for me, which was to be tired. I usually had the energy of three people or more. The sensation of not being able to do anything physically. I would move, I was exercising what I could, but there was just not much movement going on. To not be able just to lift my head or my legs or anything. Not to be able to talk. And at that point I would say I was too exhausted to even cry.

The return to consciousness is described as a "snapping to," a coming back from or a waking up[5] to the world. Time is that to which his conscious self returns, as if the self has been away, and "snapping" to is the condition of returning. The body he found upon emerging into consciousness was drastically different from his familiar body. Exercise now was defined as small movements, to move just a little was an accomplishment. It is as if he woke up to find himself inhabiting a different body, and indeed, this was the case. "Coming back into it" represents a return to the world of the living, a coming back from unconsciousness. This represents a return of self to the world of consciousness from a place where the self was unavailable to Eric. Interestingly, while he did not exist for himself during his absence from consciousness, he did exist for others through rantings, ravings, and talking, both nonsensical and otherwise. For the cleaning staff, he was very funny, while for his family, he was out of it.

D: I assume you were splinted?

I had pins and bolts, tubes, wires... I looked like a machine.

D: And you were still trying to exercise?

Exactly. I think I was trying to look and see what kind of motion I did have. And in the process I was working. So it was just trying to examine my body and see.

D: Where were you burned the worst?

I would say my chest, my arms and my face. At the beginning they used cadaver and pig skin. And then I was a test case for a synthetic skin or dressing. And so, fortunately again, all the forces came together at the time where I needed it.

D: What do you recall about the hospitalization?

Well, you're a twenty year old, athletic guy who all of a sudden has to have nurses help you pee, get dressed, feed you, and you can't put on your own gown. That's a very big thing. There was a time with the physical therapist, where she was doing something I disagreed with. We got into arguments, so I blamed her. She didn't know what she was doing. Then the occupational therapist: her job was to help me find out what I could do. And my ego wasn't willing able to accept the fact that I couldn't do what she said, she laid out a gown for me to put on. And I couldn't even put on the gown. And I felt like I was a little worm, squirming. I couldn't even get it on.

Exercise, which had been a critical part of Eric's life, became a feature of his stay in the burn center. His movements were severely restricted, and discovering what motion he still retained was a way of assessing his body. Exercise, even if it consisted only of slight movements, was also a way of maintaining his connection to his previous life. Eric stated that all the forces came together at the time he needed them. He had setbacks, there were numerous crises with which he was confronted, but what he suggested, throughout the interview, was a resolute determination that he was not going to be overcome by the injury. He projected a positive, future-anticipating orientation, which was not lost in the face of crises, failures, and depression. He was able to transcend these situations and find hope.

Eric's statements also reveal the degradation and humiliation he felt, the loss of control and autonomy and the loss of the world he had known. He has no privacy and no autonomy; nurses must help him urinate, eat, and dress. He has lost all privacy as his body is assaulted on a daily basis and he feels like a squirming worm.

D: Were you often angry?

Yes. But I couldn't accept the anger, so I blamed them. I was angry at you, I was angry at them.

D: Did you lash out?

No, I didn't. There were times, especially with the drugs, when I went from highs to lows. The people who would clean up would say, "You were the funniest guy, I've never heard anything so funny." And sometimes they'd go, "Well, I've never heard so many dirty words." You're pulled beyond the normal stretch of endurance of anything. Physically, mentally, emotionally, you're pulled to the extreme. And that's where a lot of people snap. So, from that point on, I was blaming everybody else because they weren't doing a good enough job, because I wasn't getting healed fast enough. Towards the end of the year, that's what I was thinking. I was going, "It's been a year and I'm not back." My conception of the burn and burn care, I still wasn't back. I felt like I should be better now.

Tacitly, Eric compares himself with those who snap, who are destroyed by their injury. He felt pulled beyond normal endurance. He finds himself in a limit situation where he is at the point of breaking. He is thrown into the most extreme possibilities, without recourse, into a nightmarish condition where others have responsibility for his being and care. He finds many ways to discover strength in the adversity of his injury. He recognizes that he was pushed to the outer limits of endurance, but, in enduring, he discovers strength, even though he also found that he wasn't healing fast enough. He was discovering just how extensively he was injured and this discovery was structured in reference to time-bound definitions about himself. From being in the hospital, he had projected himself into a future state of assumed and anticipated conditions, where he would be healed and well, but in reaching that future point in time, he found himself still not healed, not better. His statement refers to a period of time after he left the hospital; he had many trips back for surgical procedures. He blamed others for the fact that he was not yet healed, but he eventually learned to take responsibility for his body and for what he wanted his body to be.

D: Did you ever think you would die?

No. It's hard to explain; I had people tell me as soon as they could get hold of a gun, they'd end it. And I know people who've been burned who say if it happened again, they would not want to go through it again. And I understand that. But to me, it was, "Well, you got hurt, you've got to get better." That's all it was. Going through all of it, I didn't know what I was going to go through. I didn't really consider that I wished I was dead. I wish it hadn't happened, but I don't wish I was dead.

When I was in the hospital after this burn, for one thing it should have killed me, but it didn't. So I knew there was more than they

[doctors] knew. Which made me curious: well, what is there about
the body? I woke up from the bolts and pins in my fingers. I woke
up with a quarter-inch bolt through my jaw.

D: What was that for?

Because of the contractures of my neck, that I was basically looking
straight down all the time, and my neck melted together. They had to
cut it from ear to ear, stretch it out, and take skin and put it there.
They took the donor site from my leg, they lifted that, cut my neck,
stretched it back, sewed it in. They put the bolt going through my
jaw from the inside, coming out the other side. Like Frankenstein
basically, around the back part of the jaw. And I woke up, and I had
this bolt here. Well, to me, I go, "Don't you have your jugular, your
voice box, your throat there? Isn't there things that are important
and wouldn't you die if that happened?"

D: What was that like, you knew they were putting it there?

Scared the hell out of me. First of all, I didn't think I could have that
there. They decided that while I was in there [in surgery]. And the
second thing they decided, when I came out, is that they weren't
going to use it. So I go, "First, why? Second, if you're not going to
use it, why did you not take this bolt out while I was under anesthe-
sia?" Whatever the reason, they decided after the fact.

D: So you were never bolted into the brace, then what?

Well, they tried to use the brace; it didn't look good, I guess, so it
wasn't going to work. So they came in again, I'm thinking, "modern
technology, we're going for it." They walk in with a Black &
Decker bolt cutter and drill,....and fear. It's like the old pictures of a
dentist, going in with just a pair of pliers. Well, he just got up there
on the bed, one knee against my shoulder, and with the bolt cutters
plopped off one end of it, put the drill on the other end, and they just
pulled it through.

They gave me a shot. But it's still the fact that I wanted to be
nowhere in awareness when this was going on. So I felt it. I felt the
teeth, the threads going through my bones, through my jaw, in my
body. And they were pulling it out. And the factor they weren't
thinking about was that metal on bone causes heat. And that was
the point I had to tell them to stop because it got too hot. So they'd
stop for a while, then they would restart it again. So I was going,
"This is bizarre. This is real bizarre."

D: So you often did not know what they were going to do?

> There's a plan beforehand, and you sign for it. And so, while they're in there, and I understand it. They have a plan, but the body does not work out like their plan. It doesn't go like a machine all the time. So, they've got to make some decisions at that point. The bolts seemed like a good idea, so I'm not going to get down on them for it. At the time I was pissed, I was very pissed and I was pissed for a long time afterwards, "Well, what else?"

From the above description it can be understood that Eric entered surgery not knowing that a bolt was to be implanted through his jaw. Finding the bolt was frightening enough. He could not understand how the bolt could be placed through his jaw without causing further damage. But the more invasive issue was the fact that the bolt had to be removed, almost as soon as it was inserted. This vividly depicts Eric's loss of control over his life. Not only does he not control what is being done to him, but he does not always even know what is planned. He understands the necessity of his care, but he must still grapple with accepting his status as a very different person, in a very different world.

D: Tell me about reconstructing your nose.

> They said it would take a month. So I also knew, with the help of the therapist [a psychologist], that I could call upon my body to increase the amount of human chemicals and allow my body to do its job. I was increasing everything. I said, whatever my body does, it's going to increase. So everything they estimated, it took me half the time.

D: The therapist, would she help you?

> I was just lying there. I had medications, which I kept refusing. I didn't need it. I had a whole collection, at one point, of all the drugs they kept giving me. I told them I didn't want it. To me, it was like the drugs were designed to slow down the body, so they're slowing down the healing process. I didn't want that. If there was pain, I didn't want to hide from that pain; I wanted to learn to deal with that pain.

While Eric lost control over what he originally felt was most of his life, he discovered, through hypnosis and meditation, that he had some control over his body. He saw the efficacy of his work in the healing time. This provided some sense of control. He still had control of his mind, and he could use his mind to control his body. Besides finding that he had no

external control over his life, Eric felt that he gave away his power; but he
slowly realized that he was responsible for rebuilding his life:

Well, I had the belief that I was gonna heal, and I was going to be
able to do things. So they said I was going to die, and I didn't die.
They said I might walk in a year, and I did beforehand. Then they
said these other things, and it was more like they were slapping me in
the face. And it was like, "Well, I'll show you." And that helped
carry me through, but I still wasn't accepting that I gave away my
power to live. It was their responsibility to do it [to care for him].

I had lots of thoughts going through my head that I wanted to do all
these things, so by the time they came and got me in a wheelchair
and took me to out, do the bandages, do the tubbing, change the
bandages, wheel me over to occupational therapy,... I was already
wiped out by then. Just sitting up and going to that place and I was
tired. Getting in the tub, out of the tub, I was even more exhausted.
What eventually happened, I was blaming the doctors; "You're not
doing your job right." But the awareness that came from that was,
"Well, then I'm going to do it." The doctor had his job, which was
the surgery; the nurses had theirs, which was the wound care. And
they did a lot of psychological work...they don't get paid for it... and
emotional supporting, and kindness. And the occupational therapists
had their job; the physical therapists had jobs. Then I came to the
realization: it's not what happened to me, but where do I want to go
from here?

So it came to a period from the past, down to the present, and the
situation I was at, and from looking where I was to where I wanted to
go. It's because I knew I was in a bad situation that I knew I didn't
want to stay there. So it's like, "How are you going to stop this, and
where are you going to go?" You're thinking that people don't get
over that "Why me?" They're also not willing to look at what's
going on right now. There's a lot that happens with the acceptance
of "This is who I am, this is the situation that I am in." Most of the
problems are, people can't identify that. They're in their illusionary
world of "This is how I want to be," and not looking at how it is. So
when you're saying "Why?" this is not what I want. "Why me?"
there is no real answer to that. The humor came back, "Why not?"
It's funny to me, not to other people. The question then becomes,
"Well, what am I going to do now that it did happen?" And that's
where my focus was.

D: You have referred to giving away your power, what was that?

I would say it was the first year I went through the main discovery of
what was going on. First, all the "I can'ts." Second, I gave away
my power. I go, "You're the doctor, you went to school. You're
supposed to know what to do, so I'm giving you the responsibility,
doctor. You heal me, you've got all these machines, now do it."

Eric elegantly presents the process of self-discovery that he was
entering and going through. In another place, he stated that the burn,
"Set me down and I had nowhere to run, but to look inside." In the
marginal situation of deep crisis, many survivors confront realities and
possibilities never seen before. In those moments of acute doubt, doubt
often framed by the most agonizing depression and despair, some survivors
discover unexpected, positive things about themselves. Quite a few
survivors found new meanings and values that helped them transcend
their immediate situation, positive values which seemed to emerge from the
heart of their anguish. Not all survivors reach this point of discovery
which leads to growth, but many do. Others go on with their lives, more or
less as before they were burned, while others wither. But Eric was
beginning to discover new dimensions of self and identity, and he was
recognizing, perhaps for the first time in his life, that he had control and
power. He had perhaps felt that he had power and control before he was
burned, undoubtedly, but this power was new, this feeling emerged from
within himself. Paradoxically, he discovered his power and control in a
situation in which his endurance and fortitude were pushed to the limit
and in which he had lost virtually all control over his daily life. He was
beginning to discover what Karl Slaikeu has appropriately labeled, the
"phoenix factor," that is, growth through personal crisis (Slaikeu and
Lawhead 1987). In discovering new dimensions of himself, Eric was
constructing a new self, and a new identity. Each was emergent in the
present; each suggested the future.

During the hospitalization and subsequent months, Eric was forced
to reevaluate who he was, who he had been and who he was to become.
Eric previously had a problem with using alcohol and drugs, and he had
led what he later defined as a fast life. He had been arrested several times
as a minor under the influence of alcohol. His father had an alcohol
problem, which Eric said caused conflict in the family, and this was one of
the things which he couldn't, for a long period of time, accept. He saw his
drinking as, in part, directly tied to the problems he had in his family, and
these were predominantly problems created by his father's drinking.

Mike Lawson: Motorcycle Accident

Mike is another young man who was very extensively burned. When
I interviewed Mike he was in the Valley Burn Center where he was to
have some reconstructive work performed. Although the burn occurred

nearly five years ago, Mike continues to have significant problems with his left leg. That leg sustained a compound fracture and was also deeply burned. He continues to have infections develop in the leg, circulation is poor, and he still faces the possibility that the leg will require amputation.

D: Were you concerned about dying?

You know, it never crossed my mind. I never thought I was going to die. After I came out of shock after the first week or so when I was going, "Go on, get out of here and let me die." The first week I didn't know what was happening, I don't remember any of it, but after that I don't remember even considering the possibility that I could die. If I wanted to die, I would have died because I have had enough experience to know what happens. I've seen so many people, I've talked to so many badly burned people when they're in their initial stage of their burn and I know what happens. If there is a physical chance to live, the doctors can keep you alive, if you want to live, if you've got the strength and if you've got the guts to do it. If you don't want to live, you are not going to live. I've seen people die that just shouldn't have died. You know, they had 40 percent burns. There was no physical reason for them to die except that they just gave up.

I met a guy, and got to know him fairly well, who was burned in a fire in St. Louis. He was from Los Angeles, and his father flew him out here to Valley. He was burned over 90 percent of his body, terrible, terrible burns. He was working for his dad, installing a padded cell in a jail in St. Louis. He had just finished putting contact cement on the ceiling and walls. Well, five cells down there was a gas water heater and the fumes just floated along, wham, the fumes exploded and the door slammed shut and he burned in there. He lived four months. He made it through everything. He was all grafted, they had amputated all his fingers. And in his mind he just couldn't handle it, he couldn't see living without his fingers. If you lost all your fingers, how are you going to feed yourself, how are you going to caress your wife or girlfriend or whatever. Your fingers are your contact with the world, that's how you examine things. But in his mind, he could not comprehend living without his fingers. He died four months after he was burned. The guy had been completely grafted, there was no reason for him to die, other than the fact he didn't want to live anymore. A couple weeks before he died, he shut up, he quit talking. He decided he didn't want to live,...he just plain decided.

One of the ways he defines his survival is in reference to wanting to live. He had the will to live while others, who might be burned far less extensively, but who wanted to die, did die. This is how he defines the situation and, defining the situation also defines himself as an object of his direct experience. The definition is retrospective; it is constituted or produced in the present, but it refers to his past. It refers back to his biographical history when he was critically ill and the definition is constitutive of the meaning that he discovers about himself. It provides knowledge about himself. Further, his statement that those who live are those who have guts, refers not just to anonymous others, but refers also to himself. His definition of others who survive embeds or informs his self-definition, while conceptions about why others die also informs his view of himself through comparison with those who die. When he speaks about what it would be like to lose fingers, he is not just speaking about another person. He is suggesting how he might interpret that reality were he in the other's place. He is role-taking or, in Schutz's terms, he is demonstrating the "reciprocity of perspectives" between himself and other, the assumption being, "Were I in his place, that's how I would feel." His definition about the other also implicitly contains his typification and interpretation of motives that explain why one would give up, motives being seen in the Weberian sense of complex meaning structures that appear to the person as adequate grounds or rationale for the conduct examined or in question (Schutz 1967, 28; Mills 1967). As he retrospectively constructs a definition of the motives for the other, he prospectively suggests possible definitions of himself, were he in a similar situation. In this way, he structures and interprets the world that he produces even though he would construe that world as external to himself, as being objective and independent of his work which has created that world. In hearing his descriptions, even when about others, we are listening to a description of his world and how he construes and constructs his world.

   That some burn patients die because they have no desire or will to live is not a unique expression confined to one such as Mike, who has survived a catastrophic burn. While chapters or paragraphs on the "will to live among burn patients" will not be found in text books on burn care, this idea is commonly expressed by burn care staff. Several nurses have related stories to me about moderately burned patients who became depressed, who wanted to die, or who didn't want to live, and who did die. Death occurred in spite of the fact that the person's clinical prognosis was good. The emotional state of the patient is frequently presumed by the burn care staff to be just as critical, and sometimes more critical, to the patient's survival and recovery than is the physical care of the patient. In spite of this, routine psychiatric evaluation and intervention are not as common as one might believe. In some burn centers, a clinical psychologist, psychiatrist, or clinical social worker is summoned only when the patient becomes critically depressed. At times, that intervention is too late.

D: So what was it like for you in the burn center?

From six in the morning until 11:30 or 12:00 at night, I was being
worked on. They would wake me up at 6:30 in the morning, give me
a breathing treatment. I'd go to the chamber [hyperbaric oxygen
therapy], I'd get out of the chamber. I'd eat breakfast. I'd have
blood drawn four times a day, have a chest Xray, then Xray the bone
in my leg. I had a fracture in my pelvis but the one in my leg was a
compound fracture with burns, which right off the bat the doctor
says, "Cut it off." Dr. Matland [his orthopedic surgeon] said,
"Listen, I'm not cutting the leg off a sixteen year old kid."

It took them two hours for a dressings change. We had to change
this leg and I did not have the strength to lift my leg. I didn't have
the strength to lift my head off the pillow. They would change this
leg and scrub and bathe it down, and then this leg had a cast, so they
would take the top of the cast off and change the dressings on top of
my leg, and the bone is sticking out, and change the packing, then
they'd put the cast on.

D: How would you describe the pain?

To describe the pain,...there is no way to describe the pain. Unless
you've been burned, there is no way to describe the pain, even a
nurse in the burn unit can't comprehend the pain. You're burned,
you're raw, exposed, and having someone go over you with a wire
brush constantly.

Do you want to make the definitive burn film? Go into the whirlpool
room at dressing change time and film with audio. The nurses get to
a point where they close off. It's not that they don't have any
feelings. In order to get better they have to put you through pain.
That's why the turnover [of nurses in burn centers]. She puts in all
this time, tortures them for three or four months after she has become
attached, he dies. My nurse took care of me Monday through Friday,
8 to 5. First thing in the morning we fought, constantly. We'd bitch
at each other and that's how we got the energy out. They have to
do it, it's hard on them.

D: How did you handle the pain?

The first week or two I was in deep shock and under heavy medication. I don't remember a whole lot about that. I do remember the
most vivid things. My back was burned second degree so the rest of
my burns weren't really that painful so I had to go to the chamber for
an hour. My back was in terrible, excruciating pain. I couldn't put
any pressure on my back so I would lay there for an hour arched up

putting all the weight on my arms. It was very painful and I couldn't comprehend what was going on. I realized that I was burned, I was aware I was burned. You're in such shock, I had never really been in such severe pain, and this is just something I couldn't comprehend the amount of pain I was going through. It was really, really hard on me and the first two weeks were weird because, in the first place I figured I would be here a couple of weeks and then I'll be back at work. I had no idea how long it was going to take for rehabilitation. I figured I'd be out of the hospital in two weeks. And instead I ended up being in the hospital three and a half months, and in a wheelchair for six months after that. It was a year before I could even walk. So that was quite a shock because I kept thinking well, this has got to end, it's not going to go on much longer.

D: Was there a turning point when the pain subsided?

No, there was no real turning point. Once they started grafting you, once they started grafting, the pain goes away. So then you have the donor site to worry about. They took skin off my butt, and peeling my butt off the bed [because it would stick], I mean ripping my butt off the bed. Of course after I got like half my body grafted, it was a little more gradual, but the whirlpool was getting worse. I was sticking three wash cloths in my mouth so they wouldn't hear me scream.*

D: Did you have support from your family?

I have five brothers and sisters, which is extremely important as far as support goes. At least one of them was there every day. I also had this one friend who is a school teacher, super close, and he came down and spent four hours every day with me, even when I was so out of it that I didn't know he was there. He read to me and kept me informed about the world. When you're away in an ICU burn room and you got nothing but looking up at the ceiling, seven or eight IV bottles running in and at least four or five running out of you, you have nothing but four walls and you are in a totally different environment than anything you have ever experienced, you have nothing to connect you to your previous life, there's no way to describe that. That's worse than being tortured. I fought for three days when I was first in the hospital to give me a cigarette. That was the worst thing they could do, but I fought and screamed, and the

---

* The whirlpool is described by many survivors as the most feared aspect of burn care for it is there that most of the localized debridement, or the removal of dead tissue, is done. It is an exceptionally painful and agonizing process.

doctor said, "Give him four cigarettes before he dies." The only reason I did that was because it was the only thing that gave me contact with life.

D: Can you tell me more about what it was like in the hospital?

I was a sixteen-year-old kid and totally independent and I grew up fast and this made me grow up a lot faster, but I was sixteen years old and I had to have all these women hold my penis in the urinal because I can't move, having to wipe my ass after I go to the bathroom. It's just totally degrading, ego shattering, it makes you feel, of course, you have no control over your life, your life is now in the hands of these women, you are totally helpless.

You're treated like a person, but you have no control over it. You're lying in your bed looking at the ceiling, and you are a mind that's just attached to this body that has nothing to do with you. You are not running your own body anymore. You're trying to keep your mind saying, every nerve in your body is going out and is screaming in pain, and the nurses are coming in torturing you and it's psychological torture.

You are sitting there being, laying there, and every bit of individual independence you thought you gained through adolescence or through your whole life,...And here I am and I have no control over any part of my life. They tell me when to eat, what to eat, they tell me, they come in and tell me when they're going to put me through the pain, what I'm going to do, how I'm going to do it. I'm no longer in control of my life. I'm totally in the hands of six women. It's so totally humiliating psychologically that you almost want to die. You're crying. You're in such pain that you're in hysterics. You're screaming. I'd be in the whirlpool and stuff two or three washcloths in my mouth so they couldn't hear me down the hall. I'd be screaming and crying and between screams and cries I'd be saying I was sorry. It's just impossible to describe it.

D: Tell me about the dressing changes.

The dressing changes were the most painful of all because we would have two a day. One would be in bed and one would be in whirl-pool. The one in bed was really bad because I had no strength. I couldn't lift my head off the pillow. My back was burned, my chest was burned, my arms were burned, hands, fingers, face, legs,... my entire body. We would do one leg then we'd do one arm then the other arm and then my fingers, individually. Then we'd dress my chest and I'd have to lean forward, holding myself up.

D: Did the Betadine cause pain itself?

Oh, yeah, even though it doesn't hurt as much as iodine. Of course, when they scrub you with it, it hurts a hell of a lot. They would pour it on 4 by 4's and then just scrub you down with those. The worst part in the whole dressing change was my leg because I had a full cast on, because I had a compound fracture of the left tibia. They would take the top part off the cast and change the packing because they had sliced open my leg because [of the infection]. The bone is sticking out and burned up and they had sliced it to let it drain. They put new packing in and changed the dressings on the top of my leg. Then they would roll me over onto my stomach, which was just screaming agony. Of course, everything is screaming agony. You're always in just excruciating pain. I couldn't even move.

Mike creates a most poignant and frightening picture of a situation where one has lost virtually all control over one's situation. There is no way, from his past experience, to understand his situation or comprehend what is going on. He is degraded, he can't urinate without help, he can't feed himself and he has been rendered helpless. The situation within which he finds himself is one of terror, it is one of horrendous pain and suffering, and for many survivors, the pain seems to be without end. The person is enveloped and overwhelmed by pain which viciously attacks, and, in the midst of pain, the person fears that it will never end. He is in a place unlike anything he could have ever imagined in his most terrifying dream and his descriptions, as cutting and as vivid as they are, cannot convey the overwhelming sense of anguish and suffering experienced by those who are critically burned.

As with several other survivors, pain is described as having raw, exposed skin scrubbed with a wire brush. Paul, the fire fighter who was burned during training, described the pain in a similar manner as feeling like his skin was constantly being sliced with a cheese grater. The exquisite, unrelenting pain was unlike anything Mike had experienced; it was raw skin being peeled off adherent sheets and, when the pain finally subsided because of grafting, he was anxious over the donor sites, which were also painful. The daily whirlpool was a terrorizing time, described by many survivors as creating the most intense pain they suffered during hospitalization.

On one occasion, I witnessed a young man being bathed and debrided. He had sustained second- and third-degree burns in a scald injury. His dead skin was being removed, piece by piece, using tweezers and a washcloth. He was continuously screaming and pleading for the burn technicians to stop. They would pause, but eventually resume until they had cleaned his wounds. I left the room with a severe headache and a deeper appreciation for what the patient must go through. The room was hot, humid, and suffocating. I also wondered how the technicians could do their work. In speaking to them, and to nurses, it was clear that they must frequently feel like torturers and that they must distance themselves from their work for it takes a heavy toll on them.

One of the ways that Mike coped with his condition was by complaining, and he saw his fighting attitude as partially responsible for keeping him going and keeping him alive. He defines himself as a fighter and uses that definition, which he suggests as an identity, as being responsible for getting through his hospitalization. Smoking, which he knew was bad for him, was one of the few things that connected him to his normal life, to reality outside his isolating environment in the burn center, as were visits by family and friends. These were the threads that linked him to the normal world.

Mike's description of depersonalization, his loss of autonomy and control, and the feeling that his ego was shattered vividly portrays the reality he was forced to inhabit and the changes forced upon a sixteen-year-old, independent male who now must have nurses hold his penis so he can urinate. He is degraded but there is no recourse. His body is perceived as detached and unconnected from self and mind. His body is radically experienced as something alien, which has nothing to do with him, and it is a body no longer under his control. He experiences self as detached from part of his own being. He cannot comprehend his situation. Like a Kafkaesque character who is thrown into an incomprehensible world of terror and anguish from which there is no escape, his worst nightmares were surpassed by the terrors of the day. Time was disrupted and he had no comprehension of how long he would be in the hospital, let alone how long the burn would disrupt his life. Like many others, he initially thought he would be recovered within weeks; he soon found it would be months and years. His description of how he assessed time is like that of other survivors. One of the ways the patient finds out how badly he or she is injured is by finding that they aren't out of the hospital as quickly as they had anticipated. One can see in his statement the horizon-like, open-ended perspective as he projects and anticipates his future.

The feeling for his body, as his and as part of him, was lost, and parts of the body that he saw exposed were frighteningly strange. His body, radically transformed, no longer appeared to be his own. Parts of the body that were exposed were perceived as distinctly alien and bizarre:

To my hands and to underneath my arms and to my legs, there were tendons literally burned in half. Down by my ankles there would be a tendon hanging down about five inches. This one time I remember when they were doing a dressing change, there was a big white band hanging down from my leg and I said, "Ooh, cut that thing off, it's gross, what is it?" They said, "We can't cut that off, that's a tendon." There was a big five inch piece of tendon hanging down from my leg and they can't cut it off, and I didn't know what it was.

One of the ways Mike gained control was to be intimately involved in his own care. For a period of time, he was given some direct control over his medications. However, on one occasion, he actually over-medicated himself, without staff knowledge, and almost died. He learned his lesson fast, but he still tried to be actively engaged in his own care, a task supported by staff. Staff members generally feel patients do better, and cope with pain better, if they are given some measure of control over their care; and in most burn centers, this approach is fostered. Still, it is the staff members, especially nurses, who must inflict pain and they often must bear patient anger.

D: Did you resent the nurses for what they had to do to you?

No, [but] I fought with anybody who came in the room. I would start yelling and telling them to get the hell out, it was a constant fight. I knew it had to be done. You knew that this person that was coming into the room was coming in to torture you whether you liked them personally or not. A person doesn't put up with that without some fuss.

D: Did the nurses try to negotiate with you?

They didn't ask me, I told them. After the first couple of weeks, at the time of the dressing changes, a nurse would come in and I would say, "I need four boxes of 4x16, four boxes of cling, and six rolls of six inch cling." I knew my orders as well as the nurses did. The nurses at Valley was the most dedicated, loving set of nurses that they could've possibly found in the world. When you're coming out of the whirl- pool bath, which is the most excruciating pain of any time dealing with the burn, that's when you stuff three wash cloths in your mouth so they don't hear you screaming down the hall. You've got to put the dressings on right now, you can't screw around.

D: Were they medicating you at the time of the whirlpool?

When I was on Demerol, I don't remember anything the first week, just the IV needle. After two weeks, I was talking to all these people that were imaginary and the doctor was watching me on the monitor, and listening on the intercom and he came in and said, "Mike, I think it's time we took you off the Demerol." After that, I refused to have medication. I had a couple of seizures so they gave me phenobarbital, which they gave me for the chamber treatments.

D: What is going on with your right foot?

They did a graft on it yesterday. I had an ulceration which had been there for four years on the ankle and finally it started getting really bad and he cut the ulceration out and stitched it up and didn't graft it and I had to walk on it 'cause I have a bone infection in my left leg, which means amputation after all these years of fighting it.

D: Are they going to definitely take it off?

No, not definitely, not if I have anything to say about it. I have been fighting this for two years. We've tried everything in the book. Once the infection gets in there it's hard to get the antibiotics in there and bone infection means amputation.

The problems with the leg were persistent. Because of his leg, and the continuing problems, his life had continued to be disrupted. Even after the passage of five years, he couldn't assume that his life would now be normal. The meaning of the burn, and what the burn did to him, was not static; it was a changing process and Mike could never really tell where he stood, what would happen next, or how his life might still be drastically changed. His identity, now and in the future, his meaning to himself and to others, was still defined by an event of the past that continued to have significant and painful consequences for him and the others around him. The future was an open possibility but it was clouded by the possible future amputation of his leg. Nevertheless, he had hope, and for him, his life was not tragic.

In spite of Mike's own problems, he has found that trying to help other burn patients is important.

When I go into somebody's room I don't care if they want to listen or not. I don't like to take any credit for it, Kenny was electrocuted. He was picking avocados and he picked an 800 volt electrical line. It zapped him damn good. Both his hands were black, and he was a star football player for Santa Siedra High School. This is a sixteen-year-old guy, macho, huge, big build, got all these cheerleaders around him and here he is zapped. Got black hands, just blew out all his muscles from his knee down. This hand, they had to amputate and the other one had no muscles in it. For two weeks he laid in his hospital bed, he did not say a word for two weeks. He just stared at his hands.

I was in for reconstructive surgery at the time. So I went over and got a pair of scrub pants, walked into his room with a big smile on my face, I'm gross, this is only about two years after my accident. I'm still pink and purple, I walk in with a big smile on my face and just started talking to him, saying hey, "What are you doing there still crying for, it's happened, you've got to accept this." And he was still in critical condition, it was touch and go, and he didn't want to live. Four days later he's out of critical care and he's my roommate. This guy is doing fantastic now. I guess my walking in kinda snapped him out of it, 'cause it shows you can live through something like this and still be functional, still lead a life.

Scott Barris is a little beast, and I had to beat the hell out of that guy at one time. I had to beat the shit out of him. Fourteen years old, he sat there and looked at his hands contracting, just sat there and watched them contract, "Oh, it hurts too much to move." I was there and it was a snap. The guy comes into the burn unit and Janice, the goldbrick, she says, "Scott was here the other day and he said he'd be dead if it wasn't for you." I didn't do anything but go in and give him a big ration of shit. The guy didn't care and had given up. I wasn't putting up with that shit.

This chapter has examined some of the themes, issues, and problems which the hospitalized burn patient faces. One of the issues that arises, either in the hospital or when the person goes home, are fears about disfigurement and scarring. People like Eric and Mike returned home with drastically changed bodies from what they had known all their lives. Scarred and disfigured, they no longer appeared as they once did. Some survivors, like Kevin Davis, reported that people they had known before they were burned no longer recognized them. In Kevin's case, one woman almost ran from him until she recognized his voice and he identified himself. In seeing him, she then broke down and cried. These are obviously profoundly significant issues which the survivor confronts. The next chapter will examine this subject.

3

Disfigurement and Stigmatization: Issues of
Self and Identity

This chapter examines self, identity, and disfigurement, as interrelated themes in the narratives of burn survivors. Particular attention is devoted to understanding how survivors conceptualize themselves relative to scarring and disfigurement and how these relate to self-definition and attribution. Central questions are: how is the self conceived for those who are visibly scarred and how does scarring relate to self-attribution and definition?

These questions elicit very different answers from different survivors. Some, who are only moderately scarred, seem to globally define themselves in terms of their scars while others, who have gross scarring, make few behavioral attributions based on their scars. It will be found here that the size and location of scars, or the differential grossness of disfigurement, as well as the extent of scarring, have no simple, unitary relationship to specific self attributions made by the survivor. In other words, "minor" scarring, even when normally hidden beneath clothing, is not necessarily easy to deal with for some survivors and, concomitantly, full-body, grossly disfiguring scarring does not result in negative self evaluation for other survivors. Some survivors with minor scarring are devastated while others with gross scarring are able to transcend their injury and construct rewarding post burn lives. Understanding the consequences of scarring and disfigurement demands attention to the survivor's subjective experience of being scarred and disfigured. Attention must focus on the meanings constructed and attributed to self by the survivor and to self by others.

The survivor's ability to find positive meanings in his or her burn experience, in spite of disfigurement and extreme loss, are a central feature of recovery from the burn. Likewise of significance is the survivor's ability to cope with and redefine the negative judgments and actions of others that would otherwise discredit the survivor. Those who are ultimately unable to find positive meaning and value, and who accept the cruel imputations by others, appear to lead post burn lives that are significantly different from most of the survivors who appear in this study. Regardless of how a particular life turns out after a major burn, the results are inherently related to self, identity, and disfigurement. Self and identity are radically effected by trauma, especially when the person is disfigured. Gergen has suggested that theories of self are theories of what it means to be human: "Theories of the self are, after all, nothing less than definitions of what it is to be human. Such theories inform the society as to what the individual can or cannot do, what limits may be placed over human functioning, and what hopes may be nurtured for future change (Gergen 1987, 54).

The conception of self utilized in this study follows the classical works of William James, James Mark Baldwin, and George Herbert Mead. The self is understood not as "personality" or as a concrete object but as an emerging process which has its roots in communicative interaction and in the historical socialization of the person. Self-as-process is located, through symbolic construction, at the center of the world that is constructed by the person. The self is understood not as a consistent, trans-situational organized core, but as the emerging, self-reflexive communication process through which the person actively constitutes his or her world and, thereby, himself or herself. Self-reflexive construction means that the person learns to treat himself or herself as an object of his or her own personal experience. The self is reflexive, emergent, and historical and it is embedded in a temporal horizon which becomes manifest through interaction with others or through self-indicating symbolic usage, within particular contexts or situations. To ignore the historical situation and context in which self emerges and within which self is displayed, both to the person and to others, is to lose any understanding of the nature of self. The person is grounded in the historical nature of the both self and situation. Person and situation are coemergent within the present of action, or reflection, as each unfolds into the future and carries with it the past.

The classical conception of self, developed by Mead but also clearly traceable to James, Baldwin, and Cooley, sees the self as emerging from the human's ability to construct and use symbols, particularly significant symbols in which meanings are shared with other persons through interaction between self and other. Most important of such symbols are those that refer back to the self and, in so doing, become constituent elements of self. Crucial among humans, as opposed to other animal forms, is the ability to be self-conscious, that is, to be reflexively aware of self as an object of one's own experience and to symbolically maintain such awareness through time. It is through a reflexive stance that the self turns back on itself, casting itself, through symbolic construction, as an object of its own experience. It is here that one is self-conscious, and it is only through language that self comes into being, or that reflexivity is possible. Mead notes that "the self, as that which can be an object to itself, is essentially a social structure, and it arises in social experience....It is impossible to conceive of a self arising outside of social experience"

(Mead 1934, 140). In discussing the reflexive nature of self, Mead is also instructive:

> The self has the characteristic that it is an object to itself, and that characteristic distinguishes it from other objects and from the body....This characteristic is represented in the word *self*, which is a reflexive, and indicates that which can be both subject and object. This type of object is essentially different from other objects....That the person should be responding to himself is necessary to the self, and it is this sort of social conduct which provides behavior within which self appears. I know of no other form of behavior than the linguistic in which the individual is an object to himself, and the individual is not a self in the reflective sense unless he is an object to himself. (Mead 1956, 199-206)

The preeminent mechanism through which self is maintained, altered and displayed is oral or nonoral language. Self-referencing visual depictions, or images are also important. Awareness of oneself as a distinct and special being in the world occupies our lives. Self and other dialectically emerge in interaction, each person acting to mirror the other. The self is therefore essentially social in origin and it is the crucible wherein meanings are constituted and negotiated. It is through face-to-face interaction with others, and self-reflexive interaction with oneself (through self-talk), that self and identity are constituted and negotiated. In discussing the genesis of self, Mead notes that

> Language is essential for the development of self. The self has a character which is different from that of the physiological organism proper. The self is something which has a development; it is not initially there at birth but arises in the process of social experience and activity, that is, develops in the given individual as a result of his relations to that process as a whole and to other individuals within that process. (Mead 1956, 199)

The self is not to be understood as conterminous with, or equal to one's body. The self is obviously impossible without a body, but the body does not require a self, nor does the body *have* a self in the sense of possession. Furthermore, self is not necessary to, nor does it exist in the person's nonreflexive action. For example, if I am doing some action, such as running in an unreflective manner, the self is not engaged in the act. To be sure, I am engaged in running, through the vehicle of my body, but it is only when I think about what I am doing, when I reflexively attend to bodily sensations, when I think about the distance I must run, or when I notice pain from having just stepped on a pebble, that the self can be said to be emergent in the situation. Prior to this, I am directly absorbed in the action without consciousness of self. Nonreflexive sensation, or the raw experience of pain, directly relates to the body; but it is upon reflection and interpretation that they relate to self. In noticing, attending to, or thinking about sensations or pain, it can be said that sensation is organized about the self (Mead 1956, 200), and self exists only in concrete situations. Yet the situation is itself horizon-like in nature: "man remains a horizon of possibilities which manifest themselves historically in concrete situations. He is what he has become; but even more, he is the transcending origin of still further becomings."(Grabau 1967, 118) Berger and Luckmann are also instructive:

> The common development of the human organism and the human self in a socially determined environment is related to the peculiarly human relationship between organism and self. This relationship is an eccentric one. On the one hand, man is a body....On the other had, man *has* a body. That is, man experiences himself as an entity that is not identical with his body, but then, on the contrary, has that body at his disposal. In other words, man's experience of himself always hovers in a balance between being and having a body, a balance that must be redressed again and again. (Berger and Luckmann 1966, 50)

The self should not be seen as an objective inner entity, but rather it is a metaphor for specific symbolic processes that are self as well as other referencing or indexing. "Self" is not a sociological name for the numerous psychological concepts of "personality."[1] Used here, self does not suggest a fixed or stable and directive core entity of contents and traits as commonly suggested in personality theories. Neither does self refer to unconscious mechanisms, needs, or drives. Self is viewed here as minded "activity which is part of the social process" (McKinney 1970, 237). The self, then, is conceptualized as the constituting process and axis for the creation of meaning (Brittan 1973, 78). Importantly, mind itself is inexorably social in origin (Mead 1934; Gergen 1985b; Coulter 1979).

The self is described *as if* it were an object. This is a way of construing the self; however, the self must be understood as a process rather than a thing. Mead, following James, describes the self as comprised by two phases, the *I* or *Ego*, and the *Me*. The "I" is emergent and active; the "Me" is reflexive (Mead 1934, 173-186; Lester 1984, 26). The "I" is the actor, while the "Me" represents the person's interpretation, definitions, expectations, and evaluations of "I" as well as others, and self as seen by others. Experientially, "I" is primary in its active emergence, while "Me" is secondary in its reflexiveness. The "Me" develops through socialization, the learning of sociocultural knowledge, scripts, norms and mores, and the subject's learning to take or assume the roles of the other. The other can be a *significant Other*, that is, one who is affectively close to the subject, or it can be a *generalized other,* representing more distant or anonymous relationships. Natanson expounds this idea, stating the nature of "I" and "Me" and, following Mead, suggesting how self is both subject and object:

> The Me represents stability and continuity by providing the matrix for the self's action. Anything entertained in consciousness, all possibilities of action, and all perceptual acknowledgements are pieced together in the province of the Me. Whatever new action is contemplated appears over and against the backdrop of the Me. The I, on the other hand, is forever renewing its appearance; it turns up each time a choice is necessary. In the moment of active performance, the *deed* is sprung by the I. Thus, the Me is the object, but the I is the subject of all action. The Me is past-dominated while the I is the spontaneity of a present which announces the future. Rather than as separate regions, however, the polarities of the Me and I must be understood as functional aspects of the self....The Me is the source, then, of what is typical and habitual in experience; the I, of what is innovative and audacious. (Natanson 1970, 18)

As noted below, there is a sense in which the I is alone, but the self is a self-with-others. Being-with-others, as a "we," is a fundamental way in which the social world is experienced. Indeed, our very identities and selves presuppose the existence of others with whom we interact and share ourselves. For the survivor, others are crucial to the process of recovery, not just medical staff, but family and friends who share the burden through which the survivor journeys. The other, both significant and generalized, is crucial to the development and shaping of self. The other is crucial to how the survivor reconceptualizes himself or herself. But it is not merely that others have some role in the process, they are actually critical to the forging of self. Tiraykian speaks of this as the *we-pole*:

> [The] subject is not just "I"; it is also "we," revealed in experience as a primary form of consciousness. The "I" and the "we" [are] coexistent in selfhood. The forms, structures, and acts of consciousness partake, latently or mainifestly, of this intersubjective component, which is an integral aspect of the self as subject. (Tiryakian 1973, 193)

The subjective sense of possessing a personal self is grounded in the deeper conception of self-as-process (Lester 1984, 25). In conceptualizing the self as processural, emphasis is placed on attending to the open, emerging, and evolving nature of self and its personal meanings as self emerges through interaction, and within a situation. The self, therefore, is not conceptualized as being of fixed, determinate or enduring form.

Indeed, the self is viewed as fluid and mutable. Transformation, flux, and change are ever present as the self evolves, emerges and reemerges in new situations. Lester, in quoting Blummer states that:

> In short, the possession of a self provides the human being with a mechanism for self-interaction with which to meet the world...a mechanism that is used in forming and guiding his conduct. We see scholars who identify with the "ego," or who regard the self as an organized body of needs or motives, or who think of it as an organization of attitudes, or who treat it as a structure of internalized values. Such schemes, which seek to lodge the self in a structure, make no sense, since they miss the reflexive process which alone can yield and constitute a self. (Lester 1984, 25-26)

Through symbols, that is, through language, humans are able to construct meanings for themselves as well as for others, and they are further able to share meaning with others. It is through language that the subject's personal world is constituted and shared with others and it is through language that everyday reality is produced, day in and day out (Brittan 1977, 37). Language allows us to construct abstract definitions of self, other, and world, thereby transcending the concrete and specific. This ability is wonderfully examined by Dr. Oliver Sacks in his illuminating study of the profoundly deaf, *Seeing Voices*. Lacking language, the profoundly deaf are unable to transcend their immediate situation; only rudimentary interaction with others is possible and, lacking language, they lack the tools required for understanding themselves and their world (Sacks 1989).

The specific interactive process through which persons construct meanings about themselves and about others, that is, how they construe each other, is role-taking. In part, it is through role-taking that we interpret the identity of the other, as self is manifested in the dynamics of role. Role, self, and identity are dynamic, situational, and sensitive to context. The person's ability to reflexively treat himself or herself as a social object, that is, to see himself or herself as others might, is dependent on role-taking (Mead 1934, 150-156, 254). It is through this process of putting ourselves in the role of the other person and interpreting how he or she views us that we learn to assess ourselves in interactive settings and to reflexively treat ourselves as social objects. This is not only done relative to others, but to ourselves as well through self-talk and inner dialogue where the "I" engages in internal dialogue with "Me" (Mead 1934, 28).

Errors in role-taking judgment occur all the time and are frequently the basis for embarrassment and misunderstandings, requiring various normalization strategies in order to salvage an acceptable definition of self within the situation. Dramaturgical sociology, particularly that practiced by Erving Goffman, and also seen in the reality breaching experiments designed by ethnomethodologist Harold Garfinkel, aptly shows how persons attempt to repair and transcend such occasions. Normally, such problems are routine disruptions which are given little notice. For the disfigured survivor such problems can be emotionally traumatizing as he or she is treated as less than normal, due solely to scarring and the meanings that others therefore impute.

In being scarred and disfigured, the survivor often encounters social situations wherein he or she must actively negotiate an acceptable identity. Not only in social situations, but also on the level of inner self-meaning, the person will have to discover new meanings for his or her radically transformed being. No longer may former beliefs and values about self be reasonable, to either the person or to others. The person's identity as a normal, respectable and whole person may be continuously challenged by others who wish to see and treat the survivor as disabled and abnormal.

The struggle to achieve normal identity and to be credited by others as a "normal" person may be overwhelming for some survivors, but it seems that most, sometimes through very exceptional diligence, effort and sensitive interactional skills, will succeed in fashioning a normal life. In burn injury, as well as in other catastrophic events that cause massive personal change, the resocialization of the person, the relearning of self and world, is often a massive and arduous effort. The payoff is being able to live a rewarding, productive life.

The self is taken to be essentially situated or context sensitive and emergent. Temporality is the background from which the self emerges. The immediate present in which the self emerges is informed by the past and suggests the future (Mead 1959). The emerging event or situation, in which the self is inherently implicated as the vehicle through which meaning is constituted, suggests both history and prophecy of self and situation. The self is always in a situation, or context; it is always surrounded by, or embedded within its world. Following Mead, the self is also viewed as historical, or temporal. This is similar to Heidegger's conception of *Dasein,* that is, human existence:*

Dasein's Being discovers its meaning in temporality but temporality is also the condition which makes historcality possible as a temporal kind of Being which Dasein itself posses, regardless of whether or how Dasein is an entity in time. Historicality, as a determinate character, is prior to what is called history." (Heidegger 1964, 41)

Similar to the singular alonenss of Dasein, there is a significant sense in which Ego is fundamentally alone in the world. Of all life forms, only the human can ask what it means to exist; only the human can ask "who

---

* Dasein will be discussed further in Chapter 6.

am I?" The past gives clues to the answer, but the past is always opaque, distant, and incomplete. The future is but a possibility, remaining yet to be discovered. All that is certain is that life is transitory, in flux, and that I am in the middle of it (Breisach 1962, 112) In situations of extreme crisis, or boundary situations, the person is most alone. It may be comforting to have others near, but ultimately, the person himself or herself alone must bear the pain and anguish of injury. In discussing the aloneness of ego, Natanson note that

> The awareness of being truely an ego "on its own" is the experience of anguish. In some ways, social existence is a means of translating that anguish into a self-acceptable form of balance. Far from being a resolution of the condition of anguish, mundanity is a constant and only partially successful accomodation the ego makes in order to mask the implications of its aloneness....In these terms, anguish may be understood as the threat of placing in fundemental question everything which assures our placement in the world. (Natanson 1970, 15)

In discussing the nature and subtle differences between ego or "I" and self, which is comprised by "I" and "Me," Natason observes that

> It is the ego which has a concrete biography, a continuous experience, and a specific orientation toward the future in terms of projects and dispositions. The self is the ego clothed with the garmets of society. The self has a twofold aspect: it is at once the unified history of its past performance and the agency which gives valence to immediate action. In one direction, the self is continuous, memorially directed, and indexed with clues and keys to past action; in another direction, it is the force which moves action at any given time. (Natanson 1970, 17)

While the "I" or ego is treated as singular and alone, the self is taken to be multiple, and joined with others. The multiplicity of selves does not represent fragmentation as might be suggested in traditional psychological theory. Rather, the plurality of the self stems from the basic reflexive and interactive nature of self, as a being-with-others. Self originally arises through socialization, and through the subject's identification with significant others, as in the reciprocal infact-mother dyad. Self is sustained through interaction with others, through role-taking, and through memory. This view is a radical departure for most "personality" theories expounded in psychology. Theorists, such as Prescott Lecky, and the later "balance theory" proponents, argued that psychological health required self-consistency and the integration of the personality. This view has been predominant in psychology and it can be seen as the basis of much work in the field of "mental health." Here, however, what is taken to be of primary consequence for the person to feel "normal" is not the existence of a stable, consistent self, but rather, it is necessary that the person subjectively construe himself or herself as consistent and stable over time. The survivor's subjective feeling of consistency over time, and through massive change, is interpretively based. It is a way of conceptualizing the self and it does not suggest the existence of an unchanging core self or structure, nor does it suggest that the person is, in fact, consistent. Rom Harré has viewed what here could be referred to as a "core self" as being "an organizational feature of experience, imposed through the power of certain grammatical models" (Harré 1987, 41), and he has observed that, "there is no 'entity' at the centre of our experience of ourselves. But there are standard ways in which we express our comments upon our own mentation"[2] (Harré 1987, 41). What Harré describes is the fact that linguistic usage and structures, at least in Western culture, provide us with a way of viewing self as if it were concrete, stable, and unchanging. The concreteness of self is possible only through symbolic, linguistic construction and such construction is provided through selective definition and memory; inconsistency is situationally ignored and the person subjectively experiences himself, or herself as "being the same as I have always been."

Many accident survivors, who have undergone profound physical change, typically still define themselves as being both consistent and essentially the same persons as they were prior to their accidents. It is suggested that in order for the person to integrate the experiences he or she has gone through in being burned and in recovering, in order to feel whole again, the subjective feeling of being essentially consistent and essentially the same person is of immense significance. The ways in which the person feels himself or herself to be fundamentally the same as before the accident are frequently unarticulated, but nevertheless real. When asked how they are still the same, survivors may have considerable difficulty explaining what they mean or what the basis for their feelings is. The survivor may answer by saying, "Well, it's hard to say but I know I'm still me. I look different but inside I'm me, I still like to play sports and I just feel the same even though I've gone through some changes." While significant others may see the person as being substantially different, especially physically, after the accident, what is important is not outside definitions even if they are completely objective and factual. Instead, what is of consequence for the survivor is his or her ability to fashion an identity that feels, and hence is, consistent, whole, integrated and connected to their pasts.

Kohli has noted that the person's biography "consists in a continuous restructuring of past events within the framework of the contingencies of the present situation" (Kohli 1981, 65). The recounted biography of any person can be viewed as the articulation of a moral career (Goffman

1961). Interactional settings, be they found in the most ordinary circumstances or in the most unusual, are very frequently the staging areas for the interactant's drama like presentation of self, identity, and history within everyday life (Goffman 1959; Harré 1976). Important to the biographical reconstruction thus produced and displayed is the person's account of possessing a particular type of moral character. The self, thus displayed in social interaction, is more generally part of the routine moral order of society. People present themselves as particular identities which are unique to themselves; but in making identity claims, they claim they are a person of this or that type, the types being culturally available through commonly shared social knowledge which is generalized. In articulating their identities, biographical accounts or stories are utilized to show who they are, and how they came to be. In recounting their burn experiences, survivors produce their histories through biography that suggests the self's journey. That journey is a moral journey. But the journey, so stated, is not rendered by recounting all events in the survivor's life; it is instead structured in terms of a specific experience, that of being burned. The recounted journey articulates and defines the self. The construction of such accounts, which might also be referred to as personal myths or stories, serve to suggest who and what the person is and how he or she got here or there. Such myths and stories provide the person with a theory of himself or herself, and they also serve to provide others with a situated identity for the survivor who is recounting "what happened." Such accounts may contain general, typified versions about personal or moral character, such as one being strong, determined, or whatnot, with particular biographical features then further elucidated as examples which confirm the typification thus made. Such work serves to frame identity and self.

In daily life, we are all engaged in telling ourselves and others what happened, recounting our actions, problems, fortunes, and misfortunes, and in doing so, we are ongoingly producing who we are for both ourselves and our listeners. Together with the routinization of roles, identities and the social world, the construction of such accounts, stories, or myths about self represent crucial ways in which personal consistency is constructed and reconstructed, day in and day out. Gergen notes that through such accounts, the "individual attempts to establish coherent connections among life events" (Gergen 1983, 255). Some sense of linear coherence and cohesiveness is given to events that might otherwise be seen as rather disconnected, random and episodic. Gergen describes one of the basic styles or motifs of self-narrative as being a *stability narrative*. This is a narrative "that links incidents, images, or concepts in such a way that the individual remains essentially unchanged with respect to [an] evaluative position" (Gergen 1983, 258). Again, the basis for such constructions is founded in memory and in language usage.

Stability narratives are commonly found in the acounts of burn survivors in this study, even in those who have undergone significant change and even when they are fully aware of such change. While, on one hand, survivors recognize massive change, they often simultaneously feel that they are basically the same person they were prior to being injured. For example, they may say, "Deep down inside, I am the same as I was before I was burned even though I've gone through a lot of change." They also might say that the change has made them "different in ways," but that they still feel like their old selves. The subjective feeling of continuity, the sense of stability in the face of overwhelming challenge, crisis, and change is very powerful. These feelings are important for recovery and the sense of being whole.

In his seminal work, William James suggested that the sense of continuity of self was maintained by thought through memoric reconstruction, and he further argued that the self was plural, a theme followed by both Cooley and Mead. Yet, the person typically experiences himself as one unitary self, even when discontinuities are recognized. Again, what is crucial is the person's subjective sense or feeling about self. In referring to James, Scheibe notes that:

> James makes the claim that despite our many social roles and the masks they require, despite our combining dreaming with planning and hoping, and loafing, and loving, and feeling both secure and afraid at the same time--despite all these discontinuities in the empirical constituents of our selves, we retain an overall conviction of unity and continuity. (Scheibe 1985, 40)

Through memory, the person is able to provide himself or herself with his or her own history. Through memoric reconstruction and the production of accounts and stories, the person is able to provide others with his or her history. The history so produced suggests the self's journey through the social world. It is not only that the self can be metaphorically understood as being on a journey, but that the self is indeed, metaphorically, the journey itself, constituting itself and its journey. At any recounted point in time, the meaning of the person's life, to him or her, is contingent on how personal history has been constituted. Agnes Hankiss notes that:

> Human memory selects, emphasizes, rearranges and gives new colour to everything that happened in reality; and, more important, it endows certain fundamental episodes with a symbolic meaning, often to the point of turning them almost into myths, by locating them at a focal point of the explanatory system of self. (Hankiss 1981, 203)

The importance of memory to self, identity, and the stability of the social world, which is perceived by the subject as being routine and taken for granted, was exquisitely apparent in a PBS television presentation, *The Mind* (1988). The case of a middle-aged man living in London, a once successful conductor, was presented. Through catastrophic disease, he sustained permanent neural damage to his brain stem. Through this, he lost all ability to remember his past identity. He retained speech and his ability to write, as well as his ability to perform music but, from moment to moment, all else about his past life, as well as his ongoing life, was irretrievably lost to consciousness. He could not remember who he was, nor could he recall those who were important to him. Moments just passed were lost forever, so that each torturous moment was like awakening and reawakening from a coma. Institutionalized, he fills volumes of books with notations on his ever-fleeting experience of "waking up." He has no identity for himself or for others. He is anchored to the world by his body and his ever-emerging immediate experience of waking up to a foreign, ever-strange world with which he has no familiarity. Like some of the tragic cases brilliantly presented by Dr. Oliver Sacks in *Awakenings* and *The Man Who Mistook His Wife For A Hat*, what saves him is apparently that, lacking memory, he has little or no insight into his most marginal situation.

The self is understood as being embodied, situational, reflexive, and characterized by becoming (Mead 1959; Kotarba 1984). Writing from an existential perspective in sociology, Andrea Fontana notes that:

> The self is embodied because it cannot transcend its physical vehicular unit, and it receives its stimulation to act from feelings and emotions emanating from the body. The self is becoming because it is always unfolding, changing and developing in response to its changing perceptions of the world around it. The self is situational because it is always dependent on its immediate contexts for a sense of grounding and belonging. Finally, the self is reflexive because it is aware of itself; it is the focal point for the social, biological, cognitive, affective, and interpretive dimensions of being. (Fontana 1984, 11)

Fontana defines identity as "the perception of self by others, the ways in which it is defined, controlled, supported and challenged by the social world" (Fontana 1984, 11). Schlenker views identity as, "establishing what and where the person is in social terms. Identity is not a substitute word for self. Instead, when one has identity, he is situated, that is cast in the shape of a social object" (Schlenker 1985, 69). Schlenker also sees identity as the process of typifying the self in a [membership] category. Here, identity is the naming or labeling of self, most commonly in reference to roles, by self or other. Identity is situated, which is to say that it is articulated in specific situations or contexts wherein the identification of the person is required or where identity is problematic for either the person or for others. For others who do not already know the subject, two important identity markers are appearance and speech. As interaction unfolds, other markers become salient such as general demeanor and comportment, manner of speaking, accent, and preverbal cues, or "body language," all of which provide the other person with criteria with which identification of the person is made. Of all personal features, appearance, including clothing, as well as the body and face, provide the most salient markers with which identity is initially judged.

Identity is an element of the self's subjective reality (Berger and Luckmann 1966, 173): it is emergent with the self in the social process of interaction and communication and both identity and self are fundamentally precarious (Berger and Luckmann 1966, 100). Identity is objectified through language, specifically through interaction with others or through thought and "self-talk" with oneself. It is maintained, modified, and altered through a dialectical relationship between self and others, particularly significant others. Natanson, quoted in Brittan, puts person, self, and identity together:

> The biographical actualization of the self is the person. Accordingly, persons are selves whose identities have achieved expression. It would be misleading to think of the person either as somehow encapsulated in the self or as developed by the self in interaction with its surrounding social world. The person is not an essence precontained in the self, nor is the self a blank slate as far as identity and character are concerned. (Brittan 1973, 76)

Brittan, following Schutz, goes on to note that: "the self moves in a dialectic of multiple possibilities between the world as assumed in 'of course' assumptions, and the world as actively experienced at the level of meaning." (Brittan 1973, 76) Further, Brittan states that there is a level of experience which seems to lie outside the socially meaningful, in the sense of self as immediately experienced, and here, Brittan is speaking of the "bodily me" and he goes on to quote Allport in recognizing the sense of the body as a lifelong anchor for self-awareness. The tacit awareness of the body supports and sustains me; it is taken-for-granted and to it there generally is not direct or sustained attention except under special conditions, such as pain, injury or illness. When attention is directed toward the body, with the interpretation of bodily experience and sensations, such experience is social because the experience is interpreted and mediated by language. Bodily experience thereby becomes reportable and has an objective quality.

Identity as a personal construct seems uniquely my own; it is part of who and what I am. It serves as a schema of interpretation that refers back to the self as its own object. Though I feel my identity to be mine, my identity is always contingent; it is related to my relationships with others and to the world about me. The identities and selves of significant others, of those emotionally closest to me, such as a spouse or child, in part defines who I am and who I can become. And not only others, but things, possessions that are tangible and those things that are intangible, such as values, beliefs, feelings and ideas, can be incorporated into self and identity.[3]

Like the self from which identity arises as a reflexive naming of the self in relation to others and to roles, identity is subject to threat, deformation, and destruction through numerous challenges and losses. There are numerous and varied threats to both self and identity[4] (Breakwell 1983), ranging from embarrassment and situational incompetence, to public berating by one's boss, job loss, divorce, or the death of a loved one. All of these directly relate back to the subject; they affect the subject's life, sometimes only fleetingly and obliquely, but sometimes the results are much more profound and injurious. In the case of divorce or, more so, in the case of the death of a significant other, the results may be overwhelming, reverberating from then on through the remainder of the person's life. Such events potentially alter the person's definition of self-worth and therefore, who he or she is or feels himself or herself to be. Burn injury represents an extreme form of loss and deep threats to self and identity. It directly affects not only the person's bodily existence but also the life of both the survivor and those closest to the survivor.

Disfigurement and scarring are significant problems for many burn survivors. For some, the issues presented by looking different haunt them for years, perhaps for the rest of their lives. Disfigurement following burns is one of the major problems that lead to psychological impairment following injury. The percentage of persons exhibiting impairment[6] generally is said to range from 20 percent to 40 percent (Bowden 1980; Cooper-Frapes 1984; Steiner and Clark 1977; Vogtsberger and Taylor 1984; Young 1974; Kudson-Cooper 1981; Molinaro 1978; Clarke and Martin 1978; Noyes and Andreasen 1971; Hamburg and Hamburg 1953).[5]

Stigmatization is the process of attributing a morally discrepant identity, to self or other, based upon features or properties that are seen as residing in the person who is stigmatized. Following Goffman, stigma is viewed as a deeply discrediting attribute.

Stigma can be based upon social or moral properties of character that are imputed to the stigmatized person, such as alcoholism (Denzin 1987; McAndrew and Edgerton 1969), homosexuality (Warren and Ponse 1977), drug use (Becker, 1963), mental illness (Szasz 1961, 1970; Scheff 1969; Goffman 1961), religious affiliation, or ethnicity. Stigmatization may also be based on physical conditions or disabilities imputed to the person such as blindness (Scott 1969) or other differences which are physical (Davis 1967; Wright 1960; Macgreggor 1953).

Stigmatization, based on the marker of scarring or discrepant appearance, involves the assignment of the person to a class of persons who are defined by others as less than normal, and who are, therefore, discredited. As such, stigma truncates the person's identity. The discrepant, imputed identity reflects a moral judgment by those who define the person as less

than normal, that is, as being deviant. Stigma, linked to a deviant identity,
becomes the basis for the attribution of a global definition of the survivor
by others. Such a definition, like "cripple," not only obscures and colors
all other characterological qualities of the person, but it also serves as a
master status as well, being the peg upon which other pejorative definitions and assessments are made by those who attribute a deviant identity
to the person. Goffman, Macgreggor, and Wright have referred to this
process as *spread* or *engulfment* of identity. Following Douglas, all such
attributions, in being moral definitions, are essentially problematic (Douglas
1967, 1970). This is to say that they are open to negotiation and interpretation and they are situated or context relational. Douglas defines deviance as "any thought, feeling, or action that members of a social group
judge to be a violation of their values or rules"(Douglas 1982, 10).

Deviance can therefore include behaviors and persons who are
morally judged as deficient, as in the case of the criminal, heroine addict,
and prostitute. It can also include those who are not strictly defined in
good/bad moral terms, but who are nevertheless negatively judged, such as
the disfigured, the blind, or those who have a disability. Robert Scott, in
analyzing the social functions and meaning of deviance, has viewed
deviance as a property of social order (Scott 1972, 35), not as something
residing in the person who is judged. Stigmatization and the attribution of
a deviant identity to a subject involves a complex social labeling process
between subject and other, and it can reflect, more generally, widely shared
sociocultural values. In referring to both the work of Kai Erikson, who
saw deviance as providing important boundary-maintenance functions by
marking the outer edges of group life (Erikson 1966), and to Berger and
Luckmann's work, Scott states that deviance is a

> property conferred upon an individual whenever others detect in his
> behavior, appearance, or simply his existence, a significant transgres-
> sion of the boundaries of the symbolic universe by which the
> inherent disorder of human existence is made to appear orderly and
> meaningful. More simply, the property of deviance is conferred on
> things [and people] that are perceived as being anomalous when they
> are viewed from the perspective of a symbolic universe.

> [Deviance] constitutes the most acute threat to taken-for-granted
> routinized existence in society. If one conceives of the latter as the
> "daylight side" of human life, then [deviance] constitutes a "night
> side" that keeps lurking ominously on the periphery of everyday con-
> sciousness. Just because the "night side" has its own reality, often of
> a sinister kind, it is a constant threat to the taken-for-granted, matter-
> of-fact, "sane" reality of life in society. The thought keeps suggest-
> ing itself that, perhaps, the bright reality of everyday life is but an

illusion, to be swallowed up at any moment by the hounding nightmare of the other, the "night side" reality. (Scott 1972, 24)

For example, in being scarred, several survivors have reported numerous instances in which they have been treated as less than competent. Several survivors have reported instances of being treated as if they were retarded, incompetent, or childlike. Mary Ellen Ton eloquently tells of such experiences:

Some people have a tendency to be overly solicitous. They lean forward and bend over slightly as they speak in a tone generally reserved for children, the very old or the sick. They want to button my coat, serve me at table and assist me up and down stairs. Perhaps with the passing of time that attitude will pass. I hope so, I don't want to be forever, "the poor lady who was burned so badly." I want to be me. (Ton 1982, 191)

Such treatment may be motivated by concern, but it can nevertheless be interpreted by the survivor as a testament that he or she is less than normal and competent. The survivor is here being cast into a discredited social role, which, for Mary Ellen, obscures who she takes herself to be. Mary Ellen's experience is not unlike that of Maria and Ralph (below), and several survivors who have recounted similar experiences. In Mary Ellen's case, her visible scars provide the grounds for others to treat her as essentially different and as less than normally capable. Her identity for others is engulfed by the imputed meaning of her physical scars. The scars provide a basis upon which others can globally define her, with the definition "spreading" to unrelated sectors of her character. Her physical scars come to stand as markers for the other's assessment or imputation of wider disability when in fact, there may be no disability.

Jones, Farina, and Scott see engulfment as the essence of stigma and they state, as have the previously noted writers, that to be marked, to be seen as having a stigmatizing attribute, does not invariably lead to stigmatization. To be scarred obviously does not lead everyone who interacts with the scarred survivor to stigmatize the survivor (Jones, et al. 1984, 9). Again, the spoilage of identity is determined not by the mark, not by scarring, or the loss of a hand, or the use of a wheelchair, but is contingent instead on the definitions and attributions made by the others within the situation of interaction/attributions. In part, such attributions may be contingent on actions taken by the survivor, and in situations where the other's definition of the survivor is discrediting, the survivor may be able to situationally negotiate an acceptable identity. In speaking about the tasks the survivor who is labeled as deviant faces, Douglas notes that

> Deviance and respectability are necessarily linked together: each necessarily implies the other; each is a necessary condition for the existence of the other. This is by no means simply a matter of abstract and arbitrary definitions given to the terms by sociologists. Deviance and respectability are necessarily linked together in the social meanings of the terms as used by the members of our society in their everyday lives. (Douglas 1970a, 3)

Elsewhere, he notes that "each individual is constructing an image of himself as a moral (and normal) member of society that is plausible to himself and to significant others, primarily because this plausible image is the fundamental condition (or ground) for carrying on everyday social interaction (Douglas 1970a, 6). And in a very similar manner, Bernstein states that

> Deviance and respectability are tied to each other in everyday life and each individual tries to construct an image of himself that is normal, acceptable, and plausible to himself and to the people who are important to him. People who are disfigured struggle for acceptable roles, *and this is part of the unification of their lives* [emphasis, mine] (Bernstein 1976, 105).

One of the pragmatic problems for the disfigured burn survivor is maintaining his or her respectability as a normal, ordinary person in the face of challenges to normal respectability created by the imputation of a deviant identity by others. For example, in ordering food at restaurants, survivors, have reported being treated as if they were not present or as if they were incompetent to order their own food. The waitress will direct attention not to the survivor, but to others who are with the person. The waitress may ask, "What does he want?" referring to the survivor, but not attending to him or her. The survivor, in speaking for himself, or his friend in stating, "He can order for himself," may insist upon a renegotiation of identity. While the survivor may have little directly to do with the discrediting definition initially made by the waitress, he or she can actively assert a credible identity. Other examples would include situations in which strangers obtrusively stare at the survivor. The survivor, especially when he or she first experiences going out in public, may find such occasions to be deeply discrediting. He or she can ignore the stares or respond; the response may serve to put down the other, but it may also serve to normalize the situation by establishing a credible identity for the survivor.

In writing about going out in public, Mary Ellen Ton experienced several demeaning situations in which she was treated as less than human. Indeed, it could probably be said that she was treated as a freak:

The strangers I encountered when Gene took me to the clinic were appalled. As I stepped onto an elevator, a heavy silence fell. Even clinic and hospital personnel hushed their friendly chatting to take furtive glances. Once when I stood talking to Ernie in the lobby, a receptionist openly stared the entire time. When I mentioned it to Ernie, he said, "That's her problem." But it wasn't other people's problem, it was mine. I had no idea how to cope with being a freak. When I had lost the familiar facial characteristics I had grown so accustomed to, I lost my identity. I felt like Jane Doe wandering in a vast no-man's-land. I wondered if this was like death when we lose our physical bodies.

Walking into a room full of people where I was singled out always sent my inner butterflies on a rampage. Suddenly, I had walked on center stage. I was the "freak,"an object for the curious onlooker. As I walked down the aisle in a discount store, I was aware that a man was staring intently at me from across the store. He continued to gawk as he approached me and passed by. I moved further down the aisle, and then turned to look around at the directional signs hanging overhead. The man had turned around too, and stood in the very center of the aisle, oblivious to the fact that he was holding up traffic.

People have driven past me in cars, and then stopped, actually backed up, and stopped in front of me to look some more. I stopped my own car once to allow two young boys to cross an intersection. They looked into the car to be sure they understood correctly and burst out laughing. One called back, as they reached the other side, "Hey, lady, what happened to you, a fight with a Mack truck?" Then there was the foursome who walked out of Sears. One of the women spotted me as she walked toward our car. She stopped, bent over, and peered directly into the car window. I turned to look at her full in the face, thinking she would back off. She did, but only as far as the rear window, where she continued to stare in. Her friends, noticing her odd behavior, bent over to have a look. Having gotten their fill, they crossed the street behind our car and walked to the parking area. Out of the corner of my eye, I saw one of the men turn and start back. *I can't believe this, I thought. I really can't believe this* (her emphasis). But it was true. His companions had apparently informed him of what he had missed and, not wanting to be left out, he had returned for a look-see. He pretended to gaze into the store window for a second and then faced the car to see the "freak."

When Gene returned to the car, I dissolved into tears. He reminded me of an experience I had had only a few days earlier when Granny Ton and I had gone to Lafayette Square. Two days before Halloween was not a good time to try my wings there. A grandmother, daughter and granddaughter walked along in front of us. The grandmother turned, and seeing me said, "Oh, Cindy, look, look." Of course, all three of them turned around to see,... and they began to laugh, and so I explained, "I know this looks funny [she was wearing a Jobst mask and pressure garments], but it's not for fun. I've been burned and this mask is part of the burn treatment." They were terribly embarrassed and began to apologize (Ton 1982, 185-187).

Several important themes emerge in Mary Ellen's narrative and these themes will be found in survivor accounts contained below as well. What she experiences, in varying degree and differing specifics, are recounted by most of the survivors interviewed in this study. Certainly, all those who have visible scarring report difficult situations such as recounted by Mary Ellen. First of all, she is treated as less than human. The grounds for violating the normative dictum, or social rule, that it is not polite to stare at another, is apparently provided by the fact that the survivor is scarred. In looking radically different, the survivor, for specific others, becomes available as an object for whom the normative admonition can be ignored. The scarred survivor becomes open or available for special treatment by others, such as staring or asking intrusive questions, which would normally violate rules of propriety and comportment. In being so treated, the tacit suggestion to the survivor is that she is less than normal and therefore not subject to common courtesy or routine treatment.

Another theme shown here involves redefinition of the meaning or importance of the surface interaction, between survivor and other, in terms of its significance for the survivor's identity. When Mary Ellen's friend Ernie says, "That's her problem" relative to the staring receptionist, he is suggesting that the receptionist's action discredits and defines her rather than defining Mary Ellen. Redefinitions of the meaning of painful interactive situations and, hence, redefinitions of the survivor's identity are frequently seen in burn recovery group meetings where survivors will frequently discuss "public problems." More experienced survivors, who have generally gotten past being significantly offended by the displays of rudeness by others, will often suggest to newer survivors that it is not they, but the rude others, who are to be discredited by their comportment.

It was during the subacute, recovery phase of hospitalization that survivors started to think about what they were going to look like. But even then, not all recalled being concerned about their appearance. Some survivors feared seeing themselves and were grateful that mirrors were not generally available to them while others became obsessed with finding ways to see themselves in mirrorless rooms. Seeing themselves typically meant *seeing their faces* rather than seeing other parts of their bodies, for those with large burns could often partially see at least limited parts of their bodies during dressing changes, baths, and debridement. Seeing limited parts of their bodies, even when they were badly burned, did not pose the intense threat to self that was caused by seeing their burn-injured faces. The face was one body feature that could not be seen except with a mirror or reflective surface, and the norm in many burn centers seems to be to preclude mirrors and reduce reflective surfaces. In some cases, mirrors are introduced when the person asks for a mirror or when staff feels it is time for the person to start dealing with his or her transformed appearance. However, in at least some cases, mirrors were never provided to the patient in the burn center. This caused some terrified reactions when the survivor finally saw himself or herself for the first time. It was in seeing his or her injured, grossly distorted face, in cases where there were facial burns, that many survivors discovered the cruel results of their injuries.

One of the critical vehicles that allows other persons to define us is appearance (Stone 1962) and the face is the preeminent part of the body that others use in identifying who we are. Persona, from which person is derived, refers to mask, the assumption being that the real person or self is hidden by the persona. It has been not only psychoanalysts such as Jung who were fascinated with the idea of the mask hiding the essential or real person, but also sociologists, as exemplified by Goffman and the drama-turgical sociologists, who focused much research on the masks and on the situational selves we create in everyday life. For Goffman there was little if anything beyond what is presented, there was no concern for deeper levels of self and there was no recognition of depth.[6] For Jung, however, there was an abiding interest in what the mask hides, in the deepest feelings of the person. For existential sociology, there is also an interest in what lies behind the mask, the deep feelings and the personal myths and beliefs about oneself. The person who is facially disfigured wears a very different mask than that envisioned by Jung. Jung's mask was that of a fictive self, consciously or unconsciously worn, because of the warpage of personality, to hide who the person truly was. For the facially disfigured person, the scarred face-as-mask is imposed as a cruel sentence and it also frequently hides who the person truly feels himself or herself to be.

> Although a disfigured face may not necessarily be unsightly or difficult for others to look at, it may serve as a misleading mask which, in spite of efforts to make impartial and rational judgment, blinds others not only to the play of subtle and meaningful expressions but to the real self behind the mask. (Jones, et. al 1984, 63)

Bernstein notes that the face serves important symbolic functions:

> The face is the part of the body most often looked at not only because, whatever else may be concealed by clothes, the face is left

exposed, but because it is a symbol, a visible index to what is by nature invisible, and the most convincing of all proofs of identity. It is the face...that presents each one of us to the world. (Bernstein 1976, 23)

While scarification of the body, including the face, may be normal or even prized in some tribal cultures as a display of beauty, in Western culture scarring has rarely if ever denoted beauty. The rise of plastic surgery for cosmetic purposes, and the world-wide, multibillion dollar cosmetic industry are a testament to a contemporary obsession with the body, beauty, and appearance. While an interest in appearance and beauty is not confined to contemporary life, it is in the current period that what appears as a uniquely obsessive interest has been very widely dispersed throughout society, often with tragic results for those who are not seen as attractive or beautiful (Millman 1980; Tolmach and Scheer 1984; Baker 1984). In large measure, this interest has been artificially produced by the cosmetics and advertising industries in their mutual pursuit of wealth.

However, the sword of beauty can cut two ways. Those who are generally defined as beautiful may also pay a very high price for their appearance as they are, in a sense, captives and prisoners of their own beauty. They may grow up feeling ugly and different. Some may feel overwhelmed by their beauty and the social myths that others think they should embody. Some may become so absorbed in their own personal myths, to the extent their entire being is invested in their physical appearance and in their bodies, that they finally come to feel estranged from both themselves and from others. Some may be haunted by their appearance, especially women in business or industry who must fight to be treated as more than just a beautiful body and face.

To be beautiful is to be many things in the mythologies of Western cultures. Fostered by the media, one may think of shallowness and vanity, exemplified by the "dumb blond" or the "brainless stud." But most frequently, those who are especially attractive are seen, at least initially, in fairly exemplary terms: those who are beautiful are good, intelligent, creative, and talented; those who are unattractive are not (Landy and Sigall 1974; Fiedler 1978). From grade school teachers to executive recruiters, in everyday life, people, at least initially, judge and identify others based on appearance, most specifically, the appearance of the face. While we may all "know" that the moron, fool, con artist, or murderer can look like anyone, in daily life we often assume that those who look good, whatever that may mean from our perspective, are credited with being okay, others may not be so defined. Those who are visibly marked as different or unattractive, due to scarring, can encounter serious difficulties in establishing positive, credible identities when encountering others.

Stigmatization is not always imposed by others however. Stigmatization may involve self-attribution by the disfigured person toward him or herself as a social object. This occurs initially when the survivor is mortified about his or her own appearance. This is seen in the descriptions of survivors such as Trisha, Eric, and Mike. Such fears may be carried by the person for years as noted by Baker in the *Beauty Trap,* when she discusses Alice Walker, the Pulitzer Prize winning author of *The Color Purple* who, as a child, sustained a disfiguring eye injury. In recalling how her injured eye affected her, Alice noted that "it was great fun being cute but then one day it ended. I consider that day the last time my father...chose me, and I suffered rage inside because of this. Where the BB pellets struck there was a glob of whittish scar tissue, a hideous cataract on my eye" (Baker 1984, 32-33).

Baker noted that Alice hated the scar and that she would rant and rave about it when looking into a mirror. At fourteen, the scar tissue was removed, but the injury still left a "small bluish crater" where the white scar had been. To Alice, this change transformed who she was. She could now walk with her head raised, something she had not previously done in public. Her work in school improved, she was valedictorian of her class, but still she was haunted by her disfigurement. Thirty years after her injury she refused to be photographed for the cover of *Ms* magazine. She found many excuses for not being photographed and then realized that it was all due to her eye (Baker 1984, 33).

In the case of Alice and several here, instances of self-stigmatization are seen. The person turns toward himself or herself as an object of personal experience, and in so doing, the person's own identity is cast as discrepant, wanting, or ugly. In this act of consciousness, informed by the deepest feelings of self-evaluation (worth, worthlessness, shame), the person defines himself or herself as less than acceptable. In doing so, the person mirrors cultural values that are widely shared. The survivor's own reflexive attitude anticipates the potential attitudes of others. Fortunately, not all will see the person negatively, in spite of extensive disfigurement. Unfortunately, many will.

In her book about surviving a very large burn, Mary Ellen Ton poignantly noted how she was overwhelmed by depression and the desire to kill herself, in spite of support by her family and friends. These feelings arose, not during her initial care, but after she was recovering, especially after she returned home from the burn center. Severe pain, numerous infections and setbacks, then terrible itching, which felt like she had hundreds of insects crawling over her and thousands of mosquito bites, along with crippling disability, brought her to a place where her self imposed destruction seemed the only way out:

> Just as it would begin to look like the end was in sight, I would develop another infection and the skin would break down all over again. Three times we went that route, and each time I sank deeper into depression. It was such a helpless, hopeless existence. Inside me

was a woman screaming just as the woman [herself] who had clung to a window ledge that fateful day had screamed, "Help, help, somebody, help me." My rage box was crammed full. The lid was about to blow. (Ton 1982, 93)

Her "rage box" was Mary Ellen's metaphor for placing her anger and rage off in a corner, some place in her mind where she would not have to deal with it, knowing all along that the box, with her consent or without, would open to reveal all the dangerous feelings, fears, and anger accumulated throughout her ordeal. The box was getting full:

Without any warning, the rage so long boxed up inside me burst out. I screamed...and screamed...and screamed. The intensity of my screaming broke open some barely healed places on my face, and the blood trickled down over my eyes and cheeks. "Monster, Monster. Ugly monster," I shouted at the horror movie character looking back at me. Hollywood used makeup to create the image I had become. Open a door, pull back a curtain, run through the rainy night, and come face-to-face with a horrible-looking creature with scarred and disfigured features. (Ton 1982, 94-95)

A religious woman, who was burned in a fire at the church school where she worked and whose husband was a minister, Mary Ellen, in asking why, was brought to a confrontation with God. Answers to why, given by others to soften and explain what happened made no sense or were absurd and she was overwhelmed by her anger:

I hate you, God, Do you hear me? I hate you for letting this happen to me. How could you? Do you even hear? Do you even care? I hate you. I felt so lost, so betrayed, so abandoned. I was amazed at the sudden fury of my attack. I had thought I was handling the situation in a somewhat calm and reasonable manner. The questions friends had tried to answer for me in their own way, I hadn't even asked. All my feelings of outrage had been carefully tucked away, hidden so well I didn't even know they were there. Could this horrible thing actually be some sort of diabolical plot deliberately executed by God as part of his overall plan for me? Is this what I must believe and accept? I could not love such a God.

"God saved your life," others told me. "He saved you from the fire because he has some work yet for you to do." I had been willing to try anything I felt God's inner urging to do. But, surely, whatever I had left to accomplish was not going to be enhanced by my scarred and crippled body. Besides, if God had moved to save me from the fire that day, he was a little late. Of what use was my life as it was now?

I seemed to sink further into despair with every passing day. I couldn't stand myself. My body became a prison. Locked inside, I scratched and clawed frantically trying to escape. But there was no escape...I was trapped forever in this monster's body, more animal than human. Some of my family had been concerned about my mind when I retreated inside myself in the hospital. Now, I began to wonder too. I couldn't make my mind think straight...I would read and not remember, start to talk and forget what I had been going to say; watch television and not know what I had seen. I was frightened by my own body and afraid that my mind had been damaged, too. (Ton 1982, 97-99)

There are numerous themes that are laid bare, as raw almost as the burn victim's fresh wounds, by Mary Ellen's vivid description of her inner life during this most anguishing time of her recovery. She experiences herself as being alienated from her body. Her body is no longer familiar; it is no longer her body. This is a common theme in the survivor accounts which I gathered. As discussed previously, in her attempt to integrate a self-shattering, terrifying experience into her ongoing life, she attempts to comprehend what happened, and what is continuing to happen, in terms of her past, which very much includes religion, but things just don't fit. The "shattering of self" evolves over time. Specific events, such as seeing oneself in a mirror or finding that routine acts can no longer be performed, come to constitute the experience of self as deformed, or shattered. Like Moses crying to the Lord in the wilderness, she feels totally abandoned by her God. Her present condition, at least momentarily, precludes the integration of her previous religious understanding of herself in God's plans. Answers become trite and meaningless as she searches to answer that most fundamental and problematic question, "Why me?" She is overwhelmed by despair, depression and physical discomfort which are at many times maddening, and she begins thinking that the only way out of this continuing hell is suicide: "I don't remember thinking, *I am going to end it all right now* [her emphasis]. I just found myself searching for my car keys" (Ton 1982, 99).

She struggled to get the keys and she finally got to the car, which was in the garage, but no matter how she tried she couldn't open the door of the car. Later that night, she thought about what she almost did:

Most of the night I lay awake thinking about what I had almost done. I was amazed at how calmly I could contemplate my own death. It even seemed the reasonable thing to do. I could not understand why

I was alive like this. The next day I went out to the garage again and I tried unsuccessfully to get into the car, but it was an exercise that only added to my feelings of helplessness and loneliness. How could I make Gene [her husband] understand what it was like? How could I tell him that I wanted to end my own life? I tried to voice my pain and only bitterness was heard. Why, after being roasted like a human hot dog, did those nurses and doctors fight so hard to save my life? Why save a charcoal-broiled body when my soul has died?

Gene's eyes filled with tears. "I don't know how to help you, Mary. I want to make it better for you, I want to take it away, but I can't. I'm glad you're here...I'm glad you're alive." But you don't have to live like this, Gene. Yesterday I went out to the garage with every intention of ending it. I couldn't even open the car door, much less turn on the ignition. I can't live and I can't die. "Oh, babe, he moaned." Please don't call me that. Don't ever call me that again. I'm not your "babe" anymore and won't be ever again. You really want to help me? Then help me die. All you'd have to do is open the car door, turn on the ignition and go to work. It wouldn't be you doing it, it'd be me. Please, Gene. If you love me, you won't make me live like this. (Ton 1982, 100-101)

With Gene holding her, and with her confession, Mary Ellen felt a terrible burden release from her. It wasn't the end of her depression, but it was the first time she was able to share her self with her husband, revealing her deepest fears and anguish. She continued to suffer from depression and setbacks, but at least she had not ended her life.

Having made the above comments on self and identity in relation to disfigurement and stigmatization, and having listened to the words of Mary Ellen, we turn toward considering how specific survivors have coped and continue to wrestle with these very significant issues. For some, there are solutions, sometimes very surprising solutions, but for others, there is only continuing fear and anguish.

Ellen Ransberg: Childhood Fire Injury

Ellen was burned as a small child, so unlike most of the survivors in this study, she grew up only knowing herself as disfigured. When I met Ellen I could clearly tell that she had been burned, but I did not feel that her scars, on the left side of her face, were especially pronounced, but for her they were. This is an important recognition. What others see in the survivor's scarring may have little bearing or relationship to how the survivor views his or her scarring. Ellen had gone through surgery a few years ago to reduce the scar tissue and she felt that her scars were now less pronounced though they still caused problems for her.

D: What do you remember about school, what was it like for you?

> Whenever anybody asked me, and kids were asking, about the scar on my face I'd just get really upset and just say, "I'd rather not talk about it." I remember being called scar face and all, you know, growing up. Always being sort of, you know, feeling invisible and very shy and I mean, you talk about a shy kid.

D: You felt invisible?

> If I was in a group that was talking I wouldn't be doing any of the talking, I'd be just sort of there. It made me feel uncomfortable even to think about it so I didn't say anything. I'd just go to school until noon and then come home and hide in the house and so I didn't, you know, have friends.

Part of Ellen's problem, she felt, went back to the fact that she was never able to talk about how she felt about her scars with her parents. Throughout her childhood and teenage years, the subject of her being disfigured was taboo, for both her and her parents. If she tried to talk about it, her parents refused to listen to her or allow her to discuss her feelings. Even after surgeries, she did not recall her parents speaking about what happened.

D: Did they have any idea how awful it was for you?

> They had no idea; it's just something to them that they cannot comprehend. Oh, we have talked since I've been in counselling. You know, we've tried. I've just ceased to try any longer, just given up. They just say, "You make more of it than it is," is their comment. I realized, hey I haven't gotten any support. It was like somebody hit me and didn't give me any support. You know, your parents don't care and its still so hard I could cry right now. When I hear somebody talk about a supportive family. It just sort of accentuates it, I didn't have that.

At several times Ellen had described herself as feeling invisible as a child. Feeling invisible suggests detachment from the situation, something like feeling oneself as being an outsider, but not quite the same detachment captured by feeling like an outsider. It also suggests feeling unreal. Her reported feeling was incongruous, a puzzle in light of her disfigurement, which, if anything, would most probably serve to make her more visible.

But it could be understood in reference to her repeated reports of how she was treated, and how her feelings were ignored by her family. She felt invisible to them; they didn't recognize or credit her deep feelings about her injury. The message to her was that she didn't matter, that what she felt and feared was unimportant and therefore, to her, she was unimportant. When she says that "it" didn't exist, I believe she is construing how she felt her parents saw her, that is, she didn't exist. She didn't exist as an important person in their lives. She was not real; she was not a person to them, and she therefore carried with her the paradox of being scarred and very visible while feeling invisible. The depiction of herself as being invisible simultaneously locates her in two different realities, in two provinces of meaning. Within one, where she is physically present with her family, she feels herself to be cognitively and emotionally disengaged, whereas her family is very much present. She is present bodily, but her presence is more apparent to others than to herself. The other reality, her "away," as a friend of mine described such feelings, appears more cognitively and emotionally available, and safe, than does the realm within which she is physically present. She is describing herself as alienated from parts of her world, and this is provisionally attributed to her scars.

That Ellen felt herself to be away is not unusual. It is normal; we all feel away or disengaged from our present at times. Fantasy and daydreams are prime examples of how we simultaneously experience ourselves as occupying divergent realms of being. What is unusual is that normally we would not find such experiences as being extraordinary or accountable, whereas for Ellen, such experiences are unusual. She notices them as a distinct breach of reality. Furthermore, and importantly, these episodes are attributed to the fact that she is scarred. For Ellen, such breaches make provisional sense only in reference to her scars.

D: Did you get the feeling that your family didn't want to know you? Is that how you felt?

Not worth knowing, you know, I'm just this ugly thing that you know shouldn't be alive and I've never had a good self image and that goes back as far as I can remember and my memory starts at the fire and goes from there. It's just like, "Hey, I'm not worth the time it would take anybody to get to know me, I'm no good and that's the way I felt."

D: What was it like in school?

Yeah, and when I was with kids and they came up and go, "What happened to your face," you know. And then I would get really uncomfortable to the point of tears and just say, "I don't want to talk about it and leave."

After high school, and after she had worked as a beautician, Ellen joined the army. It was after this that she had several additional corrective surgeries to reduce the scar tissue on her face. After leaving the army, she underwent hypnosis in an attempt to uncover the roots of continuing depression, depression so intense that she has been hospitalized several times since leaving the army. Besides depression, there were physical problems which became compensable under VA benefits. These were not related to the burn, but resulted when she had a seizure during a reconstructive surgery on a knee injury that occurred in the army. First defined as having a conversion reaction with hallucinations, she was rediagnosed as having a seizure disorder by neurologists at a VA Hospital. Her seizures involved a reaction in which she depicted herself as being rather catatonic. She would be motionless, staring into space without any recognition of what was occurring around her.

Like I can just freeze. When I freeze I'm somewhere else and I don't know that I'm here and I'm seeing a picture like a hallucination, like in my car behind the wheel going over a cliff into the ocean. I keep falling and I just fall and fall and fall and I never hit bottom until, like somebody shakes me and then I come out of it. There is another one, in a burning building, trapped in a building corner window up high. The flames are coming to get me and I can't get down. I don't know if that has anything to do with the fire, why I have that one. When I come out of it, it was like I was really there. And I shake and I'm scared just like my body reacts to being in a burning building.

It seemed interesting that her seizures mirrored her feelings of being "away" or invisible, as if she were not, as a person, *there* and that the imagery conveyed a deep sense of isolation, of being totally alone in an overwhelming situation. Many of her descriptions conveyed this feeling, often mixed with the image that she was still a small child. Through hypnosis and therapy, she felt better able to understand some of her underlying emotional pain, but she still found it hard to openly talk about the burn. Indeed, while she was aware of her scars, she had never, until recently, thought of them as a problem in her life.

Ellen was in therapy for several years, yet her burn injury never came up as an issue. During five years with one psychiatrist, she was never asked about her burn. She didn't understand how it was affecting her life and the therapist, apparently, never thought that she might be repressing deep feelings relating to her scarring. Hospitalized for an acute depressive reaction, a new therapist at the hospital suggested that the burn might be of consequence to her recurring emotional problems. He suggested that she attend a burn recovery group. She stated that when the therapist suggested the burn was a problem, she didn't understand what he was talking about. The therapist replied that she had repeatedly stated how upset she was about her scars, yet she could not remember saying anything about them. Then, during a group therapy session, while another patient was talking about being raped, Ellen dramatically recalled several incestuous episodes with her older brother, something else she had blocked out of her awareness for years. She also began to recognize the profound effects of her burn. She felt alone and unsupported.

D: From a lot of what you've said, you seem to feel very alone.

> Yeah, and I have to take care of myself. I don't know how. And I'm just not capable of doing it. And it's like because I was burned and all, I'm scarred, and nobody wants me and I'm not worth loving; I'm not lovable because I'm scarred.

She is talking about how she feels now, but this also refers back to how she felt when she was three, in the hospital when her parents "walked out" leaving her alone, crying to come home. She felt abandoned to nurses and she felt that her parents didn't care about her:

> And I can feel the bandages and everything and I just wonder how I'm going to take care of myself, all by myself. There's nobody here. Nobody that loves me. There's nurses but nobody that loves me. I'm too much to really love.

D: How long have you felt this way?

> For a long time. It comes and goes since my mother wanted nothing to do with me. It's become more real since then and since I got in touch with the feelings and I don't like feeling three 'cause so many bad things happened then.

Ellen's world seems bleak, lonely, and frightening, for she has little if any support and love. There was little sense of anger or rage against her parents and family, but the limited anger that was displayed was for them. There was more of a feeling of desperation, futility, and of imposed self-pity (Charmaz 1980). She seemed to have tremendous burdens to bear, but it also seemed that she was now starting to recognize and release some of what she had carried for years. There was also the expression of grief and loss expressed for her broken relationship with her family. She seemed resigned to this loss, still feeling abandoned like she felt when she was a young child. There was hope also, since now Ellen was actively trying to build a family of friends to replace what she lost and still sought. In a number of ways, though less dramatically so, her feelings appear to parallel those expressed by Jeff Asmore who is discussed elsewhere.

Kevin Davis: Chemical Burn

Kevin sustained a chemical burn to his face. One badly damaged eye was eventually removed and Kevin is beginning to consider returning to work. While his disfigurement is not extensive, it is obvious that he was burned. Kevin feels that his identity has been changed by his injury; and he has noted that, because his appearance has changed several times, through surgeries, he must keep getting used to his face. At first, he did not know how extensively he was injured though he was, for a while, concerned that he might die. He was blinded by the accident because of direct damage to one eye and his good eye was closed because of swelling. Once he regained some vision, which allowed him to see only shadowy images, he was less frightened about what would happen to him. In talking about first being in the hospital he states:

> I felt it was really serious because my family came to see me in the hospital the first night. One of my brothers started crying and I didn't want my girlfriend to see me because I didn't know how I looked. Then they told me I was really a sight because I started swelling up bad then. I sensed the pain of them for me [from] their voices, just their feel. It felt like they were paining for me. As people started coming to see me, people would start crying. Like I say, I could hear them crying, I could hear all the emotions, stuff like that.

Kevin's determination of his condition was contingent on actions and behavioral displays made by family members, friends, and nurses, which he assessed. Clues knowingly or unwittingly supplied by them became information bases upon which Kevin could judge his condition and what he must look like. In essence, he became a detective, searching for clues in what others did and said, to ascertain what and who he was relative to his injuries. The contingent process of his decision making, of how he constructed knowledge about himself, is visible. For example, that his brother started crying, a brother who was involved more in hard drugs than in family matters, and that there was a lot of "emotion" when others would come to see him served as evidence for his own understanding of his condition. The statements of nurses also provided clues as noted below, but sometimes the information provided was confusing, creating further puzzles. Finding out how he looked, when he was finally able to glimpse himself, was horrifying for Kevin. It was as if he saw a monster from a horror movie, a fairly typical reaction echoed by many survivors.

> It's weird. When they was taking the bandages off my face my nurse would come in and say, "God, you really hurt yourself bad." A few of them I got to know, would tell it to me like it is. And I couldn't really figure it out. Each day, one would come in and say, "You really look

great today." I couldn't figure that out, what they meant by "I look great." And I knew something was wrong. I knew from my girlfriend. They say, "God, man you hurt yourself pretty bad."

D: Could you see out of your good eye then?

I could see down [with one eye] and that's how I held my head-- down. Now, when I took a bath they would put the bandages on either there or back in the room. Now this nurse didn't want other people to see me, she put a towel on my head to cover my face a little, cause she knows I can look down and get around. I thought God, something must really be bad because, I guess she put the towel over my head so they wouldn't see me, because I guess I looked that bad.

OK, this day I say, "I'm gonna look at myself." There's the bath- room, there's a mirror straight ahead. So as I approached the door to the bathroom, I could start to focus in and see in because I couldn't see that much further as far as real clear. So as I got to the door, I could start seeing my face. And everything was just drooped down, you know, discoloring here, discoloring there and this eye, it didn't have no lid on it, it was just white, I pictured it as a fish eye.

And then I got scared. Because I looked like one of those horror movies that I had pictured a long time ago and I was kind of afraid of them when I was small, so that automatically kicked in and I backed out.

D: Was a nurse with you then?

This was something I was gonna do by myself so I didn't say nothing. It scared me enough for me to back up. So the next day I say, I'm going to look at myself, go into details, look and see what's happen- ing with me. So the next day was allright. I just seen I was hurt real bad on this side. Now it really felt like mud on my face, like a blob or something. It didn't have no feeling and I couldn't get rid of it, it was just there.

D: What did you think when you saw yourself the second time?

I thought the surgery was going to put it all right. I know I was going to have plastic surgery. You know, the thirty-three years of looking like Kevin. You know, the Kevin Davis I know. I'd lost it. I didn't know the extent of losing it, understand, until later on, not really. I didn't know the extent that I lost it. I just know I lost my face, and everything was going to be allright.

More directly, perhaps, and more clearly than in the descriptions by other survivors in this study, Kevin shows the linkage between identity and facial appearance. The loss of "it" was his appearance and this was also, in part, his identity. While he knew that he had a drastically altered appearance, he assumed that plastic surgery would return him to his normal appearance. It was only later, in discovering what surgery could not do, that he realized the extent of his loss. His bad eye was still in at this time and for a while his surgeons thought the eye could be salvaged, though with a loss of sight. During his second surgery, the eye had deteriorated so much that it was feared the optic nerve might be destroyed so it was removed. He had not known that the eye was to be removed when he went into surgery. Indeed, his surgeons were themselves unaware of the necessity of removing his eye until they actually performed surgery and found the increasingly serious degradation of the eye. This unexpected experience is similar to that of Eric when, during the course of surgery and without warning, his surgeon decided to place a bolt through his jaw.

D: How did you find out about the eye?

My girlfriend said, "I have something to tell you." So she told me. I didn't have the foggiest idea. So she says, "They took your eye." I says, "took what eye?" 'cause I couldn't see out of it anyway, and it didn't feel like it. And she says "Yeah, it was really bad." So I accepted it. You know, since it was bad, I don't need it.

Acceptance appears situational and provisional, and while his interpretation may suggest his future integration of this consequential loss, in fact he came to more fully comprehend the seriousness of his loss only over time as he discovered what losing the eye meant in terms of his appearance, future surgeries, problems with infections, and so on. Right after the surgery, Kevin was able to "accept" this loss because, in fact, he did not know the full consequences and ramifications. Later, through the passage of time, the loss became greater. While losses may be initially experienced, both cognitively and emotionally as profound, the survivor will understand the full impact only over time as he or she reconstructs his or her life.

When I got home, I had to be with my girlfriend. Now she knew this guy, but he had a strange face. But she didn't see him [that is, she didn't see his face which, for Kevin, is *Kevin*] for three months. But all the prettiness was gone, all the handsomeness that she liked was gone.

After I got out, she had to get used to me. My lip was all weird, she didn't want to kiss me, we didn't hug. A lot of intimate stuff was gone. She was sort of scared, not used to it. She just couldn't handle it yet. Even to this day she can't handle it. Because of, I guess, the trauma that she went through. I don't think it really started getting bad until I seen how people started looking at me. Then I had to go into a way of just saying to hell with it.

Kevin had to wear a hard plastic mask used to reduce the formation of hypertrophic scars. This restricted his movement and, together with damage around his mouth, precluded clear speech. He then used a Jobst mask, which is a tight-fitting, elasticized garment. This was more comfortable for him and he could move around more easily.

D: What was it like when you first went out?

When I first went out people would just not understand, and stare and stuff. Because they don't know what's happening. My girlfriend was driving me then, everywhere we go I had people looking. So that didn't bother me. Because now, I wondered if anybody liked me outside my family. As I got out more, I started seeing people I knew. I would see them, some girl I was talking to back then. Nobody knew me. Some of them, I could say a few words and they knew my voice.

D: The woman you scared when she saw you, she had known you?

Knew me quite well. Another lady I knew, and I just said my name and she said, "What happened?" God, she just broke down crying on me. That was, I think, one of the saddest things. Seeing somebody else feeling, that something had happened to me. That was,...weird See, I had several different things that was wrong. Here, *I had lost my identity, lost my dignity, then lost my girlfriend first thing* [my emphasis]. So I had so many losses all come down on me at the same time.

In another part of the interview relating to how Kevin coped with his injury, he stated that he had always been rather shy and "hidden," but because of his injury, he could no longer be shy, he couldn't be hidden in the background of social gatherings as previously. Like it or not, he now felt more visible than he had before he was burned.

I was kinda shy and hidden. Which I can't be anymore because my face says "Hi" before I get there. A lot of people get in the background all the time but [they are] always there. And that's how I was. But now my face says "Hi" before I get there.

D: You have talked in group about your face and identity changing, what about that?

> It still happens. It's the strangest thing. I don't really consider myself having a face. It's like I don't have a face because deep inside, I don't particularly care about this face. It's just something I have to live with because it's there. It's been changed so rapidly in these five years so that I can't get used to my face. Now [after his surgeries have been mostly completed] I can almost settle down to a face that I can get used to and care about. But I know it's going to change again.

What separates Kevin from Ellen is that there really is little sense of self-pity in Kevin's descriptions. While Kevin went through significant depression and problems of drug abuse, his story is not a tragic tale, real as the tragedy indeed is. On one occasion when Kevin and I got into an elevator at the hospital, a young man made a comment that Kevin could have taken as an insult. This man, who was with three other men, each of whom looked like L.A. street gang members, said something like "Hey man, what happened to your face. It's all fucked up." One of the other men said "Shut up, can't you see he was hurt and has enough problems." After we left the elevator, I asked Kevin about how he felt about what happened. For Kevin, this episode just wasn't construed as being degrading for him. Instead, the comment turned back on the one who made it and served to degrade the other rather than Kevin. If this had happened with some other survivors, such as Ellen or Jeff, I believe the statement would have been received much differently, as a threat to the deep feelings of self. While Kevin is still learning to adapt to his injury, he seems more secure in himself, even when he recognizes real problems and issues which have yet to be resolved. Also, there is no sense of constriction as Kevin recounts his problems. In returning to previously enjoyed activities, such as skating and basketball, he found accreditation of himself.

In having his face change, Kevin felt he didn't have a face. There was a sense of disowning and being affectively unattached to the face he had, as if it were an alien object that had little to do with his identity. Yet he realized that his face made him uniquely available or visible and he described his face as saying "Hi" because it was so readily noticed by others. What made him begin to feel he could accept his face was the installation of his prosthetic eye. Because of various complications, the fitting and use of the eye was delayed for a long time, during which he had to wear a patch. The prosthetic eye allowed him to feel that he had a complete face. Slowly, as he go used to have the artificial eye, he felt more comfortable in public places. He also became more accepting of the way his face looked even though he knew it would change as additional surgery took place.

Sharon West: Flaming Drink Injury
(Interviewed with her husband, Paul)

Sharon was burned in a restaurant while having dinner with friends. The burns involved her face, chest, arms, and hands. She has minimal scarring on her face, but her neck and chest are scarred. Because of the swelling of her face, her parents didn't recognize her when they first saw her in the hospital. Like virtually all the other survivors, Sharon did not realize how badly she was injured at first. She kept thinking she would be out of the hospital in days, but the days turned into weeks, with the necessity for several returns for reconstructive surgeries. Part of adjusting to her injury was the recognition that she was not going to ever be exactly as she was before and while she realizes that she has progressed, accepting the scars has been difficult.

> I know it's not going to be back to the way it was, perfect skin, it's not going to be that way. God, I mean I know the first time I looked at myself in the mirror I said I looked awful. I do remember going, "Yucch." I just looked awful. *This was not the person I knew.* And I know when my parents came to see me, Paul explained, "This isn't Sharon, the one you know, she does look different." My father, I'll never forget the look on his face. He just couldn't believe it. He just walked in and sees his little girl lying there and not looking like myself. A year later my mother said if they didn't know it was me in that bed they wouldn't have thought it was me.

D: What did you think when you saw yourself?

> I was not pleased at all because on my face it was real blotchy. We entertain a lot and I think, gosh, Paul has to take me out and I think, God, is he going to be embarrassed by me, which he wasn't. And you know, you don't like people staring. You look in the mirror and you don't like what you see. 'Cause you look back, and how you were. You want to look the way you were.

Sharon found who she was in the present by referring to her past. Sharon is a very attractive woman and she was grateful that her face did not sustain deep burns, but accepting the damage, and the scars that remain, took time and she is still involved in learning to accept how she has changed. She finds herself putting herself down and she wonders what would have happened if her accident had occurred when she was single. Being married, and knowing that her husband is still there, seems to make it a little easier.

I put myself down and Paul gets so mad. 'Cause I guess I'm not as nice looking as I was, and he gets mad. I can't imagine if this happened to me when I was single, how are you going to meet someone, tell someone that? I think it would be very difficult for those people that are single and kind of have to start all over again.

D: Were you very depressed about this whole thing?

Yes. You have moments. You start feeling down but the kids, they pick you right up. But you do feel [depressed]. I went through all my clothes last summer and got rid of everything I couldn't wear. I had been just keeping them in my closet. I just cleared my closet out, that was very difficult, especially some brand new dresses. It's hard, very difficult.

In a sense, in giving away dresses, articles of clothing she had worn and some which she had yet to wear, Sharon was giving up part of herself, part of her past and part of her former identity. Clearing the closet, as much as it represented a pragmatic act taken in order to rid herself of clothes she no longer felt comfortable wearing, was also symbolic of recognizing a part of her that no longer existed, and the preparation for what was to be, what she would become as she selected new clothing that would not reveal her scars.

Paul and Sharon, while not wealthy, were solidly within the middle class. With a large, very attractive hillside home and a good income, they were still facing severe financial problems because of Sharon's burn. There was continuing medical care needed, and perhaps, future surgeries down the road. Her burn occurred at an insured restaurant but since Paul had not accepted the initial offer to settle (an offer made immediately after Sharon was burned), the insurance company would offer no assistance to them until after a court decision was made. This left them owing, and trying to pay, 20 percent of the charges, $100,000. They had always paid all of their bills on time, but now they were having real problems meeting their obligations and this was potentially stigmatizing. Sharon and Paul were facing the discrediting fact that they frequently could not pay their bills. More than once they had to borrow from family and neighbors just to pay routine bills. Paul had to go to the city to plead for an extension on his utility bills. While the hospital and doctors were very understanding, he found he was treated like a disreputable person by a clerk at the city hall, and by other creditors who had little sympathy for the problems the family faced. Fortunately, Paul's boss and fellow workers were understanding, and he was often allowed time away from work to handle these tedious and frustrating problems. The family in this sense became stigmatized as creditors demanded payment and threatened legal action.

Paul: I think this has a psychological effect on the family. Besides the devastation of the accident and the physical and psychological things, you have to change your ways a little in the way of life. This accident was brutal for us, besides the physical and psychological stress that it has put on us, financially [it] has been devastating to us.

Maria and Ralph Porter: Residential Fires

Maria was very critically burned in an apartment fire and Ralph was burned in an arson fire in his home. Both have extensive facial scarring with Maria being the most severely disfigured woman in this study. Maria and Ralph met at a surgical/burn rehabilitation unit when Ralph was having some surgery. At the time, Maria was a volunteer in the unit. Through a little matchmaking by another burn survivor, they started dating and, after a short separation, married.

Both of Maria's hands were amputated because of the very deep burns that extended down to bone. It was hoped that her hands could be partially salvaged, but the destruction was too extensive. Even with the loss of her hands, and the fact that she was in the hospital for months, Maria did not comprehend the extent of her devastating injuries until she finally saw herself. After seeing herself, she became deeply depressed and virtually stopped eating. When she was able to eat, she frequently regurgitated. It was an extremely agonizing time period and she sometimes wonders how she got through it all. After she learned from her cousin that she had almost died, she became concerned with how she looked.

Then I started worrying about seeing myself in the mirror. I wanted a mirror and no one would give me one, no one. I asked one of the nurses for a mirror and she said, "I'll be right back." I saw her whispering to another nurse and then another nurse came by and I saw them whispering and looking at me, and I just started worrying more.

Even with the amputation it didn't sink in that it was that bad. It was like I wanted to escape from reality. I didn't want to see things. An amputation is a real serious thing and I just didn't want to look at it like that. I just wanted to go home.

I tried not to think about it. Mostly every time when I would think about things was when I was in school, about my friends, about things I used to do. I tried not to think about my hands being amputated, I tried really hard not to think. It didn't sink in.

Maria's ability to not think about the consequences stemming from the loss of her hands would, from a psychological perspective, represent denial. There is no doubt that she did, in a real sense, not recognize the massive implications of this loss, but this fact does not necessarily imply the existence of unconscious defensive processes, namely denial. Her response can be seen also as reflecting a conscious, active coping technique that is contingent, not only on the moment, but which is also temporally bound toward a future that is indeterminately available to her. Recognizing what the loss means, in any real sense, must await the future; by thinking of her past self, she actively blocks dwelling on future possibilities that may be truly devastating.

Seeing oneself for the first time after injury can be especially traumatizing for burn survivors, especially for those who are facially burned. This can be shocking even when they are prepared by medical staff for what they are about to see. Some survivors become acutely curious and search for ways to see themselves in their mirrorless environments, while others accidentally see themselves. In some cases, they are steeled for the experience, but in others, they are not. In Maria's case, seeing herself was a planned process. The burn unit psychiatrist and social worker were sensitive to her need to see herself and they prepared her for this crucial experience. For Maria, even with support, seeing herself precipitated a turning point and crisis. Prior to being burned, she was a very attractive young woman; she now had to cope with the loss of her hands as well as her drastically altered body and facial appearance.

> I asked her [the social worker] what I looked like, and she told me. She said that I was going to look very different. She said that if I went out on the street people would stare at me. She said that I wasn't going to be pleased with what I saw. I was totally different.

D: How did it go as you started learning how badly you were burned?

> It was like sinking into depression, real bad depression. When I got to look at myself in the mirror, Karen and the psychiatrist were there. It was planned. The psychiatrist, Dr. Goldman, I gave him a real hard time because I wouldn't talk to him. I didn't want to talk to anybody. I was very quiet. He was there. The night before, he came and said "Tomorrow," and he told me the time. He and Karen were there and they asked me if I wanted my sister or my mother there, and I said no. I wanted to be by myself, with them. And they brought a big mirror, a long mirror.

> I didn't see myself for long. It must have been a couple of seconds. But what I saw..., I screamed and I wanted to be alone. I wanted them to leave and from then on I didn't eat, I didn't talk. Nothing. I

was closed in to everything. Every time they tried to feed me, I threw up. I was like that for four months or more. I had a tube in my stomach and they would feed me through there because I wouldn't eat anything, I threw up everything. I wanted to forget. I didn't want to think about anything.

In her reports of dreams and hallucinations, Maria saw herself as whole and unburned. Even several years after she was burned, in her dreams she would see herself as she used to be. She reported a recurring dream in which she saw herself approaching a wall with a mirror. She would approach very slowly and see herself, unburned.

After seeing herself, Maria continued to be cared for in the burn center and she received intensive support from Dr. Goldman and Karen Hobart. It took a long time for her to recover from the image she saw reflected in the mirror, but very slowly she began coming to terms with herself. While seeing herself was overwhelming, she still thought that, through surgeries, she would look normal again. Understanding that she would not look as she had previously was yet another devastating experience; it was another way in which she and her world were shattered. Yet, as horrifying as it was for her to see herself, her condition was then understood by her as temporary. She believed that she would eventually be normal looking, but this was not to be.

I had this idea that I was going to look the way I looked before, after all the surgeries.

D: Even after you saw yourself?

Yeah. They would say, "You'll look better." But by that I understood, "You're going to look as good as before." Even my family thought that, so they would talk about it. They would say, "Oh, they're going to do all this surgery on you. You're going to go through a lot of plastic surgery." We had this idea that, "Oh, yeah. Plastic surgery. It's going to make me look the same." I never thought when I was home I would have defects. Even using a prosthesis; I didn't think about that. I would think about going home and having a normal life and taking care of Maria. I never pictured me going through all this trouble, not being able to dress myself, not being able to do a lot of things at first.

Again, her inability to conceptualize the future reality of her situation reflects, I believe, not simply a naivete born of denial but also an active coping strategy of focusing on future perfect possibilities and ideal conditions, while using this projected future to block present realities which would be potentially consuming and overwhelming.

It is apparent that covertly or overtly, others, including medical staff and family, provided Maria with the clues she sought in order to construct an acceptable version of reality as discrepant and fictional as that reality turned out to be. A script was written here, a tale or fantasy about how things would be, and the coauthors who enabled Maria to thereby "deny" the reality of her loss were several. It can only be conjectured that family and staff may have many pragmatic reasons for knowingly fostering such a fantasy. Most of us have been in situations where, to placate and reassure someone, we have quite consciously bent what we felt was the probable truth of the situation, sometimes hoping against hope that we are somehow correct because we ourselves cannot face the expected consequences. In the case of the disfigured survivor, the most typical reason for fostering a fictional tale probably pertains to the feeling by others that the survivor has gone through too much to accept reality, and that it would be better to delay the inevitable discovery of truth.

Depression was directly related to Maria's conceptualization of her present condition and her recognition that she would not be the same again. The root of depression, at least here, is not seen as stemming from a mysterious psychological process, but instead from information that was communicated to her by others, which told her that she would not be the same again. The information was deeply discrediting for she was now told that she would not again be who she was, and who she thought she would again be was no longer a viable image to which she could cling. Hope was shattered in the cold truth of a mirror and brief statements by burn center staff. Part of her was gone forever. We can only wonder the extent to which, in her silence, she may have feared that this would be the case after she first saw herself in the mirror.

She was surrounded by clues that, from an outsider's perspective, may have certainly suggested to her the devastating nature of her injury yet she didn't see the clues. This was in part explained by what she was told by others. All of us, when confronted by discrediting information or bad news, are frequently adept at not seeing what is laid before us. Psychologists and sociologists have numerous labels, such as selective perception, selective inattention, and denial for this uniquely human ability to disregard what others clearly see. It often seems, when the person finally sees "reality" that, in retrospection, he or she finds that they were suspicious all along. Patients often refrain from asking what they fear and suspect; the avoidance of confronting her fears was at least partially dependent on the erroneous statements made by family members and medical staff that, essentially, gave Maria hope that all would be well in the future; finding that it wouldn't be was devastating.

D: Do people ever say anything to you in public?

Maria: I have met people, this one lady. I see this lady standing right in front of me. I'm afraid of meeting weird people that can do something to me.

Ralph: She gets a lot more of that too, because she has the prosthetics.

Maria: Finally, she came up to my sister, she says, "Can I give her a hug?" and my sister says, "Ask her." She hugged me and started praying. I thought, "Oh my goodness. Why do these things happen to me?" I don't like people to do that to me.

Ralph: A lot of people treat us like that, too, like you have a really low mentality because something happened to you.

Maria: People who treat us like we're mentally retarded.

Ralph: [Like in going to a show when people say] "Please take your money and put it here. Then you get your ticket for the show. Go right through that door, if you get lost...."

Maria: We met a man like that in Philadelphia, Trisha and I were at a conference. The doorman—Trisha was just going along with him. He was saying, "If you go out here, you'll see a taxi. If not just wave and the taxi will come up to you. Now this is your room, and the number is this, and you use this key to open it." When we left, we said "Can you believe this guy?"

Maria: People treat you like that. They come out with that voice, you know, how you talk to a one year old. They treat us like we're retarded. Then a lot of people will ignore you all together. Like if you're with somebody else, they'll look at the other person. One time I was going to a concert. I got out of the car and this guy says, "Oh, shit. What happened?" He looked like he just saw someone from outer space. I looked at him and just gave him a dirty look. I just kept walking.... Sometimes I get upset because sometimes people really do react. I was at a dance with friends. I felt so strange there. These two guys were coming towards where we were and they looked at me, and pointed at me, and they laughed. That's the worst thing. I felt bad.

To be disfigured is to be on public display. It is, in a sense, to lose anonymity in terms of the actions of others who sometimes appear to be exceptionally insensitive. While some people do not want to get near those who are disfigured, others treat the disfigured person as if they were publicly available for touching or for intrusion into their lives; they are treated as objects rather than as persons. Some of the occasions can be exceptionally traumatizing for the survivor; some are odd or humorous. Maria believes that she has caused at least one traffic accident when a motorist, who was staring at her, hit another car. On another occasion, she saw a teenager walk right into a lamp post, as his head was turned to look at her. Both Maria and Ralph, as well as other survivors, described situations where strangers came up and touched them, made rude comments, or asked intrusive questions. They also told of witnessing the following situation with Kim Lann, a young Vietnamese man who was very severely burned when he was a teenager.[7]

> **Maria:** You know Kim Lann? We were driving down Colorado and he was at a bus stop. We stopped to see if he wanted a ride. We saw this lady approaching him very close, extending her hand. He's backing up and he's going, "No." I got worried that it was some type of weird person. She was trying to put money in his shirt pocket. He didn't speak English. I said, "He doesn't need your money; he has money of his own and he's upset." So she took the money and we turned our backs on her. He was relieved.

Eric Mathews: Vehicle Accident

It was like for women, "Well, no one will ever want me." So that part of me just lay down and said, "Why try?" Then part of the healing process, it was three years that I spent at home, doing a lot of intro-spection and figuring out how I'm going to survive, what can I do? I went through all the things I couldn't do first. "I can't, can't." Then again, you're disoriented. My identity of who I was, I was no longer. So then it's a complete search. What can I do, where am I going to go. When I go outside, other people are going to look at me. They're going to laugh and they're going to think "it's ugly." I go, "Well, before I would have looked and I would have thought it was ugly." I knew I couldn't change all those other people. People are going to look. People are going to notice you look different. Some are going to say, "Ugly." Therefore, what I can control is how I am going to deal with that. I'm more than just my body.

In going through his list of things he could no longer do, Eric referred not only to things that seemed physically impossible, but also to things that seemed out of reach socially, like dating and partying. In seeing himself as no longer being capable of taking part in various activities which were once important to him, he was reinterpreting his identity; what and who he had been, he was no longer. His search was for identity and self, identity and self transformed by fire. He understood the anticipated, projected reactions of others to himself as being not unlike how he believes he may have reacted to others who had similar injuries. In this way, he conceptualizes himself as stigmatized as he takes the role of the other towards himself as a social object. When he anticipates the reactions of others, he is role-taking; he is interpreting himself as he anticipates how others would view him. In role-taking he is typifying himself; he is projecting himself toward an anticipated future from his present, and his interpretation of the reactions of others refers back to his own social experience within the everyday world.

D: Do you recall some point where you looked at yourself and were horrified?

Oh, yes. I was at home, they keep mirrors out of the hospital. So when I came home I thought I'd go take a look at myself in the mirror. And I went in and I looked, and it's like my insides just collapsed. The deepest feelings of knowing that, I said, "I'm so ugly." My nose was burned off, my eyebrows were gone. My eyelids themselves were from other parts of my body. I walked in, looked at the mirror and had this feeling, then I just went, "I'm so ugly." I did understand the pain of what I looked like, but I also know it was more important not where I was, but where I was going to go. It's not, "What happened to me," but "Where do I go from here? What is my job in all this?"

In other sections of the interview, Eric recounts how he got past the terrible problems of his injury, which included substantial disfigurement. For the first time in his life, he started feeling like he was in control over what he knew he had to accomplish and further, he believed that he could overcome his situation. The fact that he was disfigured was accepted with the attitude that, if that's how it is, so be it. He saw that he had power over his life, regardless of what had thus far happened. He believed that he gained this appreciation through meditation, therapy, and prolonged reflection on his past life relative to where he wanted to go. For the first time, he felt free to choose what was going to happen in his life. It was a time of anger and depression, but it was also a time of significant discovery and growth. This is not to imply that what Eric went through was easy; it wasn't and he had many fears and concerns about how he looked.

D: What was it like when you started going out in public?

Well, I went out covered in bandages. Still the cream and all that stuff. It was my own thinking, that people are going to look. They're going to be shocked. I go, "I might as well go out before I think I'm ready, to get used to it, so that when I think I'm okay, I won't even notice them." Seemed logical to me. I went to malls, because where are the most people? In malls. It was an intentional purpose for me to do those things, to go out in public so I'm used to it.

D: What happened when you went out?

From extreme rudeness to extreme kindness, the rudeness of people walking by, just shocked. Their eyes bulging out, their mouths hanging open. Some people say, "Oh my God." Some say, "Oh, shit, what an ugly dude."

In restaurants, people notice. My brother, he was more aware than I was. For the rudeness, I just accept it as their immaturity, not as my problem. So I put it upon myself to cross that bridge and say, "Hello. How you doing? Yeah, I was in a fire." There's as many reactions as there are people. The worst was the first time I went back to the night club and these guys were looking at me. When I walked by, they intentionally tried to trip me and do weird stuff like that, which got me very.... And I was at the beach just this year, and these people were riding by on bikes. And as they were riding by looking at all the scars, they were like, "Oh, boy." And they stopped [to look more]. I saw him coming back, and I waited until he was close. And I go, "I was in a fire. I was burned. Anything else you want to know?" I was willing to talk and explain it to him. I try not to get angry. He just got embarrassed and rode off. So, they're going to look. What are you going to say? I like to be in control of the situation. I can't control the situation or another individual, but I can control myself.

I was always a doer, and I paid for it. It's like jail. Once you go to jail and get out, you're supposed to start all over again. And I paid my dues, I paid a heavy price for what happened. So why should I lock myself up again, or exclude myself from living? It's from doing those things, exclude myself from living? Find out what you want to do and do it.

As with other survivors who were facially disfigured, the loss or damage to other parts of Eric's body did not appear as overwhelming as the recognition that he was facially disfigured. He had often, every day, seen other parts of his body during his stay in the burn center, but at home he came to finally see his face and the extensive damage to his face was the most traumatizing result of all.

One of the processes that occur in burn recovery group meetings for survivors entails the reconceptualization or redefinition of meanings involving issues and problems that the survivor encounters in being disfigured. For example, a newly arrived survivor may report having problems with people staring or making rude comments. More experienced survivors may provide alternate definitions of what such intrusive behavior "really" means, suggesting that staring is okay and normal, but that those who make rude comments are simply ignorant, uneducated, moronic, or asses, whatever label fits. The new survivor may be told that he or she will eventually get used to such episodes and that, no matter how painful it may at first be, they must continue going out in public. Eric's attitude displayed this type of reinterpretation. After all, should his life be further damaged just because others have problems in seeing him? The meanings of the injury and all that goes with the injury, which become significant to the survivor as self-referencing, are contingent on definitions and attributions made by others, both those who are known by the survivor as well as those who are not known, such as anonymous others who stare, gawk, and make rude comments. These shape and inform the survivor about the social and personal meanings involved in burn injury and they inform the survivor about himself or herself. Shown by the comments made by Eric, Maria and Ralph, the survivor can redefine those situations wherein their identities are discredited. In part, it is through this and similar attributional and interpretive processes that survivors can reconstruct new, acceptable identities. The process is ongoing and open to further elaboration and change.

A significant turning point in the survivor's experience entailed seeing himself or herself in a mirror. For a few of the survivors, this only confirmed what they already knew or suspected, but for most of those who were facially burned, the mirror, or reflective surfaces, provided shocking evidence of who they had physically become. Virtually all of the survivors assumed and believed, supported by reassuring statements made by family and friends as well as by medical staff, that they would look better, but the question was, "Better than what?" The extent to which anyone other than medical staff realized how marginal improvement might be, when judged from the nonmedical standpoint of the survivors or family members, remains unknown. None of the survivors interviewed, who sustained any significant facial burns, felt that they turned out looking as good as they had believed they would and none felt that they looked the same as they had before they were burned. All survivors who sustained full thickness facial burns, or partial thickness burns where scarring resulted, were at some time very disappointed with their final cosmetic appearance. I suspect that even those who have ostensibly accepted their appearance have periods of time when they still feel considerable anguish when they see themselves in a mirror or photo. Of consequence is the fact that they do not allow such feeling to consume them.

Surgically, the appearance of such survivors may be outstanding considering the extensive destruction of facial features, such as nose, ears, chin, and eyelids, which some survivors sustained in the moments of searing fire and heat. Nevertheless, for the survivor, and for others also, what is medically "beautiful" may be insidiously horrifying. I recall witnessing a vivid confrontation between a plastic surgeon and a woman who was badly burned in an apartment fire. The woman had been burned five months previously and she had just undergone some reconstruction on her face and neck. She was doing well physically; she was free from infection and all grafts that had just been stapled in were taking, but she still had some open, moist wounds, and she was still very reddish. When the surgeon entered her room, he commented on how beautiful she was looking. Without warning, all the rage and frustration she was feeling came out. She accused the surgeon of lying to her; she had seen herself and she knew she wasn't beautiful now and she knew she wouldn't ever be beautiful again. I felt painfully sorry for both her and the surgeon and I felt like a voyeur who had just witnessed the shattering of a woman I hardly knew. I was a witness to the destruction of a fragile self and the collapse of normal interaction, which caused exceptional embarrassment to all who were present. For the surgeon, the gloss of "beautiful" represented reference to medical/surgical criteria, typifications and judgmental properties that had nothing to do with her understanding of beautiful. For her, the term was a mockery. And for the physician, while I do believe he was referring to his "surgically informed" perception of her, the use of "beautiful" may have had an element of subterfuge, representing the construction of a facade designed to sustain interaction and the appearance of normality in a situation that was stressful for both he and his patient. If that was the case, in this instance he was called on it, and the whole setting collapsed in tears and embarrassment.

For all survivors who were facially burned, mirrors provided the ultimate visual proof of just how badly they were injured, regardless of how often they had seen other parts of their bodies. In the cruel reflected images provided by mirrors or other reflecting surfaces, survivors confronted the brittle, disintegrating realities that some had feared, others had ignored, and none wanted to recognize. This, together with the discovery of disability and the finding that recovery was not to be as soon realized as each had assumed, provided the evidence for the survivors that their lives had been invariably transformed. The survivor's sight of himself or herself was typically horrifying, yet for many, there was still the hope that they would eventually look normal again. Hope was not woven out of imaginary cloth; the survivor's belief that all would eventually be right was fabricated through attending to, and believing in, statements made by medical staff, family, and friends. To be sure, many survivors probably had doubts and fears about what they would look like, but like the terminally ill patient who hears of a new, mysterious wonder drug, it is understandable that some survivors could interpret anything that seemed positive as a basis for hope and expectation.

Recovering survivors may be required to wear tight fitting garments which reduce scarring. For those with facial burns, a mask may be required, made out of elasticized fabric or clear plastic. In either case, such devices are uncomfortable to wear. In hot weather, they are especially uncomfortable and they are generally intrusive.

For some survivors, however, the masks can come to provide a sense of insulation and security, even if people did stare at them while they were in public. This was exemplified by Trisha:

> You know, there is a side of me that says I'm ready to get out of this thing, just dump it, and there's a side of me that says, "Oh, boy, now everybody is going to see my scars," and they are going to say, "Oh, how ugly, is that how you look?" and "Oh, her face is really terrible."

For Trisha, the mask that she had to wear, which caused some identity problems in specific settings, became part of her identity more generally. Over time, the mask was incorporated into her self-image. Like clothing, it served as an identity prop, more or less becoming routine over time. At the same time that it made Trisha more visible to others, it also served to hide her scarred face. The mask was visible, but in a personal sense, part of her was hidden by that very visibility. This was clearly noted by Trisha, and was experienced with concern and misgivings when it came time to finally remove the mask and go into public without it. In removing the mask, Trisha expressed the fear that others would now really see her and, in so doing, would be repulsed. Others have expressed similiar concerns, not only with masks, but with Jobst garments, which may cover most of the body. Here there is a direct parallel with Jung's interest in the mask. Trisha's mask, which obscured her appearance and hence, her identity, was literal. For her, the plastic mask became camouflage, an identity prop. For Jung, the face-as-mask was the camouflage for hiding the self.

An interesting problem can arise for some survivors who go into public wearing either a fabric mask or a plastic face mask. During burn group discussions, over a period of three years, at least two people, both males, reported being stopped by police because of their covered faces. In both cases, the police were apparently suspicious of someone driving down the street while wearing such a device. Both men were seen by the police as possible criminals, due not to conduct, but solely to the unique or discrepant appearance of each as seen within a particular environment wherein such an appearance for the police is problematic (Stouffer 1970A, 1970B; 1971). Not only does the mask look strange, but the strangeness can provide others with the grounds for interpreting the survivor as potentially criminal or threatening. For the police in these cases, the mask provides warrantable grounds for attributing a discrepant identity to the wearer. Dianne Bringgold, who was burned in a plane crash in which her husband and two young children perished, experienced this type of problem as she was returning to a hospital for therapy,

> One day two policemen were driving by just as I was entering the side door of the hospital. Seeing me duck in the door, they became concerned. When I was leaving the hospital after my therapy session, a friend at the desk stopped me. "Boy, did you cause some excitement! Two policemen came rushing in here about an hour ago, ready to pull their guns. Said they were looking for a masked woman. Thought they'd catch her red-handed robbing the hospital. After I explained to them that you were harmless, they went away." The last close call was at the Jack-in-the-Box drive-in. I'm afraid I almost scared the cashier to death. I drove up to the window, completely forgetting about my mask. When she turned to hand me my order,...the girl's mouth dropped open. Gasping, she threw her hands in the air. (Bringold 1979, 91)

Dianne was able to quickly normalize the situation and renegotiate her identity by making a joke about not robbing the drive-in. Nevertheless, this demonstrates the importance of discrepant appearance relative to assessments of identity made by others and it also indicates one of the more unusual public problems that a survivor might confront.

Besides risking the degradation of being stopped and questioned by police or having the general public stare or point, the person who must wear a mask may also be subjected to very rude comments. When Trisha went to a nightclub with several friends, two males yelled at her that it wasn't Halloween so she could take off her mask. As I recall, this may have been near Halloween; nevertheless, this was humiliating for Trisha. It was one of those publicly visible acts, where she was thrown momentarily onto center stage, and where her identity was called into question by two idiotic males who most probably had no idea of what they were actually seeing. To go out in public, to a crowded gathering place, was difficult enough for Trisha. Fortunately for Trisha, like Eric and many others, these experiences did not lead her to shun public contact. Survivors may have had some second thoughts. Trisha and others may have gone home quite depressed and in tears, but they continued struggling to build a normal life and they continued to insist that others treat them as normal. Other persons who are disfigured have reported being told that, looking as they do, they shouldn't go out in public. This type of experiece has been reported by a number of survivors. Fortunately, it seems to be an infrequent expression of callous disregard. But one can wonder, if some express this attitude, how many others, in seeing a grossly disfigured person, feel the same way? One female survivor, in going into an expensive, fashionable restaurant was asked by another woman patron how, looking as she did, could she ever go out in public! This was a devastating experience, but one she eventually got over.

Surprisingly, not all burn survivors found disfigurement, even gross disfigurement, to be all bad. Several people expressed, in differing ways, the fact that they would go out of their way to explain what had happened to them to curious children or adults. This was done because these people felt some responsibility for trying to act as spokespersons for the community of survivors. More importantly, each felt that, especially with children, telling a little about what happened might prevent a future burn. I think many survivors could identify and accept this statement without difficulty for virtually all the survivors said that at one time or another, they had told strangers a little about what had happened, thinking that such revelations might build some understanding and, perhaps, help prevent a similar accident.

What was even more unusual, and unexpected, was finding a few survivors who felt that their disfigurement was an asset in some important ways. Trisha felt that she became more open to others whom she did not know when she met people in social gatherings. She felt that she became less shy and introverted than she had been before she was injured. Because she is facially disfigured, she believes that some people are reluctant to approach her. Because of this, she will go out of her way to say hello to strangers, a sentiment expressed by Eric and several others as well.

Alan Jeffery Breslau, mentioned previously, described how being facially disfigured has been positive for him. Initially believing that his appearance could be restored by plastic surgery, Alan discovered that this wasn't to be. He was especially concerned about his nose which had been destroyed by the fire. His plastic surgeon had discussed the process of rebuilding his nose and Alan thought that he could finally have the type of nose he wanted: since adolescence he had considered plastic surgery for the correction of a bump, something that he had considered a defect. Like many others, he didn't fully appreciate what plastic surgery could and could not do:

> Little by little I became aware that it wasn't going to be like that at all; when all was said and done, I would be unpleasantly disfigured. Soon, I began to discern some satisfying advantages to this condition. For one thing, recognition is instant and total. As a result of that plane crash, I have become a personality; I am no longer anonymous. When most people return to a place after a few days, they are generally unnoticed nonentities. But now when *I* [his emphasis] return even a year or more later I am greeted with, "Hey, where have you been?" Wherever I go I get the feeling that a red carpet is being rolled out for me; the receptions I get are warmer and friendlier than any before the accident. This familiarity makes people feel more

comfortable and it makes it easier for me to form bonds of friendship with them....Since my disfigurement, men are considerably more open and friendly with me. They accept me more now because they think that since I'm disfigured I'm not a sexual threat to them.

Women are more receptive to me since the accident than they were before. It isn't fair to say that they find me more or less attractive now than before, but they notice me because I am disfigured. Once they have picked me out and we get to know each other in a more informal way, they see what they want to see. *Since they know this is not me they're looking at, the only real me they see is the one in their mind's eye* [my emphasis]. They paint that picture themselves and they react to my personality rather than to my appearance. (Breslau 1977, 216-217)

While those who are psychologically inclined might define Alan's and the others' statements as positive proof of rationalization as well as denial, I feel that such a definition, while possibly warranted in some cases, demeans the experiences of these survivors. By viewing their experiences and statements as rationalizations for deep, unaccepted losses, the implication is that resolution has not been achieved and that acceptance is necessarily fictive. I do not believe that this is the case here; the statements made by Alan, Trisha, Eric, and others represent real growth. This acceptance represents the discovery of positive meanings in the midst of terrible losses. Again, what is critical for the survivor is interpretation and meaning; to suggest that what is tragic can beget only that which is tragic is to grossly misunderstand the human capacity to create meaning and transcend adversity. Growth here reflects the survivor's ability to reconstruct self, a self not of tragic isolation, but of forward-seeking growth with others, and the formation of a new identity out of the broken remnants of what had been.

To be sure, not all survivors can find positive meanings in their injuries. Four of the survivors interviewed in my research, in varying degrees, feel that the quality of their lives has been adversely affected by being burned. Ellen is one who feels that much of the trouble in her life stems from the fact that she was burned and, more importantly, that her family never would acknowledge the reality of her injury. Three others were similar in having families who, in different ways, seemed unable to accept the significance of the burn in the survivor's life. In the case of Jeff Asmore, the only person in his life who seemed to be of importance to him, his mother, died in the fire, as did one brother, a fire that Jeff believes his stepfather either set or caused. Jeff, more than any other in this study, reported many distressing experiences which he attributed to his gross disfigurement. Everything from being evicted from municipal buses, to losing jobs is seen by Jeff as being directly related to his appearance. I am sure that some of what he reports is related directly to how he looks, but in his case, there are other confounding issues that aggravate his life.

The next chapter will examine the survivor's relationships with others and specifically focus on issues which arise when the survivor returns home. He or she may no longer be perceived by family members as the same person they once new and there is a sense of strangeness for all when the survivor comes through the long familiar door. The meaning of being home may be very different. Home may no longer be the welcoming place it was and the survivor will have new demands with which he or she must learn to cope.

4

The Homecomer and the Stranger:
Relationships with Others

This chapter will examine the survivor's relationships with other people. Consideration will be devoted to family and friends and how being burned affected the lives of these others and how, reciprocally, they affected the survivor. Of concern here are the ways in which others facilitated or hindered the survivor's reconstruction of a normal life. Some attention has already been directed to this subject in the discussion of Kevin's and Ellen's cases. But here I will concentrate on issues of interpersonal support and what was faced by the survivor when he or she returned home.

All of the survivors looked forward to going home from the hospital but most also felt at least some concern about leaving the burn center. Some, like Eric, Maria, and Mike had spent months in the hospital. When Maria left the burn center, she went directly into a special rehab unit where she remained for three more months. The hospital, even with all the pain and trauma which the survivors experienced, had become a known environment, and in some ways a place of relative security. The task of going home would mean change and new demands and, for many, going home was another experience which was shattering to the self in which the survivor, on his or her own ground, had to contend with disability and issues not directly confronted within the hospital environment.

In going home, survivors were again forcefully reminded of how much they had lost to flames, chemicals, or electric current. It was in returning to life outside the hospital that some found additional evidence showing them just how badly they had been burned and that what they had sustained was not just a serious injury. It was, instead, a massive destruction of who they had been. The effects of the burn were encompassing and enveloping and the consequences of their injuries overtook and foreshadowed all aspects of their current lives. And like the initial experience of being burned, there was, for many, no simple retreat, no escape from serious, threatening consequences that followed them. For some, like Eric and Trisha, the discovery was visual when, for the first time, they saw themselves in mirrors. For others, the discovery was one of disability; they could not care for themselves and they had to rely upon others at home just as they had in the hospital.

Demands were necessarily made on family members; in some cases spouses became surrogate therapists and nurses, roles they felt were imposed on them and for which compliance was required. Most spouses were able to carry out their new roles with only limited difficulty, but a few found it very difficult to dress open, sometimes weeping wounds, and it was especially difficult when care meant the infliction of pain. The necessity for wound care at home and continued exercise is an area burn care staff seem quite able to relay to patient and family. Other realities, such as that of the patient seeing himself or herself for the first time in a full-length mirror, or problems involving sexuality and intimate relationships, seem to be more commonly ignored or glossed over by medical staff. The realities of returning home often turned out to be very different than expected. In significant ways, the homecomer returned as a stranger to both self and family.

Mike Lawson: Motorcycle Accident

Mike probably went home before he should have. Like demanding that he be allowed to smoke, he became increasingly insistent that he be allowed to leave the hospital. His weight had dropped to ninety pounds and he was still very ill, but he felt that he would die if he didn't get out of the hospital. He had reached the point where he felt that he had to get out of the hospital regardless of the problems thereby created. He had a large family, at least one, two, or more members of which visited him every day at the burn center, driving some 140 miles to see him. Because of the dedication of his family and Mike's insistence that he be allowed to go home, his doctor released him:

> I had had nine surgeries and it was taking me five days to wake up after a surgery. I was all covered, grafted, but I had a lot of open areas, raw open spots. If you touched me the skin would rip open. I was skin and bones, but it was time to go home. They carried me into the bedroom and put me on the bed. I was in a lot of pain: if you touched me, the skin could come off. Now I'm home and its different, it's not the way it was before. It's a different environment, I'm not myself. I'm a burden to everybody. My friends came over that night. I was bald, blue and red and gross looking. I didn't have any dressings on. I was the picture of a concentration camp kid. That's exactly what I looked like. It was quite a shock to them and quite a shock for me. It was humiliating and embarrassing, and very strange.

My little sister couldn't come in and talk to me; she couldn't look at me. She's just two years younger than me, fourteen, very emotional and she just couldn't talk to me. Of course, that hurt psychologically and my little brother didn't understand.

D: You said that Phil took care of you. He had just returned from Yale?

Phil is two years older than I am, he's the one who took charge. He would pick me up, carry me, put me in the bath tub. He would [try to] put me in the tub, land flat on his back, I would cry. He really took a lot. I didn't want to do anything but lay there and be comfortable. I didn't want to move or exercise. I didn't want to do anything. It felt so good to lay there, in a comfortable bed and not have to do anything, and to not have to hurt. And within a week I was contracted up into a fetal position.

D: You knew you were supposed to exercise?

I knew I was supposed to wear splints on my hands and I fucked up; at the time I had to rest. My whole body was physically exhausted from the ordeal. I couldn't take any more. I'd sleep eighteen hours a day and I just had to do it, just eat, rest, and sleep. I had to rest. I guess you can say I kind of gave up and just stopped trying.

Mike saw himself as being emotionally at the end of his rope. He felt that he would be emotionally destroyed if he didn't get out of the hospital, but he realized that being temporarily comfortable had high, long-term costs. His understanding of the meaning of his present condition was contingent upon the meaning that he assigned to his past experience in the burn center, an experience in which he was fully depleted of energy, tortured every day, and exhausted by the rigorous demands of intensive medical care. His present situation made sense only in reference to the past. The meaning of himself became a time contingent accomplishment and that meaning was provisional. What turns out in the future may be very different from what was initially anticipated in the present even when the present informs the future. Mike knew that he had "fucked up," but the full consequences of his failure were fully understood, not merely when he saw that he had contracted;* the full implications of his failure were realized finally when he had to undergo difficult therapy and further surgery due to serious contractures.

---

* Contractures commonly occur in burns as scar tissue develops. Splinting and diligent exercise reduces contractures. If the person fails to wear prescribed splints, or follow exercise requirements, debilitating contractures can result. Further surgery may be required in such cases.

D: Tell me about how people reacted to you.

> The one thing I vividly remember was my little sister sat at the side yard with a couple of her friends, and one of her friends looked in the window and said, "Who is that weird looking bald man in there?" It just put me in tears. That was the first time I realized how bad I looked.

D: You had really not gone out in public?

> Yes. Nobody ever had said anything. I went home and saw my face in the mirror, and it was just shocking; it didn't even look like me. My face didn't look like me, I was bald.

D: How did your sister react to this?

> It really hurt her, but it hurt her more when I got pissed. I was really upset, I started crying when she said that. I got upset, and I started yelling at her. I have really gone through a lot of head trips. I can't really explain, it was more like getting used to myself and adjusting to what I was, and realizing that *I was still who I was* [my emphasis]. That's when it hit me that I was scarred and deformed and *not the same person* [my emphasis].

D: You saw yourself in the hospital?

> I could see everything but my face and it didn't affect me that much. Seeing my tendons hanging out and my muscles exposed, it really didn't hit me that much. Once I was outside in the world a little, it hit me that I was scarred and that I had changed, *but I still felt that I was the same...I was me, I didn't feel any different. I was still Mike* [my emphasis]. My friends never let on that they felt I was any different.

D: Did any friends have problems with seeing you?

> Yeah. The first one, when I got home, was a friend who helped put me in the bath tub the first night. And it just freaked him out. When they got me up I was crying and in pain. When they picked me up they ripped some skin off. It just grossed Tim out. He didn't come back for a while, he couldn't. That's when I thought, "I don't care what other people think, I'm going for it." I went back to high school in a wheelchair the second semester. I weighed one hundred and five pounds and looked terrible. I didn't give a damn. I didn't care what I looked like. *I was me and I was out to prove that I could*

show everybody that it doesn't matter, that I was still the same person, that I could still be who I was [my emphasis].

D: When you returned to school, what happened?

Nobody really came up to me and talked to me, I was really alone. Now it was different because I couldn't go out and seek those friends. My real close friends were still close but my social clique, we didn't associate anymore because things were so different.

March of my senior year, I was walking on crutches and the night of graduation we had to walk all the way around the track in front of the bleachers up to the front and sit. Instead of using crutches, I used a cane. This was stupid but I wanted to prove...I wanted to graduate without crutches. I made it all the way around the track and I was getting tired. I fell back in the line but when they called me up to get my diploma, I made it up there without the cane. *And it was like graduating from this mess. And it was thrilling for me because it had been one year from the time I had the accident* [my emphasis].

Mike discovered how he had changed when he was confronted with seeing his face and when his sister's friend reacted to his appearance. Regardless of how gross his other injuries were, it was the appearance of his face and another's reaction to him that were the most shattering and threatening in terms of his subjective sense of identity. His inner subjective sense of self, of his identity and who he was, remained resolutely firm.

Nurses have often stated that how a person does after being burned is dependent on their "personalities." Here, how well a person does is attributed not to "personality," but to how the person has learned, over time, to reconceptualize him or herself. Critical are the meanings that the survivor attributes to self and, in many cases, such meanings are suggested, at least in part, by others. It is also contingent upon how the burn experience itself is construed and whether the survivor sees him or herself as a helpless victim or, as someone who can surmount such challenging events. The support of those who are closest to the survivor, such as family members and friends, is also of consequence. How well a survivor does following injury turns out to be not an individual accomplishment. Instead, the post injury quality of life for the survivor is an achievement that is social in origin. Reflected by what the individual appears to accomplish, a whole range of others have been of consequence in enabling or disabling the survivor as he or she recovers from injury. In no sense does this mean that the survivor is not of paramount importance to the process, but it is recognize that other people are of immense consequence to the recovery process.

Strength for the survivor is displayed in resolute decisions made in the confrontation with devastating, overwhelming possibilities. Mike could see his strength in the fact that he was able to graduate with a cane instead of with crutches, and in being able to get his diploma unassisted by even a cane. A simple task was made painfully complex by his condition, a simple task that took on extraordinary significance and suggested just how far towards recovery he had come, and how strong he was. It is in such experiences that the survivor discovers who he or she is and learns how he or she has transcended the injury. For some people, the discovery of strength within overwhelming adversity radically changes who they feel they are. Some of those who survive never could have imagined where they would be taken by their injury or how they would be so drastically and positively changed.

Peter Shrader: Vehicle Accident
(Interviewed with his wife, Lynn)

Several burn survivors and their spouses, during support groups, have discussed problems occurring when the survivor returned home and expected his wife (these were almost always men) to care for him as had the nurses. Sometimes this problem reached crisis proportions and became a central focus for accusations made back and forth between both parties. The husband would make ceaseless demands for attention and assistance on his wife, while she felt overwhelmed and quite unable to cope with someone who was supposed to be learning to care for himself. In turn, he felt abandoned and not understood, and he accused his wife of being insensitive and indifferent to his plight. In at least one witnessed case, this in part provided the stated reason for divorce. In the case of Lynn and Pete, there was some resentment for Lynn over the fact that Peter was stubbornly independent. The fact that he was minimally demanding, which is really the way physicians and nurses would like to send their patients home, was distressing for Lynn. Lynn saw her role as that of care giver, but that role was tacitly threatened by Peter's independence.

> **Lynn:** He's that stubborn to where he'll do whatever he thinks he can do until he finds out he can't do it before he will ask for help. When he came home I took two days off work. I was going to take a whole week off, but I just went back to work because he's so stubborn. He wanted to do everything for himself. I said, "What do you need me here for?" I got mad at him because he wouldn't let me help him. Like he couldn't button his buttons. He'd still try everyday to do it, and until he got frustrated, he wouldn't ask for help.

Nevertheless, the spectre of being confronted with a husband who still needed care, including daily wound care, was disturbing to Lynn. In a significant sense, Lynn was facing a stranger and there were misgivings about what life would be like.

> And now, he was coming home, and I had to take care of him, freaked me out even more. Because I had to sleep in the same bed with him. I'm getting better at it, even a year after the injury, of touching him. I'm afraid I'm gonna hurt him all the time.

There was also a difference in how Lynn and Peter first viewed the prospect of going out in public with Peter wanting to go out before Lynn thought he should.

> **Peter:** The day I came home I asked her, could we go out to dinner? And she looked at me and said, "What!?" I wanted to get out in front of people 'cause I wanted to prove to myself that there was nothing wrong. I wanted to be sure I could be around people, that it wouldn't bother me.

D: What happened when you went out?

> **Peter:** I was treated as a freak for a while and I still am. [They] just stare at you and gawk. I guess in your subconscious you think they're talking about you. They were very curious why I was wearing gloves and I had a lot of people ask me about the accident. I always feel people are staring at me, but it doesn't bother me to the extent where I worry about it because I know it's doing a good job for me.

Several survivors alluded to their feeling that their significant other, while not physically burned, was nevertheless a burn survivor. Kevin stated that several times during both my interview with him and in support group meetings: his girlfriend was also a burn survivor. What happens to the one partner, through identification and role-taking, as well as the daily involvement in being concerned about the other, happens, in a sense, to the unburned partner as well. Lynn also expressed this feeling about what she had gone through while Peter was in the burn center.

> **Lynn:** He doesn't remember the first four weeks after the accident. I do! I am a burn survivor too, but I don't have any scars. I just don't have the scars. It was my spouse that went through all the pain and the burning part, but I went through it with him, and I remember the first parts of it and what he went through. *You feel, if you're married, you feel a part of that person and it bothers you. You are*

feeling what's happening to him. You're going through everything with them, step by step [my emphasis]. I think I suffered more mentally with all this than he did, but nobody offered me a psychiatrist. Basically I was alone through all of this, except for my daughter, Marci. I had her.

This also obliquely suggests what Kevin said about interpreting his condition through what he perceived to be his brother's reaction to him in the hospital. Kevin couldn't see, but he could *feel the pain in his brother,* through his brother's crying, pain he knew was for him. For Kevin, that interpretation served as a basis for understanding how seriously he must have been injured. Lynn here describes the recognition that what exists between them as separate individuals, as entities, is something which transcends both. Her identity and self are shared with, and contingent on, Peter's identity and self just as his self is contingent on Lynn. There is a reciprocal interdependence between Peter and Lynn. What is seen here is a cogent example of role-taking in the development of self between two interactants who are copresent to one another over time. The self is shared; it is contingent and accomplished through identification and interaction with the other. The threat to Peter's existence was a threat to Lynn as well; it was a threat to her being and life as part of his life.

There were two significant losses that Peter and Lynn still had to face when Peter got out of the hospital. One involved Peter's job and the other involved friends, or those who had been considered friends. The job loss was anticipated; the loss of friends was not. Peter had been very concerned about getting back to work and he feared losing his new job, a job he hadn't actually started. He was surprised when his employer kept calling to ask when he could come to work. When he got out of the hospital, he called his prospective employer. He was to start light work a month later.

> **Peter:** I called them and I was told "don't worry about coming to work," I was already terminated. They had terminated me a month ahead of time and hadn't told me and I was home recovering, thinking in my mind that I would be able to go back to work. I knew I wouldn't be 100 percent, but I knew I could do the job.

D: What did that do to you?

> **Peter:** It kinda wiped me out. I think it drained everything. It was like, here I spent twenty-three years getting the job, and then, because of the accident....I got to the point where, "Was it really worth living?" I didn't see any future. "What am I gonna do now?" At that time, I was getting close to my forty-second birthday. I don't

have a job, you know? I kept saying to myself, "What am I going to do?"

At the time of the interview, Peter was still on disability and Lynn was working. They were getting by; they felt they were doing all right but it was difficult at times, and they were not able to live as well as they had before the accident. It was increasingly becoming economically difficult. It was a frightening position to be in. He had supported his family for years and suddenly he was out of work. He was disabled, at least temporarily, and Lynn needed to return to work just to keep the family going. They were able to get through very difficult times on the hope and expectation that Peter would be able to return to work. The threat of job loss, in terms of stigmatization and feelings of self-security, here seems to be more significant to Peter than was the burn itself. Peter seemed to accept his burn very matter-of-factly. The loss of his job and friends was something else.

A significant part of both Peter's and Lynn's hope that all would eventually turn out all right was founded in their strong, mutually shared, fundamentalist religious convictions. It was their religious beliefs that gave them courage on the darkest nights. But it was their friends at their church who gave them their most disheartening experience since Peter was out of physical danger after his accident.

D: What were the problems with the church?

> **Lynn:** It was Seaview Baptist Church. We quit being members. When the money started being gived like it was [they were not making normal contributions], it's just like the whole church turned against you and says, "Sorry!"

> **Peter:** We were Sunday school teachers for years.

> **Lynn:** We were very active members, we both were. He was a commander and I was a director in the youth program, which is every Sunday night. We'd go on Wednesday nights for parents that were in the choir, that needed care [for their children]. Just about anything they really needed, they would ask and we would do it.

> **Peter:** What was funny to me is, we thought we had a lot of friends. And until you go through something like this, you really find out who your friends are, your true friends. And we found out we didn't have hardly any.

D: I would think it would be close knit.

Peter: That's what we thought, too. I got out in August and there was only two weeks left in [Sunday] school so I went ahead; I went back to teaching. I taught for two weeks, for three weeks. Then I said that was it, because of my body. I was pushing. I realized I was pushing myself too hard, too quick.

Lynn: They thought he was fine because he was getting back into all this.

Peter: They felt they saw me getting around, that was it. They thought I was healed.

D: Did anyone ask if you needed help?

Lynn: Not once. We wrote letters explaining why we quit, putting our problems on paper, and sending it to the pastor there to see if he would do anything. Peter went in personally and talked to him and was made promises this, this, and this is gonna happen, and nothing never did.

D: What did all this do to you?

Peter: It was just gone. It was gone. I loved working with the youth. And in a three-year period, we had brought seventy boys and girls into the church ourselves, just by recruiting. And when I got back and asked the pastor why nobody called, he couldn't give me an answer. And it really upset me. There was at least one hundred women and not one of them called Lynn. And I just couldn't understand why. The trust in people just went downhill.

D: Did you have any support, even at first?

Lynn: When he had been in there about a week, I called the deacon, I called the pastor of the church and had the deacon come up and they laid hands on him. They anointed him with oil and prayed over him, in there. And the nurses didn't want to let them in and I said, "You better step aside. You have no business telling me I can't let them in, they're going in." And they left me alone. Then you know, I never heard from them again. It's really strange. You think with something this bad happening to a very active member of the church, there'd be a lot more people calling, asking. They didn't care whether we were there or not so we just broke away.

D: Did you have other friends outside the church?

Peter: We really didn't have other friends because of the church. Our life, for eight years, was the church and when you're committed, that's what you do. It's your life.

D: Did you feel that these people were uncomfortable because you were burned?

Peter: They all knew what I had been through. But they really didn't know. They thought they knew. Until you've been through it, nobody knows what a burn patient feels like.

Lynn: That's what made him the angriest, when people would come up and tell him, "I know what you're going through."

Peter: That would upset me.

Lynn: He would always get angry and say, "No you don't." Lots of times he would really get angry at people telling him that.

It is very apparent that both Lynn and Peter felt isolated and alone in going through Peter's burn experience. Several times, Lynn stated how alone she was when Peter was in the hospital. She had very little support except from her daughter and one woman whose husband was in the burn center. There is a strong sense in which Lynn's world, as much as Peter's, was shattered by his being seriously burned. Tremendous responsibilities fell upon Lynn and she had no friends to whom she could turn. Her family wasn't in the area, and while her brother was described as very wealthy, he called her only once and offered no financial support. Peter's family was also far away and they had not been close to Peter for several years, though they did visit him after his accident, and have become closer now.

The problems with the church only intensified Peter's and Lynn's feelings of alienation and abandonment and neither could understand the reasons they were treated as they were. Their identities, in large measure, were tied to being dutiful members of their church. Their belief in God, in part, carried them through the trials they endured with Peter's injuries. Their belief in their church, in what it meant to be active participants in the work of the church, and their reliance on friends in the church, a reliance which had been taken-for-granted, was destroyed. Personal identities (selves if you will), were shattered as much, if not more, by this than they were from the accident. Also destroyed was Peter's initial belief that he could return to work, taking up his new job shortly after he was released from the burn center. All of these experiences fragmented and splintered long-held beliefs which both Lynn and Peter held about their personal worlds, worlds that in many ways were reciprocally or intersubjectively created over a period of years. The unexpected realities they faced cut deeply into their fundamental understandings of their worlds and themselves, calling into serious doubt basic tenets about who they both were, who they could trust, and their importance to those whom they had considered to be friends.

Many burn survivors recounted the importance of religious beliefs to their recovery. For many, it was through religious faith that they found hope and that they were able to make some acceptable sense out of what happened to them. All of the survivors who felt that their religious faith was an asset, except Peter and Lynn, were supported by others, to varying degrees, in their respective churches. Peter's and Lynn's experience with members of the church is distinctly different from what others reported as their experiences with friends and fellow church members. Lynn's and Peter's experience with members from their church, while perhaps representing an extreme case, provides insight into what such losses personally mean to survivors.

In a significant manner, Peter had become a stranger, not only to himself by being incapacitated, by being removed from the central roles of family provider and church member, but he became a stranger also to those persons who had been considered friends. In not understanding what he had gone through, they didn't understand Peter. He was no longer the same Peter. In others saying that they knew what he had gone through, his own understanding of what he had gone through and how he was changed was for Peter demeaned.

Several survivors have made it very clear that they also were angered by people who presumed to understand what they had gone through. Several survivors have commented on this issue, including in their condemnation, nurses, therapists and doctors as well who, from the survivor's standpoint, can never understand what pain and anguish they have suffered, no matter how many burn patients they work with. The transformation created by the burn does not end with only the survivor; it sends out ripples like a stone cast into a placid pond. The extent to which lives are shattered by the injury, the degree of loss of roles, identities and fundamental beliefs, none of these may be apparent initially to the person or to his or her family. The consequences of the injury, as discovered and defined by the survivor, and those close to the survivor, emerge over time. For many, the subjective feeling is that the burn goes on and on, never ending as it changes their lives long after the original accident.

The meaning of the burn, both retrospectively and prospectively, changes over time for the survivor as his or her life changes. What doesn't generally change is the fact that the burn and its results continue to foreshadow the survivor's life. The burn remains concretely available, always there, minimally in a background sense, in an unfolding variety of ways, as both topic and resource, in the emerging and unfolding biographical history of the survivor as his or her world is produced through daily life.

In a related or parallel manner, the burn also remains present for those who are close to the survivor, if not immediately as a problem or concern, it is nonetheless present as a background condition or feature which is situationally contingent. Existentially therefore, the meaning of the burn exists within an open interpretive horizon, the meaning of which is never fully deterministically available at any point in time except in the most provisional manner. For many survivors, the burn goes on and on reverberating throughout the course of their lives.

Sharon West: Flaming Drink Injury
(Interviewed with her husband, Paul)

When Sharon finally came home from the burn center, she also was a stranger. She was not the same woman who, on the night of the accident, had kissed her two young children good-bye. The most difficult and wrenching experience for Sharon was the reaction of her children when she returned home after six weeks in the hospital. At the time she was burned, she was still nursing her daughter, Bridget. Paul was suddenly confronted by the need to help care for his wife. He still tried to work and care for two young daughters. It was a very difficult time for all. Family needs were met through the hiring of a house-keeper/babysitter. She took care of the children all day until Paul returned home in the evening.

One daughter, Amanda, had problems accepting Sharon and, in turn, this created emotional problems for Sharon.

Paul: But Amanda recoiled from her mom. She would not go near her mother's side or give her a hug or welcome her home. Sharon cried when she saw the kids, of course, just out of joy. Amanda took one look at her mother, saw some of the bandages, saw some of the scarring on her wrists, and she wouldn't let her mother get close, touch her, give her a bath, or dress her. She was afraid that whatever her mother had, she would catch. It took about three weeks, and of course, Sharon went into the bedroom and cried and I went in and asked her what she was crying about. And she said, "My daughter has recoiled from my touch, my hugging," whatever. But I said, "Sharon, you have to understand, you've been away for six weeks. What she remembers when you left for dinner that night and what she sees of you today are two different things, and it will take a little time to adjust."

Sharon: Oh, God. That was so painful. They saw the mom dressed up, and now you come home and nothing too tight because your bottom is got,...because that's where they took the grafts from. You know, mom wasn't the normal way she always looked.

Paul: But eventually, it worked itself around. Of course, Sharon never went back to breast feeding. I think the trauma was more for Sharon; she breast fed Bridget for seven months and then not being able to breast feed was very traumatic for Sharon.

For Sharon, there were also difficulties in realizing that in coming home, she could not fulfill her normal role as mother in caring for her children, and in finding a housekeeper doing what she normally did.

Sharon: Paul did a fabulous job with the children, with everything. He's been great. But gosh, I don't work. I stay home with the kids,...no one takes better care of the kids than I do. And Paul told me that we got a housekeeper, and I mean, "Who's this strange lady taking care of my kids, cause no one can. Who can take care of them like I can." Here you are, laying there, not being able to do a thing. It's hard. Amanda was going to have little valentines and she couldn't sign her name so I said, "Amanda, do you want me to sign them for you?" And she said, "Well, the housekeeper will help me." I was crushed. I wanted to sign them for her and help her. She didn't want anything to do with me. And I thought, "Gosh!" I was crying. I felt kind of rejected. Here's mom who is with her twenty four hours a day. She went with me everywhere; we're together constantly and all of a sudden she wakes up and calls me and I'm not here. I'm sure she looked at it as abandonment. I looked awful. This isn't the mommy she remembered. I looked completely different.

D: Was she withdrawn during that time?

Sharon: I'd have to bring it out of her. She was thrilled to death when Paul got home. Boy, she'd hear Paul's car and she'd go running to daddy, happy as can be. It's awful. You're giving your life to the children and all of a sudden, nothing. This is heavy duty stuff for a three year old to understand what happened. All our lives were turned upside down which, I mean, they still are. We're starting to get back into a normal routine, but it's very difficult.

Coming home wasn't the end of hospitalizations for Sharon. She had to return for further reconstruction eight months after she first was discharged. She was to have some replacement of scar tissue with new grafts. It was going to be a two day surgical process, with Sharon getting out of the hospital in about a week or ten days. But there were complications. After the first surgery, the grafts became infected overnight. She was put on high doses of antibiotics and was placed in isolation for ten days. The whole area had to again be surgically excised and regrafted after the infection cleared up. Donor tissue was taken from her back, creating what was, in effect, a painful second-degree burn.

> **Sharon:** Right after the accident, he [the surgeon] asked me what my life-style was like. I said I was very active and I wear a bikini and stuff and he said OK, and he really did a nice job. Well, when that time came again [to harvest donor tissue] he said he could do it again, take it from the same area [from her buttocks]. Then the infection set in and he had to take it from my back, so it just went all down my back. So that was doing well. So I got up and I was walking a little bit and I turned completely white and I thought I was going to pass out. They put me back to bed and a couple of nights later, I started to get these high fevers that wouldn't break. My temperature was 104 degrees and not breaking. This was four days after the second surgery. So Dr. Frankel came in and ordered chest X-rays and tests. My blood level was down to zilch, it was 6.8 [hematocrit], which they said was very low. They sent in a hematologist and she said I was very critical. I said I feel bad but not as bad as everyone thinks I should. Everyone said, "My God, 6.8." They were calling Paul to get his permission for transfusions. I thought, "Poor Paul, he's going to die when he hears this one!"

For Sharon, this setback was another indication that things were not returning to normal. It was eight months after she was burned and, again, she was critically ill, facing the need to redo surgeries, becoming infected and needing to stay in the hospital for several weeks when she should have been home in ten days.

> **Sharon:** I was at that point where, you know, it's something else. Everything had gone bad, everything went wrong. It was like I couldn't take it anymore. Everything went to junk.

D: Until that time, how were things going?

> **Sharon:** No. I couldn't work out, I couldn't play tennis. I couldn't do anything. And then summer came and I'm a very outdoors person. I love being out in the sun. I can't go in the sun now. It's hats and I hate hats. It was awful. Everything went wrong, and then the blood problems on top of all that. Whether someone gets cancer or what's happened to me, like we all say, this isn't supposed to happen to me, it's supposed to happen to someone else. Granted, I know it's happened, but I still cannot believe that this has happened to me. It's so hard to comprehend. I still have a very difficult time saying this happened to me.

D: Paul, what was it like for you when Sharon developed all the complications during her second hospitalization?

> **Paul:** I was upset, I was angry as soon as I got the word from the hospital. As soon as I got the word from the doctor and I went to the hospital, I saw the sign on her door. I was angry, frustrated I guess. While I was there, Dr. Frankel was making rounds. He met me in the hallway and he was obviously disturbed by this. And he said he had no excuse for it, it was just one of those unexplained things, a staph infection, the graft wouldn't take, and he was going to have to regraft it when the infection was under control. He apologized profusely. Those things happen. And by this time, you get a little stoic. You figure, what else can happen? But you say, "We'll pick up our skinned knees once more and plod on from here and see it through. It's unfortunate but, hey, we'll just regroup and fight it off from here." And then we had the setback of the anemia, and you know, again you get angry and you get frustrated and you say, "When does it end?" It's tough, but at this point in time, you have no choice.

D: So Paul helped you get through all this?

> **Sharon:** Oh, most definitely, kind of the light at the end of the tunnel. I know Paul, a lot of the things he went through which at times I did not understand exactly what he's going through. But even the nurses would say Paul always has a smile on his face. I kinda lived for his visit. He'd always say, "Sharon, this time next year it's going to be better, the year after it's going to be better," which it has.

It was difficult for Sharon to believe that all of what happened was really happening to her. Her past life had been healthy, she was young; it was all unexpected. Where previously she had been active, she now found herself debilitated. Even after she first got out of the burn center, she was not well. Her world continued to shatter, to "go to junk." Surgical procedures, which should have been relatively straightforward, turned into ordeals. She became seriously infected and gravely anemic. When she was home, she was beset by pain, and the repeated use of analgesics became a further problem. When I interviewed Sharon, her life was slowly returning to normal. There would be more surgeries, and these were of concern because of the serious complications which she had experienced. The financial problems just made matters worse. At the time of the interview, however, both Sharon and Paul felt that the entire experience had strengthened their relationship.

Jeff Asmore: Residential Fire

When Jeff got out of the hospital, he was cared for by one of his sisters. There seemed to be little love in Jeff's family between his brothers, sisters, and himself. The only person Jeff claimed he loved was his mother and the last memory he has of her is seeing her charred body lying outside their burning house. He, along with his mother and younger brother, were transported by air to a large burn center. Both his mother and brother died in the hospital and Jeff says that he knew when they died; he could sense it. Nurses acted differently towards him and he was soon visited by several remaining family members who told him of the deaths. In many ways, Jeff seems to have never made peace with himself over the fire and the deaths of his mother and brother. He continues to appear tortured and haunted, embittered by catastrophic losses that he could never understand.

I met Jeff at a burn recovery group meeting he came to with an older brother who was then visiting him. I gave him my phone number and he called me three times or so before I interviewed him. His calls were always about problems. He seemed to have more trouble in daily living and in getting along with others than did any of the other survivors I have interviewed and, at the time of his interview, he was the most disfigured person with whom I spoke. His ears were destroyed, as was much of his nose; his face and hands, which are missing digits, are badly disfigured. His nose was reconstructed, but he is still missing ears. He speaks gently; sometimes it is hard to hear what he says, but it is clear that he remains very angry. Much has not been resolved. Jeff, along with three others, represented those persons whose lives were truly damaged, perhaps irreparably, by their journeys through fire. There are significant elements of paranoia in Jeff's account. From his standpoint, it seems that virtually all others, even those who befriend him, turn out to be against him. He feels used and abused by others, frequently for money. While this account is about his interpretation of his postburn life, it also provides a glimpse into the construction of a paranoid world and into abuse for abuse stands out as a theme throughout his account. Unfortunately, the interview was only with Jeff. The other family members, who are so prominent in his anger, were not available. There was the suggestion, by two clinical social workers who had tried to assist Jeff, that his problems predated his burn and this is suggested in his interview as well.

When Jeff's mother died, he felt that he was dying. In many deeply personal ways of the spirit, I believe Jeff did die when his mother died. He is still struggling to become whole again. His descriptions are especially painful. As I listened to him, it was not possible to distance myself from his anguish, from what I believe he must have suffered and continues to suffer in a world that he experiences as often hostile and indifferent. While this section is not about the hospital phase of care, I provide some material on his hospitalization as background material for understanding some of what Jeff has gone through.

D: Tell me about when your mother died.

> I wanted my mom. That's what I wanted. I really didn't care about my brothers; she was the one that cared for me. I knew when I saw her outside of the house that she was hurt real bad, but I wanted to see her and I wanted her to be in the same room. After three days my mom died. She died first then my brother died. Then I got a strange feeling that I started to die.

D: Did they tell you about your mom?

> No. They didn't tell me anything. I just felt empty because the attention wasn't there anymore. It was just the hospital staff theirself. When I was laying in my bed I could see through the window. I could see a lot of the staff moving, going by the door. I just knew something was wrong.

D: How did you find out?

> Well, a brother Richard, really Ricky, him and my sister Cathy, they came in and stood over at the door. They just stood there and they didn't even come over to me. It was just, just the way they reacted. I knew something was wrong. When I saw my brother and sister standing there I knew something was wrong: they were more quiet. When it comes to death, the people they don't know how to keep it hid. There's always something that changes in a person after someone passes away, someone close to you. But I just knew.
>
> After being bandaged up and left alone I didn't feel anything. And all this time the doctors kept telling me everything would be fine,...which I believed. But after I started to feel the pain, a lot more pain when I'd go to surgery and they would stick me with needles. I mean, it was just really painful. I didn't want to live. I even asked the doctors to let me die. I wanted to die, I didn't want to live.

D: Because of the pain?

> That was part of it. It's just that I had seen all the times they had taken the bandages off. I had seen the way my arms and my hands

looked and having pins* sticking out of my fingers. Things like that. I knew nothing was going to be the same again. And I didn't want to be part of the world they were trying to keep me in. So I asked them to let me die and kill me, to put me to sleep and just give me an overdose. I had no control over my life, I had no say in any matters. The doctors were wrong, wrong for keeping me alive. My sisters and brothers had control of my life.

D: Did they [family] know you wanted to die?

Yes, everyone knew. Some of them agreed. Some of them told me after I got out of the hospital, they say, "Yeah, you should have let him die." Because they were selfish. My family and the doctors were selfish.

D: You have seen psychiatrists and psychologists but you feel they don't understand your problems?

That's right. I can tell them what I'm feeling but they still don't know. All they do is hear, but they don't feel. Why don't you take ten men and ten women and put makeup scars on them, have a camera and have them go out to singles bars, have them go to discos and go to theatres, and walk down the sidewalks, and film the reactions you're going to get. And let them try to pick up someone or sit in school and see what happens. And they would most likely end up tearing it off their faces. They could not wear it.

D: At anytime since you were burned have you been glad you're alive?

I still feel they should have let me die or killed me...because the way I'm living now and the way that the world has changed, they have created a disaster. I know when I do wrong and I know there are times when I could...I feel...to where I could actually kill someone. But I won't because before I can take someone's life, I think of what I've been through and why should I take it out on this person because they're so ignorant.
Just recently when the doctor placed these large balloons under my scalp [tissue expanders] to blow them up, well, great. I'll be glad to have this bald spot covered up for good. And I won't have to wear a hat ever. And he said it was painful. But I didn't really know how painful it was gonna be, what it would be like when I go outside.

---

* Surgical pins were used to splint his fingers. This technique aids grafting by imobilizing the newly grafted area. It can also reduce the development of contractures as the area heals. Intensive therapy and exercise will normally follow.

And they say, "Well, you have long hair, nobody will hardly notice." Well, that's not so because a lot of people notice and I ended up being locked up inside my apartment because it was too noticeable. And it was very painful. They didn't tell me I wasn't going to be able to sleep. I had to take pain medication and I overdosed on my pain medication and I still couldn't sleep. And a lot of times I would sleep with my head hanging off the bed or off the end of the sofa. They didn't tell me anything like that.

D: Let's go back to what it was like when you first got out of the burn center, after the fire. How did your brother's death affect you?

Not much. I didn't like him. He was my younger brother and there was a lot of jealousy there. When I was the youngest, I got all the attention. And that's probably why my brothers threw me in a tub of hot water [he had been previously burned, not seriously, but he reported that two of his older brothers threw him into hot water when he was around six or so]. I think about that. When Tim was born [who died] and my mom would have to care for him more than for me, it seemed I would feel neglected and left out and that's why I didn't like him. He had red hair and I don't like people with red hair. I think they're the meanest, cruelest people of all, people with red hair.

At twelve, Jeff had not resolved the sibling rivalry with his younger brother and now he despised the other members who remained of his family. More than once he mentioned his hostility for red-haired people. His anger often seemed especially acute. Anyone who had red hair seemed to stand for all he hated in his younger brother and perhaps, in his older brothers as well. He felt robbed of his mother by Tim and even in death it seemed that he was cheated by Tim. His description of his preburn life suggested long-term problems that were physically resolved only in the dissolution of his family. Emotionally, the problems were not resolved.

D: Do you have any contact with your family?

I don't. It includes everyone. I spoke to Phillip. I called him and spoke to him. I told him I was feeling depressed and things I was thinking about. About how my family had taken advantage of me and how I really despised them. I was just telling him that whenever I do die that I'm going to hell and I'm going to see everyone of you suffer there '"cause I'm going to have fun seeing you suffer." It's just something I had to get off my mind. He understood. I can't forgive them. They've done me wrong too many times. When somebody makes a mistake, you don't try to repeat it twice. And my family has repeated things over and over and apologized over and over. You get tired of hearing just an apology.

D: Where did you go after you got out of the hospital?

My sister Cathy's. She's the eldest in the family and she got custody because my brothers and sisters were all fighting. Not for me, but because to get the money that was coming in.

D: Insurance, or money from the state?

I don't know. I never saw any of it. That's what they fought for. Since my sister Cathy was the oldest she got custody. She took care of me. I was out just one week and I knew I was gonna be taken back for more surgery. I didn't want to go back and I asked her if she would let me stay and don't take me back. She just told me she couldn't do that. So she called the doctors. She told them what I was going through and she was afraid I was going to run away or something. So they had her bring me back to the hospital. I couldn't walk that well, and I couldn't do hardly anything. They said they were going to some amusement park but instead we ended up at the hospital. I went in there and they were examining me. I had told my sister not to leave me there. So I was in the examining room and they were putting my clothes back on me. And I was in a rush to get out before my sister and them left. When I got out there was nobody there...they had already left.

D: Why did the doctors want your sister to leave?

Because they said it was going to be hard for them to see me start screaming and crying and asking her to don't leave me there and take me because they're going to hurt me again.

D: Did they keep you there? How did you feel about your sister?

I was mad at her from when I was in the hospital and it was getting time to leave. I felt we were playing a game of hide and seek. I couldn't walk very well and I tried to bend down and hide behind a wheelchair and I fell down and tore a graft on my arm. So I had to stay in the hospital a bit longer. But my sister came and the doctors talked to her and I said, "I want to go home now and everything's okay and I'm fine." My sister and them went out. They couldn't handle it, my sister and her husband Gene. I would cry. Here they had told me to pack my things. And here I was, trying to get my things together and while I was doing that they had already left. The doctors, they caught me; I was going out the doors. They even had guards at the doors downstairs so people wouldn't run away. And that's how to not treat people in my position. I saw her, outside the window. I hit the window, I started banging on it. I was calling her name.

D: So you were mad at your sister?

I didn't like any of them. Even my brother Clive,...I was transferred to Cincinnati about a month after it happened. I could see my brother being wheeled around in a wheelchair. I was in isolation. So they,...him and my sister, it was like favoritism in the family. He wasn't disfigured like I was. He also had red hair. He could feed himself which I had to be fed, even when I left the hospital. I got the reaction from my sister that she was getting tired of having to care for me.

Then I thought maybe I could do something about it. After I started learning to feed myself and going to the bathroom on my own, my sister hadn't really believed how I had managed doing this on my own. And my sister and them didn't like this. They didn't want me to be able to take care of myself or do anything. Because they still wanted the money that was coming in to be in their name.

D: You still had to be cared for by someone, you were only twelve.

No. They could have at least left me in a hospital or put me in some facility of some sort to where I would have someone around to care for me.

D: You didn't feel you had proper care?

Not at all. She didn't even want me to learn to ride a bicycle. They were afraid I was going to go to the City of Owensplough and tell the police how I was being treated.

D: You didn't like her from before?

She was a total stranger to me. My sister started pulling some foul play on me. They started telling the doctors that I had psychological problems and the doctors were taking their part. Even the police, my sister had told them, "He's been burned, he lost part of his mind, because he's not the same again." I didn't lose part of my mind, I knew exactly what was going on but they took her word over mine.

Like psychiatrists,...I resent psychiatrists because they say, "Well, if I were in your shoes, I think I would be suicidal or I would try to kill myself." He even said that I,...I did this, that I killed my mom, I killed my brother, that I did this to myself. I said, "No I didn't." He was a fat, sloppy, disgusting man. This was at Becton State Hospital. This is how the system out here has done to me.

D: He suggested that the fire was your fault? Why do you think he said that?

I don't know why anyone would say that. It was a complete accident, it wasn't my fault and I was twelve years old when it happened and anyone's to blame it's my stepdad and my mom. I don't like blaming my mom, but she was responsible for what happened. I still say my stepdad, he did it purposely because it was an argument. My mom sent us out of the house [Jeff and two brothers] and my stepdad made us go in. And my stepdad just happened to be out of the house when it took place.

D: How long were you with Cathy? Did you go back to school?

I was there about four years. They suggested a tutor because I wasn't able to do a lot of things for myself. My sister said the school would arrange for my brother Clive to be in the same classrooms.

D: What was it like at Cathy's? Who was there?

Cathy, her husband Gene, and her five kids. My brothers and sisters, they came to visit me. One of my sisters, Peggy brought a camera. I was upstairs. I was still in bed. This was the day after I just got home. I had my braces on and I didn't have 'jama tops on but I had the bottom parts on. Peggy, she came up to see me. She pulled off the sheets and started taking pictures. And still today, she shows my pictures to total strangers. If anybody in my family is psychologically disturbed, everybody else is except for me. I'm the only one that has common sense to know that something drastic has happened. I've learned to adjust but they haven't.

D: Do you think any of them care about you?

They don't give a damn. None of them does. I was just a bad reminder for them. They didn't want me around, and I hated them for what they did to me. If it wasn't for the money, they woulda got rid of me.

D: How did Gene treat you?

> He was as bad as her because when these guys picked me up and took me back, she threw me in the basement. They put a bed down there, a bucket and some toilet paper and they locked me down there. I had a light. I was down there for almost two weeks. I tried lots of times to get out but I had no way to get out. When she would feed me I would always wait beside the door. When they would open the door I would grab the door. And lots of times they would slam the door on my hands. I would end up falling down the steps. I started yelling that there were rats down there so she sent her husband down. If there weren't no rats I would still be down there. So she told me if I ever did anything like that again, she would throw me down there with the rats.. I was scared. I had no one 'cause everyone around was told I had a psychological problem. *This is because I'm a burned person* [my emphasis]. My own family took advantage of me and turned everyone against me.

D: Did your other brothers or sisters know about this?

> I told Ricky but he didn't believe it. He asked her these questions,... she always had a story, "We had to punish him. All we did was send him to bed early, not let him watch TV." They didn't believe me, they just thought I was lying, so I had to stay there.

D: Your sister did put you back in school?

> Yeah, and to me I thought it would all be the same [like before the fire], everybody would treat me equal. And it wasn't that way. There was a student in the class and he was making remarks like, "It sure is hot in here." Then he would wipe his forehead and unbutton his shirt and say, "It sure is burning up in here," and the kids would giggle. And the teacher just sat there like a fool. As little as I was, I didn't weigh no more than seventy pounds, I picked up my desk and threw it across the room at him. I was just mad, I was crying, I was frustrated. I knocked over the bookshelves, the large divider. I left the school, I walked right out of there. No one would even touch me or tried to stop me. I had control. Everyone was just stunned to see what I was doing. Another teacher came out behind me. He was running and I was headed to the street where the trucks were. He caught up to me and he didn't touch me and talking and telling me to calm down. "Where are you going?", he asked me. I said, "I'm going to the street, I'm going to jump in front of a truck." He goes, "You can't do this." I go, "Yes I can." And he picked me up and

carried me and I was crying and he even started to cry. And it was just,...he seemed to feel what I was going through at that time, a real emotional time for me.

D: Did you have friends in school?

I didn't want friends. I did have them before but I didn't want them anymore. It's mainly because of a girl, Kelly Jones. I knew her when I was a little kid and we grew up together practically. We even talked of growing up and getting married. We played husband and wife. But after the accident,...I came back and she changed a lot. And I had completely changed differently. And she,...what really hurt was she didn't even know who I was at first. And she pulled away. When she was assigned the seat next to me she would scoot her seat away from me and she didn't want to sit near me. It was just that everything was changed, everything was different.

D: After you had problems in school, were you accepted then?

I knew they had to accept me. I resented that a lot. I don't think anyone should have to be told to accept a person or treat him equally. They shouldn't be so stupid. I think that my whole classroom should have been punished, that they should have been expelled. That was including my brother, he was in on it. One time we were at the cafeteria. We were standing in line to go into the auditorium for a movie. And there was a guy named Jimmy Stowers that was standing next to him, they were making remarks about me. I started using foul language,...I would call those kids bitches and bastards and mother-fuckers. I kicked my brother because he was in on it with Jimmy Stowers, right between the legs and they had to take him to the hospital.

My sister got on me for that also. She said I caused a lot of problems and she was placing me in a home because I was getting out of control. I even kicked her down the stairs. I kicked her down the stairs from upstairs, this was about the braces. I would get her son Thomas to take them off me during the night, she wasn't doing it like she was supposed to. I would sleep without the braces. She would wake up in the morning and she would pull the blankets off me and she would see I didn't have the braces on. She would get down and start putting them back on and start yelling at me. She didn't punish her oldest daughter or her youngest. Her other three kids, she didn't like at all. So I got Thomas to take the braces off again and she came up and was trying to put the braces on and I was fighting against her. And we were at the top of the stairs. She had already put the face mask over my head so I couldn't get it off. So I just kicked her, I kicked her in the stomach and she went back and down the steps. It scared me for a moment and then I thought, "Well, you deserve it, you bitch." They took her to the hospital because she was unconscious a few minutes.

One can only imagine the tormented feelings of abandonment and isolation that Jeff must have felt when he stood alone, miles from his sister's home, realizing that she had left him at the hospital, a place that represented the death of his mother and months of physical pain. Abandoned by his mother in death, abandoned by his sister who lied about where he was to be taken, it is not hard to understand where his bitterness comes from. His view of his family remains conspiratorial, and in this single instance, one can gain some appreciation for how he must have felt at twelve years old. He also disdains doctors, for he feels that they learn to care for those who are burned by experimenting on other burn patients. And his family, it was someone in his family that felt he should have been allowed to die.

The material presented on Jeff is a small fragment of his interview, but it is clear from this that he has experienced a very distressing life, the problems of which are not attributable to only his burn. There are numerous contradictions in his account, wanting to go home and wanting to be placed in a hospital, resenting inadequate care but kicking his sister down the stairs when she tried to put his braces on him (a painful process), wanting to be accepted but rejecting children who tried to be friends, and resenting the fact that they didn't accept him without being told to do so. The picture that emerged from his interview was one of a young man who had a horrible life; the burn was another overwhelming fact, clearly the worst and most destructive experience for a child who had probably been emotionally and physically abused before he was burned. His feelings about Kelly Jones, the girl he liked in school, were expressed with sadness. She seemed to symbolize, for Jeff, many of the losses he faced after he was injured. With her, there was not anger but resignation. For others, there was considerable anger.

Jeff was finally removed from Cathy's care by another sister, Cherri, who brought him to California. His other brothers and sisters finally had become suspicious of his care at Cathy's; they alerted Cherri who agreed that Jeff could come to California and stay with her. But life at Cherri's was not much better; perhaps it was worse. Cherri was periodically involved in drugs as was her live-in lover. Jeff believed that Cherri, like Cathy, took him only to get his disability payments. Jeff was placed in special education classes where he also had problems leading him to be institutionalized for short periods of time. He has continued to have many problems, from apartment evictions, to being thrown off buses, to losing jobs. Throughout Jeff's account, there are paranoid, abusive, and suicidal themes. His world appears bleak. He seems to be enmeshed within a hostile, unloving world from which extrication is impossible. He is exceptionally angry, and there is no suggestion of warm relationships with others. Instead, what is portrayed is a truncated life, a life of one who is in considerable agony, lost his moorings and is floundering without saving assistance. In other parts of his account, there is the clear indication of abuse, abuse that predated his burn. Now, abused or not, his relationships are tainted and tortured.

Jeff has been placed in protective police custody more than once when neighbors or others, including hospital staff, felt he was suicidal. In the interview, he mentioned suicidal themes, but he stated that he could not kill himself because he might fail, and thereby end up worse than he is already. Suicide appears an option, if only it could be final. He has continued to report asking doctors to put him to sleep, and an article, that appeared in a metropolitan newspaper, quoted him as saying that he just wanted to die because of the pain of living. The article generated considerable public interest, including several job offers, but none of the jobs were anywhere near where Jeff lives so nothing really happened for him after the article appeared.

Jeff attributes all of these problems to his appearance and the fact that he was burned. While he is exceptionally disfigured, so are several other survivors who were interviewed. When compared with Maria, Eric or Mike, Jeff does not seem more remarkably disfigured. No other survivors report problems of the magnitude that Jeff encounters. Unlike the others, there appears in Jeff tremendous underlying anger with little insight into how he seems to often set himself up for ill treatment. He has found nothing of value to replace what he has lost through abuse or the fire. He clearly seems to represent someone who had a horrible life long before he was burned. His disfigurement has become the peg onto which he hangs all other problems and it is painfully clear that his scars are exceptionally deep, not just the scars of burned skin but the disfigurement of warped development. When I tried to assist him in various ways by suggesting programs that might be of use to him, he always found numerous reasons to disregard the suggestions. He has dreams of being accepted as a ballet dancer or stage performer. He realizes he is disfigured and he says "knows" that he would not be accepted in such a role, yet at the same time he feels that he should be accepted by the public. There is, in what he says, almost a demand that he be accepted, and anger is close at hand for the fact that he has not been accepted. Ultimately, Jeff appears to lack the mature coping strategies and the social support necessary to overcome the horrendous challenges imposed by his life and his injuries. His adjustment to the tragedies imposed upon him has been the construction of a marginal life and for him, no other possibility may have existed.[1]

The Theme Of The Homecomer And The Stranger

Throughout the above accounts, with all the specific differences between the survivors, the theme of homecomer and stranger emerges. The person who comes home from the burn center is not the same person he or she was before the injury and home is not the same place it was before the injury. The injury leads to a radical transformation of personal and social identity. In being seriously burned, the survivor's personal as well as social identity is dramatically transformed. The transformation may ultimately be of only marginal significance for some, and the person's life goes on much as it had before the injury. For others, the injury may be interpreted not only as having negative consequences, but also, it may be seen as creating positive changes. For others, the meaning of the injury may seem essentially positive, as that which created the grounds for significant transformation and transcendence. For others, the injury is construed as causing, and continuing to cause, overwhelming problems.

Hanus, Bernstein, and Knapp have aptly used the metaphor of the immigrant to depict the social-psychological problems that challenge the reintegration of the facially disfigured into society. Writing about children who have craniofacial abnormalities, their use of "immigrant" metaphorically captures the status of the disfigured-as-stranger who attempts reentry into the world of the nondisfigured. Their discussion pertains to children who are brought into the world as strangers, the status of stranger being due to the child's discrepant appearance. For the burn survivor, the status of stranger is acquired. It is a status over which the survivor may feel little control, though others, such as Eric, Maria, Mike, Ann, Kevin, and Trisha, do feel that they can significantly control who they are (their identities) for other persons through such techniques as being assertive, by insisting on how they shall be defined, or by ignoring those who are intrusive and rude. As in Hanus et al., the traumatically disfigured survivor can be understood as an alien in terms of the society of normal-appearing others into which the survivor is transplanted. Quoting Handlin, it is noted that:

> [As] strangers, the immigrants could not locate themselves; they had lost the polestar that gave them their bearings. They would not regain an awareness of direction until they could visualize themselves in their new context, see a picture of the world as it appeared from their perspective. (Hanus, Bernstein, and Knapp 1981, 40)

Further, Handlin noted that anonymity was not available to the immigrant; he or she was easily identified by clothing, speech, manners, and culture as being different. In being different, the immigrant was conspicuous. And so is it with the burn survivor who is disfigured. Kevin's disfigured face says "Hi"and, in different ways, other survivors reported having similar feelings about the obtrusiveness created by their visible scars. It remains the task and challenge of the disfigured person that he or she must frequently, and actively, negotiate his or her identity as one who is acceptable and normal, that is, that he or she is not a stranger after all.

But there are other ways in which the metaphor of stranger and homecomer can be compared to the burn survivor as suggested by Alfred Schutz in two of his papers. Schutz also referred to the stranger-as-immigrant, considering the immigrant as the person who tries to be accepted, or at least tolerated, by the community in which he or she dwells (Schutz 1964, 91). The stranger is in some significant sense, unknown. Throughout this and the last chapters, the burn survivor frequently appears as the unknown stranger, not only to others but to himself or herself as well. The survivor must redefine and reconceptualize who he or she is, new identities must be forged and new ways of being at home with oneself and others must be discovered. The task can be arduous, and it may be fraught with contradictions and dilemmas at every turn (Billig et al. 1988, 24).

Through injury, the survivor has become, in various ways, a stranger to himself or herself and to significant others. Schutz's stranger and the immigrant described by Handlin, understand that they are strangers, they know their status as outsiders before they attempt to enter the group. It may come to pass, in knowing their status, that such knowledge is only suggestive or anticipatory; how they are concretely different, how they are specifically "outsiders," may fully be grasped only as they conduct their lives in the new culture, group, or social order. Their initial "knowledge" pertaining to themselves as outsiders is very general or provisional, a loose typification which will be filled in through actual experience. In essence, the stranger must discover or learn just how he or she is a stranger and, in so doing, the stranger simultaneously learns how to become a member of the group, clan or society. The burn survivor does not anticipate his or her forthcoming status as a stranger. There may be haunting fears, there may be suggestions in the night, but preeminently, the survivor discovers, with a shock, how his or her status has been transformed to that of stranger. Sharon did not anticipate her daughter's reaction and, for Sharon, Amanda's reaction was more than distressing, it was personally discrediting. In coming home, the presumption for the survivor is that he or she is finally *Home*. Yet what home meant before the accident turns out to be different from what is encountered by many survivors. Home for many represents a place of security, a place of some comfort, a place of acceptance, and a place away from the intrusive procedures and terrible pain of the hospital. But home frequently turns out, at least initially, to be alien, different, and even threatening.

Previous roles and identities, abilities, needs, and interests have been transformed by the concrete exigencies of the injury. The returning mother is perceived as threatening by her children; the husband can no longer fulfill the role of family provider; the athlete is no longer able to perform; and home is no longer the familiar place it once was. Home is now a place to discover, in more detail, how much has been personally lost. It is a place no longer secure, because of rising medical bills which threaten to bring about foreclosure, the need to do painful exercise, or have wounds cleaned by a family member. It is a place where one is no longer self-sufficient, but where one must be cared for as an invalid. The meaning of one's status within the relationships of significant others is altered. No longer can previous ideas and attitudes about oneself be taken-for-granted as they had previously been. The survivor emerges as one who does not fully comprehend where he is, or who she is. Previous schema for interpreting his or her immediate world no longer work. The stranger, states Schutz,

> is about to join a group which is not and never has been his own. He knows he will find himself in an unfamiliar world, differently organized than that from which he comes, full of pitfalls and hard to master. The homecomer, however, expects to return to an environment of which he always had and, so he thinks, still has intimate knowledge and which he has just to take for granted in order to find his bearings within it. So he feels; and because he feels so, he will suffer the typical shock described by Homer. (Schutz 1964, 106-107)

In this chapter and in the next, cases have been presented that show various ways in which survivors cope with being cast into the roles of stranger, how they negotiate and find meaning in transformed worlds in which their identities are called into fundamental question, and how they attempt to redefine themselves as credible and normal. The next chapter will examine intimate relationships between survivors and significant others.

5

Intimate Relationships and Self

> Sometimes I sit alone at night
> And think about my life
> Both the past and the future
> I miss the happiness I had
> I wonder if ever there will be someone
> Someone to hold this broken body
> And see the woman beneath the scars
> (Linda R. Fraser, January 1984)

I had the same fears, I cried the same tears, I had the same disappointments as many of you. And what other people reflect on when they're seeing me, that's not something I can control. I've had men admire me, I've had men that didn't admire me; I've had women that admired me, I've had women that didn't admire me. Before my electrocution in 1984 when I lost both my hands, my wife and I had a very, very good relationship sexually and in other ways, communication and things. And coming home without arms, without hands, I found it very difficult, you know, without having the sense of touch, not being able to stimulate my wife in the way she was used to or in not being able to feel her breasts. And it took a long time, a hell of a long time, for myself,...to feel confident that I was maintaining my role as a male in that aspect. And it took time, but eventually as you compensate for the hooks you compensate for other things. And I think the very important thing that everyone in this room has to remember is number one, you have to feel good about yourself. If you feel good about yourself and you're satisfied with yourself, then you have it beat...because what's in here [self] and up here [mind], that's the bottom line. Those that accept you,...accept them; those that don't accept you, you don't even want to know anyway. (John, May 1988)

The last chapter introduced the metaphor of the survivor who is viewed as both stranger and as homecomer. This chapter will continue to examine this theme, specifically in relation to intimate relationships and sexuality. Problems involving intimacy, love and sexuality are of concern to many survivors. It often matters little whether the survivor is married, single, dating, not dating, involved, or uninvolved with another person. As noted previously, scars can be very discrediting, and nowhere is this more clear than when the topic of intimacy and sexuality is introduced.

Alfred Schutz in "The Homecomer" states that "to feel at home is an expression of the highest degree of familiarity and intimacy" (Schutz 1964, 108). For one's own feeling of being at home in the world, for one's feeling of security as a complete and whole person, few things seem more crucial than the acceptance of one's being *as sexual*. A basic, most fundamental way in which humans are existentially in the world involves their being *sexual beings*. I use sexual here in a broader sense than that defined and limited by physically intimate acts such as coitus. While obviously significant, such acts represent only one important aspect of sexuality. By sexuality I refer more broadly to the acceptance of one's bodily being and, importantly, to the human need to develop intimate, trusting, and loving relationships with others. It is very possible to live a rewarding life in the absence of coitus or acts of physical sex; it is not possible to live a rewarding life in the absence of loving relationships with others, relationships involving communication, understanding, and trust within which the deepest sense of self, as taken-for-granted being, is given birth and shape in the copresence of significant others.

In a very pervasive sense, burn injury threatens one's sexuality. It globally threatens the security of self in taking oneself for granted as lovable and as worthy of the love of another. More specifically, burn injury threatens the most physically intimate, interpersonal relationships, which the survivor might seek to continue, renew, or establish. Disfigurement and scarring are centrally important to sexuality and intimacy. None of the survivors in this study, regardless of how extensively they were burned, had sexual problems that resulted directly from physical damage. For all, the existing problems which they reported resulted from social-psychological issues. These issues represent such themes as trust in and acceptance of self, the belief that the survivor is or is not acceptable to others, fears of rejection by others, and fears of touching or being touched.

Existing research on "adjustment" to burns is contradictory relative to the importance of the location and visibility of scarring for the survivor. Yet also as noted, some researchers have found that the location of the burn, with visible scarring on such locations as the face, neck, hands and arms, presents more of a challenge to survivors than would scars that are normally covered by clothing. Obversely, other researchers have found that the burn location has little to do with the survivor's adjustment to the injury. From my research, it is clear that both answers are correct and both are incorrect. It appears that the location of the scarring is definitely of consequence to some survivors such as Ellen, Darrin, Jeff and James.* Equally, for survivors such as Maria, Eric, and Mike, there was little concern about the location and visibility of scarring. The latter all have extensive scarring with no location being unscarred, while in the former group, which happens to be comprised of those who seem to be having trouble with adjustment, scarring is limited to publicly visible areas of their bodies. The one exception is Jeff, whose disfigurement is extensive. Among several other survivors who had scars which are normally covered by clothing, many stated that they believed they would have had more problems in accepting their injuries had the scarring been visible. Several said that they were fortunate that their scars were not visible. At least three stated that they would have wanted to die, or they would have contemplated suicide, if their injuries had been facial. One survivor, Jim Gonzales, also ascribed such feelings to his friend who died, saying that this man, had he lived, would have wanted to kill himself since he was burned extensively on his face.

What is to be made from such contradictions and confusion? First of all, and most simply, there are no rules and there are no hard answers. Visible scarring, even when it appears to an outsider to be relatively minimal, as in Ellen's case, can have lifelong, devastating consequences. Rather mild scarring can provide the publicly visible peg upon which the survivor hangs all failures and shortcomings in his or her life. The survivors may seem overwhelmed by their scars. Much of their life's activities, and the negative meanings they ascribe to themselves, are referenced back to the self-attributed consequences of being scared. Self-attribution is not, however, an esoteric, solitary achievement of the individual, that is, it is not purely psychological. Attribution has a social dimension, one where the evaluations made by others are frequently utilized by the survivor in negatively conceptualizing, defining, and judging himself or herself. It often represents being rejected by others where, correctly or incorrectly, the survivor believes that his or her scars are the reason for rejection. Attribution need not be pejorative, however. Others may facilitate the survivor through acceptance and affirmation, thereby assisting the survivor in the construction of an acceptable and positive self-image.

For those who are scarred over much of their bodies, there is little choice in being overwhelmed by the consequence of scarring at one location. Except for Jeff, the most massively disfigured survivors who appear in this study have done reasonably well in achieving normal lives or in trusting themselves and others, and in believing that they can achieve what they desire. With Jeff as the exception, the others, though also substantially disfigured, do not focus on scarring as an issue which prevents them from having normal lives. In Jeff's case, the problems he

---

* Darrin and James do not appear elsewhere in this study.

reports have historical roots that go well beyond the fact that he was burned. All of those who felt they had serious problems caused by the burn also were survivors who felt that their injuries were not accepted by their families. All were burned as children and only one person, whose case is not included here, felt that his relationships with family members were loving and generally accepting. But even for him, there was the distinct feeling that his family could not specifically accept the fact that he was burned. It was an issue which simply didn't exist for his parents, though it very much existed for him. His story was different from the others who felt devastated by the consequences of their burns, for the others all felt unaccepted, in general, by their parents while he felt loved as he was growing up.

In speaking to many survivors, it seems that several issues, especially those involving physical intimacy, are the most frequently ignored topics by burn support staff, yet they are issues which are very frequently troubling to burn survivors. In doing the research for this study, only one article was located which addressed sexuality specifically (Cooper-Fraps 1984). One recent book (Bernstein, Breslau, and Graham 1988) written in part, for burn survivors and their families, has addressed this issue, but for the most part, sexuality apparently remains taboo, an area where the survivor must often chart his or her own course without assistance from burn center staff. The burn survivor, like others who have experienced disfiguring trauma, may equate disfigurement with ugliness, and they may feel that they are no longer lovable (Cooper-Frapes 1984; Steiner 1977; Griffith 1975).

That sexuality remains closeted is perhaps not surprising. Some survivors had problems discussing this aspect of themselves yet it was of singular interest and importance. It was clear that survivors themselves, frequently had trouble, even among other survivors, in bringing up matters that referred to their most intimate concerns. When the topic came up in group, it usually seemed to be suggested rather than being directly articulated. This is not surprising. Being burned doesn't facilitate communication about deeply personal and potentially discrediting matters, even among a group of relative strangers who have been on the same journey. Similar to the patient who doesn't ask to see a mirror, staff apparently leaves well enough alone if the patient does not raise specific questions about sexuality. This chapter will examine some of the issues, feelings and fears which survivors stated in the interviews. It will examine the construction of self and meaning in the lives of survivors who find, or who wish to find, that they are acceptable as sexual beings and that, as before they were burned, they can be loved by someone who sees past the scars and disfigurement and will accept them as whole.

For most, the self is experienced as continuous rather than discontinuous or fragmented. Discontinuous sectors of the person's life are subject to explanatory remedy through his or her construction of accounts, excuses, or justifications which serve as bridging devices between what is and what should have been. Through the construction of accounts, involving biographical reconstruction, troubling discrepancies are made sensible and coherent, at least for the moment, and until further notice. Memory is crucial to biographical construction; memoric reconstruction of self, the filling of gaps, recasting the self in a specific light, ignoring some details while stressing others, all of these are commonly utilized to produce what seems like a continuous self.[1]

Biographic reconstruction is situational; it is not every day that the survivor, or anyone else for that matter, is called upon by self or other to reestablish who he or she is. Most of the time the survivor, like others, goes about life without needing to examine the past. Special situations, such as discrediting and embarrassing confrontations with rude or inquisitive others, may necessitate identity repair, but these situations are certainly not continuous problems at every turn in the survivor's journey. They are, rather, special occasions in which identity becomes problematic, and sometimes massively so, and they may involve intimate relationships between the survivor and others. The person who is visibly disfigured may have deep concerns about being rejected initially and in total, while those whose scars are normally hidden below clothing have the problem of deciding when and how to tell the other about their scars, fearing that when the normally hidden scars are seen, they will be rejected. In either case, each survivor faces the possibility of being rejected by those with whom he or she desires to establish an intimate relationship.

Most importantly, what the person takes himself or herself to be is, in a deep sense, contingent upon how others define the person, on how they "mirror" the person's identity. In particular, significant others are especially crucial in this process. Significant others are those with whom we are most familiar and intimate, those with whom our most important relationships are forged. Referring to the reciprocal interpenetration of selves and lives, Schutz notes that:

To each of the partners the Others's life becomes, thus, a part of his own autobiography, an element of his personal history. What he is, what he grew to be, what he will become is co-determined by his taking part in the manifold actual or potential primary relationships which prevail within the home-group....The partners in a primary relationship experience one another as unique personalities in a vivid present, by following their unfolding thought as an ongoing occurrence and by sharing, therefore, their anticipations as plans, as hopes or as anxieties; it means, finally, that each of them has the chance to reestablish the we-relation, if interrupted, and to continue it as if no intermittence had occurred. (Schutz 1964, 111)

Catastrophic burn injury therefore threatens not just the burned person's physical and emotional life, but it also threatens primary group relationships. Lives are interrupted and plans are placed on hold. The relationships between the survivor and significant others are placed in doubt. The survivor may believe that his or her scarred body will never again be attractive to the other and that he or she will never be loved again. A spouse may recoil from seeing or touching scarred skin; there may be fears of inflicting pain or there may be revulsion at the sight of the loved one who still has raw, open wounds. Such untoward reactions serve to confirm and amplify the doubts and fears that the survivor harbors. The survivor may fear undressing or being fully seen, even by a marriage partner who has shared the same bed for years, and the fears may not be openly expressed. The fears, doubt, and anguish may be kept secreted away, hidden to all but the survivor himself or herself. Even talking about these concerns can be threatening, and potentially discrediting, to many people. Those who are not married and who are young, may conclude that they might as well forget even thinking about intimate relationships for no one will ever be interested in their scarred faces and bodies. These are the disheartening issues that face many survivors.

Eric Mathews: Vehicle Accident

One of the first concerns expressed by Eric when he reached the burn center was whether or not his penis had been burned. In males who are burned near their genitals, this concern seems relatively common and intense.

D: You were extensively burned. Did you have any concerns about your penis?

> Yeah. That was my first question; my first conscious question was, there was a nurse there and I didn't know how to put it to her, "So, what about my family jewels?" She goes, "What?" "My balls. How are they?" And she says, "Oh, I don't think you're burned, don't worry about that." And then I go, "There is a God." That was a tremendous security. I don't know especially for men, but for me it was. At least that's OK.

Initially reassured that his penis was intact, Eric later became concerned about how women would relate to him. Athletic, attractive, and very sociable, he had previously dated many women. At home, after he left the burn center, these were issues of some importance.

It was like for women, "Well, no one will ever want me," so that part of me just laid down and said, "Well, why try?" Then part of the healing process,...it was three years that I spent at home, doing a lot of introspection and figuring out how I'm going to deal with this, how I'm going to survive.

Eric went through lists of "I can'ts," but he didn't stop there. These lead ultimately to lists of "I can" and to his conclusion that he was much more than his scarred body. He concluded that he could control much in his life even if he could do nothing to undo all that had happened to him. He was involved here in reconstructing himself through redefinition, but there remained genuine concerns about women. Fortunately, a friend helped him understand that he was still attractive sexually.

D: Did you have a girlfriend before the accident?

No. I had several acquaintances, and I had certain long-term relationships. But that changed. For me, I figured it's over. The ones that I did have a good relationship, they came and took care of me and had no problems with it. I consider males and females friends so it didn't seem strange if girl friends came to see me that I wasn't really involved with. But ones that I had a long time ago came and things like that.

D: So you decided that intimate relationships were over?

Well, yeah. I just figured there would be no one who would want me; even though it was wrong, it was my logic at the time, and it helped me get on with other things.

D: So, you didn't think about it for a while?

Right. Well, when I was first in the hospital, the first thing I said to my brother was, "Don't let any girls in here. Don't let them see me like this." So I did have this awareness, but later on it was just like I was ugly. I mean, it's obvious. No one's going to want me, not taking into account that other people would look at the insides and stuff. And there were desires, desires I wished I could remove from my mind, and things like that. But there was the realization that when the time was right, it'll be there. But no one abandoned me; no one really laughed.

D: So what happened? What did you find as time passed?

I got on with other things that I could; again, it's not where I am, it's where I want to go. How am I going to do it? This is what I can do right now. If I can't take care of it, let it go.

Eric actively focused not on what he couldn't do, but instead, on what he could do and what he could try to do. He became actively committed to rebuilding himself and what he had lost to the fire. He took control of his life and, for the moment, he set aside issues and concerns that he couldn't deal with or control. This orientation, of taking control, was a basic theme throughout the interview with Eric. It is a theme found in other survivors as well and it seems to be one of the distinct differences that separated those who appear to be doing well from those who continue to have significant problems in coping with the massive changes they had undergone.

D: And what has happened now?

I have had some experiences that have shown me that it doesn't matter if you're burned. Pretty much by the woman's initiating it, which caught me off guard. There were some girls that I knew beforehand who would come out and we would have some intimate situations even though I was completely covered in bandages. I'm sure it bothered them, but there was enough love there, which blew my theory right there.

D: Did you solicit this, did you ask them?

Right. Then they would comply. I'm sure it was love, but also feeling sorry. But that ended eventually, because they were starting other relationships. Believe me, I wouldn't have stopped it. The fantasies go on; they're female, they're there. Because of the kindness, that's an attraction in itself. So I had an awareness that there were people who loved me that I knew, and then with that love there were other women, other relationships.

Then there were the first intimacies with someone that I had not known before. It's not like there's a lot, but yeah. This one individual, where I was at a lecture, and we were talking, and I needed a ride home so she gave me a ride home. And we were talking the whole time. I needed a ride and I had never met her before. So I said, "Let's have dinner." So I bought her dinner because she was giving me a ride home, and she was dropping me off. At that point...I give hugs and kisses just because that's all I could do then, to communicate friendship. And so I was going to give her a kiss on the cheek [and she gave me] a real aggressive kiss. That shocked me. I backed up, and I just like, "Did that just happen?" It was bizarre but she gave me her name and number and I went ahead and called her, and went over to her place for dinner, and ended up having a great time and spending the night. We had a few more meetings. It was just a surprise.

Eric's experiences demonstrated to him that even with his injuries and scarring, he was not beyond being sexually acceptable to women. The first woman with whom he had intercourse, after he was burned, told him, "Once a stud, always a stud." This, and his subsequent relationships, though limited, led him to conclude that his life with women was not over. At present, he does not have a girlfriend, but he is confident that, when the time is right, he will find one and she will accept him.

Mike Lawson: Motorcycle Accident

Mike was not dating when he was burned, but he had previously dated a few young women. Even with scars, he was a very handsome young man. He was intelligent, and a good conversationalist, yet he had deep concerns about whether he would ever find a woman who would accept him. Like Eric, one of his very initial fears, expressed to nurses at the emergency room, was whether or not his penis had been burned. Also like Eric, it was some time before he became concerned about what his injuries might mean relative to dating and being accepted by women. As he slowly recovered, these concerns surfaced.

I had some heavy sexual problems, up until last year. I was a virgin until I was twenty-one and that was seven, eight months ago. Heavy sexual problems, not due to any girl, but I should have treated my own fears of what she would do and what,...I was pretty much sexually impotent and I have never really talked to anybody frankly about this. I could go out with a girl and feel pretty comfortable but,...we would get our clothes off, get in bed, and I was just too uptight. I could not get an erection. I was too uptight, too scared. I don't know whether I was too scared to perform, or what she would think, but I was totally scared shitless,... shaking. It was hard enough getting in bed with someone. It just scared the shit out of me, but I knew I had to do it. I wanted somebody to be with, and I wanted to prove to myself I was okay.

D: Was this something that would build up?

Yes. I started getting really scared. It would really build up to where we would get in bed, have our clothes off and I would literally start

shaking. I don't know why, just scared shitless. Then I finally just
came across the right girl who, the first night we went to bed, calmed
me down to where I could feel the feelings, and get an erection. And
I had to be really soothed and calmed down all the time.

I had three sexual relations before the present girl. I had sex with
three women, but I never really achieved an erection or had an
orgasm. This girl, the second or third date we were in bed. It was
natural, but I couldn't perform. I was just shaking and she held me
and talked to me and calmed me down. We just talked, we talked all
night long. We went to sleep and the next night the same thing
happened. The third night I got a full erection and had an orgasm. I
needed a woman who would talk, and take it a little slower, and care.
And that's the way I would have wanted it whether I had been
burned or not.

D: It helped you, to find someone?

Yes. It did help a lot, but at the same time we had been going
together I had reached a point with my leg,....the doctors kept giving
up on my leg, and my infectious disease doctor says, "Sorry Mike,
there's nothing more we can do for you. We are not going to do
anymore surgeries on it, we're not going to put you on IV's to try to
cure the infection. It's just going to stay there until it gets better or
the leg comes off." It's been a trying six months for me. It's all set;
I've got a fantastic woman, but I'm up to here with this bullshit, with
the leg. And my burns, after all these years, I really can't take much
more.

Mike found someone who would take the time he needed in order to
feel secure during physical encounters. Even then, the burn continued to
overshadow his relationship with his girlfriend. Facing the possible loss of
his leg, he cannot escape the consequences of his injuries. It is not
possible to say whether the fact that he was burned affected his first
sexual encounters which were rather terrifying experiences, but there is
little doubt that being badly scarred, and his fears of possible rejection,
significantly contributed to his anxiety in sexual encounters. His fear was
overwhelming; he was absorbed and enveloped by fear that precluded
him from "feeling the feelings." The possibility of having intercourse was
an occasion for being fully seen by the other and being fully seen
presented him with the possibility that he would be discredited. The fact
that he was unable to have an erection was also discrediting, yet he
persisted. Backing off, not because he could not achieve an erection, but
because he was rejected for another by his girlfriend, he ultimately

concluded, as have several other survivors, that he had nothing further to lose. In having nothing to lose, he had much to gain.

This same attitude was expressed by several unmarried survivors. Two of these were women who finally decided that they had "nothing to lose" in their attempts to establish an intimate relationship. In making this decision, both went to singles bars specifically to be picked up. They both were successful. Of interest was the fact that both felt this conduct was "out of character" for them. Both disdained one night stands, but both also felt a desperate need to affirm themselves sexually and this desire situationally overrode their ethical standards. Seeing if they could get into someone's bed was construed by each as a necessary experiment, an exceptional behavior, not as part of their normal identities. Furthermore, both women described their interest, not so much in physical terms of sex, but in terms of a need to know if they were still lovable. This seemed to be another way in which each woman accounted for conduct which she might otherwise feel was discrediting to her.

Mike now knows, regardless of what happens with his leg or his current relationship, that he can be accepted. The women mentioned above, through their intimate encounters, knew that if they could find one person who would sleep with them, they could find others as well, regardless of the fact that they are scarred. The importance of finally achieving orgasm for Mike, and finding someone who saw past the scarring and disfigurement, went far beyond immediate sexual gratification; the significance of this experience was in finding that, regardless of his appearance and possible disabilities, he was a whole person even though he sees his injury as totally screwing up his life. For the women, it was similar. In having intercourse, they realized that other men would accept them and that they weren't untouchable lepers. This was an important lesson.

Sharon West: Flaming Drink Injury
(Interviewed with her Husband, Paul)

Sharon's scars are mostly hidden beneath her clothing. There is some visible scarring on her neck, but this is hardly noticeable. She is careful in the selection of clothing and she takes some pride in dressing meticulously. She is very intelligent and personable and I am sure that many people, both men and women, consider her to be very attractive. She had always considered herself to be physically attractive, but there were now doubts. Athletic and enjoying her time spent in the sun, she had always placed some importance on her appearance. She feels very fortunate that she was not facially disfigured; had she not turned her head to the side, to look at a friend, her face would have been badly burned when a flaming drink, being prepared by a waiter, exploded at her table.

D: There are still concerns about how you look?

> **Sharon:** Most definitely, yes. I know I don't look the same as I used to. I can't wear the cute little nighties,...well you can, but it doesn't quite look the same. I just feel like a new person, but completely different. Paul, he was always the perfect husband; he was great! When I came home from the hospital,...I think you [Paul] felt the same way,...we had to get to know each other again. Just with everything,...didn't you think.

> **Paul:** Yes, there was a period of time,...I did not pressure her into a physical relationship. We sleep in the same bed,...I didn't want to hurt her; I didn't want to cause pain. She was still taking pain medication and she was still bandaged. She wasn't in the mood, I could tell that. And, of course, that wasn't a priority with me. I guess as time went on and the bandages were removed,...it's like when you're dating, you just don't go to dinner and jump into bed. And it was, again like she said, kind of like relearning each other again. I wanted to be sure she was comfortable, and I guess it just spontaneously happened.

> **Sharon:** I don't know a lot about these things...whether he was going to leave me or...but, it's difficult. You look so different and here you're looking so different to someone, it's hard. It was very hard, but then everything just flowed together and then it was okay. Besides the devastation, you have to adjust to and change your ways a little bit in the ways of your life. So it was kind of a redefining ourselves and finding out where we were.

D: Did you discuss this with each other, your concerns?

> **Paul:** I guess, a little bit, but I think I probably really waited for Sharon to bring it up or at least talk about the subject. We started talking about getting away from the kids to be by ourselves. Then Sharon and I stole away to Santa Barbara for a weekend, just to be by ourselves, and we had a wonderful time.

D: Was there a reluctance to physically touch because of pain?

> **Paul:** I'd hug her very lightly, at first. Maybe the second time, I'd hug her a little bit harder. And I know with her wrists, I'd reach down to grab her hand and I'd get her wrist and she'd recoil and it wasn't a recoil of, "Don't touch me" but, "That smarts." And that was kind of my approach to finding out where I could touch her and where I couldn't, where it did hurt or where it didn't. I changed her

dressing and I could still see open areas so, obviously, I would stay away from those areas. It took a little time.

The themes of homecomer and stranger are exquisitely clear in this material. Sharon and Paul were both the same people as they were before Sharon was burned, yet, in significant ways, each was different. The newness of Sharon was compared by Paul to her newness to him when they started dating. In returning home, they had to reorient themselves to each other and they had to get to know each other again. There were areas of Sharon's body that could not be held and caressed, and to freely touch Sharon could cause pain if care was not exercised. Sharon's body, with which Paul had been intimately familiar as Sharon's lover, became problematic. Common, intimate familiarity with her body was transformed, not only due to physical appearance, but because of pain. Sharon's body had become for Paul, as well as for Sharon herself, problematic and unfamiliar. Paul's desire to be physically close to Sharon, and her desire to reestablish physical intimacy with him, presented a dilemma. What Paul could previously take-for-granted, such as hugging Sharon or grabbing her hand, now became something that could cause pain or reinjury. For Sharon, there were significant fears of possible rejection. She was scarred, would this man still want her? They had to rediscover who they were, in themselves and for each other, and where they were in their mutually fashioned world. In Paul's words, they had to redefine themselves. The process of establishing intimacy again involved restructuring an interrupted relationship; it involved a reconstruction of selves and identities. In conceptualizing the emerging relationship, the survivor comprehends the relationship, and makes sense out of what is happening in the present, in terms of time, and through his or her reinterpretation of their past relationship.

Following Berger and Kellner, marriage is viewed as meaning or *nomos* building: within the social construction of marriage the individual creates a social order in which he or she can experience life as making sense (Berger and Kellner 1970, 50-73).[2] Within everyday life, marriage, as a subuniverse of meaning construction, is one of the major institutional vehicles for ordering, or constituting, primary relationships between individuals. Within marriage, biographies, identities, and roles are intersubjectively constructed and legitimated (delegitimation can also occur, most particularly noted where marriages dissolve). Berger and Kellner state that:

> The individual is given by his society certain decisive cornerstones for his everyday experience and conduct. Most importantly, the individual is supplied with specific sets of typifications and criteria of relevance, predefined for him by the society and made available to

him by the ordering of his everyday life. This ordering or nomic apparatus is biographically cumulative. It begins to be formed in the individual from the earliest stages of socialization on, then keeps on being enlarged and modified by himself throughout his biography. (Berger and Kellner 1970, 51-52)

Marriage is one of the institutional cornerstones to which Berger and Kellner refer. They go on to note that,

> Marriage in our society is a dramatic act in which two strangers come together and redefine themselves. The drama of the act is internally anticipated and socially legitimated long before it takes place in the individual's biography, and amplified by means of a pervasive ideology, the dominant themes of which (romantic love, sexual fulfillment, self-discovery and realization, etc.) can be found distributed through all strata of society. (Berger and Kellner 1970, 53-54)

In this account by Sharon and Paul, and in the last chapter, the problem of reconstructing a shared, intersubjective world-together is apparent. Through marriage, a new reality is dialectically and reciprocally constructed between the marriage partners. The partner's work of constructing a world-together is an ongoing, evolving project that is objectified over and over again "from bed to breakfast table, as the partners carry on the endless conversation that feeds on nearly all they individually or jointly experience" (Berger and Kellner 1970, 61). Having one partner seriously injured, ill, or disabled threatens the world that has thus been constituted. The process of constructing a world together generally occurs in the most taken-for-granted manner. Like the individual who is unaware of his or her own biographical history until problems or crises arise, so the partners in marriage are unaware of the process of constructing a life together until problems, arguments, or crises threaten that which has been created over weeks, months, or years. Sustaining the marriage through routine disruptions or major catastrophe requires the renegotiation of identities and roles and this process can be seen here. The task for the marriage partners is problematic, ongoing, open, and evolutional over time.

D: Did both of you talk about the concerns you each had?

Sharon: Yeah, we did some.

Paul: I told her I would stick around for a while. I did everything I could to assure her that the scarring of her outer personality, I guess you could call it, or body or skin, was not primary in my thinking. And that due to it or because of it, my concerns, feelings, love for her, hadn't changed. I went through, obviously, some thoughts about why it had to happen, why to us, why to her, and if it happened, why did it. I mean, here she is twenty-five. Why? You have a talk with God. You say if you're going to do it, why not to me?

Sharon: See, I would rather have it happen to me than Paul. I think I can handle it better happening to me than to him.

Paul: See, I come from a very Catholic background, so you have talks with God often, very strict with nuns and Jesuits. I was looking at it and saying, hey, I'm the one with sin, if that's a criteria for this kind of thing. And those are the things you think about. She's an innocent girl, I took her out of her home. I can look back at my life and I can't throw rocks. I can't open my closets because there's a few skeletons in it, kind of a thing. Hey, I'm the one that deserved to be punished if you're punishing someone,...then I'm the guy, not her. But I have to say now in retrospect, that this tragedy has brought us a lot closer together. We're still physical, but I feel we have a far more spiritual strength between each other. I'm talking about a spiritual feeling for each other mentally, emotionally, and those kinds of things.

Sharon: We were always very close. After this, boy, you can make it through anything.

Paul: I mean, nobody asks to have a boiling pot of water on you, or in her case, a flaming drink. It's the will of the gods I guess, or fate, it's whatever label you call it, but it happens. But you need each other in those times. What happens to those relationships when they dissolve? So how shallow were they? At no time did I have the feeling of leaving this lady. She's given me two beautiful children and she's physically and emotionally been through a lot. My feelings from the onset was to give her as much support as I could, both physically and emotionally. She went through some valleys, she's dropped off the ends of the earth, into depression and tears, from crying in the middle of the night to crying in the middle of the day because of her physical appearance, and her concerns. I did everything I could to assure her that it would not affect our relationship. I've loved her in spite of this happening and I mean it sincerely.

Sharon: When the chips are down, you really find out what kind of person you're married to. Some people just can't take this kind of thing. I know this has made us stronger. We were always close and had a very good relationship before, but this has just added something. We can make it through anything. There are worse things, but this is up there.

In the above narrative, Sharon and Paul continue to describe their process of rediscovering each other and in reconstructing themselves. Sharon, like many survivors, conceptualizes herself as a new person and she recognizes that the changes through which she has traveled also affect Paul and how he may relate to her. Both find in the injury, and in the evolving process of recovery, that they have been strengthened as both individuals and as a couple. There is no denying the very high costs of the injury, but in spite of such costs, they are able to discover or create positive meanings out of their deep losses. They retrospectively have found that they are spiritually closer than before. This suggests a redefinition of their identities and it further suggests a redefinition of that which binds them together.

Sharon and Paul had a great deal of social support from friends, family, and their church. This was mentioned by both of them. Two major factors seem to separate those in this study who felt themselves to be doing well from those who felt that they were having significant problems. One factor is perceived social support, or the lack of support, while the other is the ability to find positive meanings or values in the burn experience. As simple as these issues seem, they appear as the central differences between those survivors who felt that they were doing well from those who continue to be vexed and overwhelmed by their injuries.

Another process that is apparent in Paul's statements is that of searching for and attributing meaning to the burn event. For Paul, who is religious, the search for meaning, as a search for "why," is framed partly within a religious context. This is not to suggest that this is the only way he made some sense out of what happened, nor is it to suggest that only answers posited within a religious context were referenced, but it is clear that religious themes played some part in his search. He sat down and talked to God, but instead of "Why her?" it was, "Why her,...why not me?" To make some sense out of what happened to her, and what he felt should have instead happened to him, Paul referenced, through memoric reconstruction, his past. His history, as opposed to how he construes her history, and hence, her identity as being "innocent," informs him and suggests that he should have been the victim if there had to be one. It has been stated that the self is emergent and temporally achieved through self-definition and attribution in the present, which refers to, or is informed by, the subject's reconstructed past. Paul's account displays this process, and in his case, his definitions of self are also contingent upon his construction of Sharon's presumed past. What is seen here is the situational, contextual creation of identities.

Sharon was grateful that she rather than Paul was burned, not because she felt she could endure the injury better than he could, but because she felt she could not cope with having him burned. Her anticipated and self-attributed emotional weakness was used to explain why it was better she, and not Paul, was burned. This seems to be a unique definition, but it shows at least three things. First, it obliquely shows self-definition: it tacitly contains a reference to her self-attributed emotional strength to deal with the possibility that Paul, not herself, was burned for in it she suggests that she could not cope with having Paul burned. Therefore, it is a self-assessment. Second, it speaks to her assessment of Paul's ability to cope with her being seriously injured. It is an assessment of the strengths and weaknesses of each of them. It also shows the variability in self-assessment and definition that the survivor can create for overwhelming situations.

Ann Saunders: Scalding Oil Injury

Prior to being burned, Ann had never considered herself especially attractive, an image that I am sure many others would have disputed. While majoring in psychology at a university, she took a course in special education. During that course, many issues relating to persons who have disabilities were discussed including the case of a young woman who, in an accident, lost part of a finger. The instructor in the course had met this woman at a lecture and he had felt that she was an exceptionally beautiful young woman. The professor commented that, for this woman, the loss of her finger was like the loss of everything she possessed, wanted or cared about. It seemed that in losing her finger she had lost her identity and self. Her world was heavily invested in her appearance and the loss of just part of one finger was a massive threat to her identity. Her continuing grief seemed extraordinary. In the absence of losing all, one sometimes seems to grieve more for small losses than for more significant losses. Ann thought about this lecture after she was burned. She questioned whether she had invested too much of herself in her physical appearance even though she had sometimes doubted her physical attractiveness.

At the time of her burn, Ann was romantically involved with a man who was her senior by several years, an engineer where she worked. They had been dating for four years, but Ann felt that the relationship was really not developing. Their relationship seemed stagnant to her, but neither of them could make a clear decision to terminate it. It was at this time that Ann was burned. While she was in the hospital, he started dating her primary care nurse whom he soon married. While bitter about how the relationship ended, Ann felt that it was best that it did end. But then, she had to consider what it would be like in the future if she sought intimate relationships.

D: So what has it been like since then?

I spent a lot of years walking around with my head down. Because I didn't want to see, not place myself in a position where I felt bad. Why invite that sort of thing? I could have walked like I owned the world, and if I caught somebody looking at me, it would have made me feel bad. So I decided I wasn't going to look at people and chances are, they weren't going to look at me. And if they are going to stare, there's nothing wrong with that. People are curious. Sometimes I look, I see myself, but I don't think I see what other people see. I know how far I've come.

D: Do you think of yourself as disfigured?

Well, yeah. It's not always easy to think of myself with a cavalier attitude. I'm uncomfortable, 'though I've been at the pool, or at the beach a couple of times, but I do the ostrich routine. I try not to call attention to it, but I'm very glad that my scars aren't worse. I can live with the way I am and not have a problem with it. There are times when it is worse, like when I'm with men. Like when I'm with men, sometimes I feel my scars, or my neck starts to pull. There are times when I go through that and become uncomfortable, but I can't let it get me down. I've had the opportunity to meet people who've been burned more severely, and I'm aware of how lucky I am. I've also met some people who've been burned who carry around emotional baggage. They won't let it go and it really ruins their lives.

D: Did you have concerns about relationships with men?

I had that question posed to me by one of the nurses as I was about to leave the hospital. She said, "Have you thought about what your life will be like out of the hospital? Having no boyfriend now?" And I said, I don't know. I'd like to think that I will, when the time is right. But again, I don't want to get my hopes up that ... It's a way I've always been, if it works it's okay and if not, it wasn't meant to be. And it doesn't mean I won't try to work if it looks like it might be falling apart because I've had to do that.

D: Have you dated?

Well, now I have, but it's probably not because of the burn. That was the hardest thing, to get comfortable in going out. The easiest way for me, in the beginning, was to go out with people who weren't a threat. It was usually types I wouldn't get serious about to begin with. Somebody might set me up with someone I didn't know, but might like as a friend but not with someone I might be serious about. I went out with one friend, somebody from work, and he was asking

me about my accident, and I got upset. Normally it doesn't bother me
but he said something, and I just said let's talk about something else.
I dated a guy [another person] for a couple of years and almost
wound up in the same position I was with Bob. I couldn't break up
with the guy. I wanted to, but couldn't for some reason, hang on, be
miserable. He was trying to change me, but I never felt burned
around him. I never felt self-conscious. I never felt like, "I look
pretty good for somebody that's been burned." It was like, "I look
good!" And I never felt like I looked good before, after I was
burned. I didn't feel burned around him at all. He was the first
relationship with someone after I had been burned and he didn't
know before. When I realized that I was staying with him for that
kind of comfort and security, I looked at it that that was nice, but not
enough. That's why it was hard to do, breaking up.

Like Darleen, described below, Ann does not locate all her problems
with men, whatever the problems may be, in the burn and in the fact that
she is scarred. Being burned causes problems, perhaps more for her
emotionally than for men she dates, but she nevertheless does not account
for or attribute her problems simply to the fact that she had been burned.
This fact is important. It shows that she is aware of her burns; she accepts
and acknowledges the possibility that scars may interfere in relationships.
But in not attributing all failures to her injury, in not blaming, she is better
able to accept herself as whole and she is better able to believe that she
has a reasonable chance of establishing meaningful relationships regardless
of her injury. The meaning of the burn does not become overwhelming for
her as it has some of the others. For Ann, the burn doesn't become the
reason for not establishing relationships with others.
It is also seen in her account that, in comparing herself to other
survivors, she feels fortunate. She could have been much worse. She
could have more significant scarring; she could have lost her sight and her
hearing. In spite of the negatives that resulted from the injury, there are
still consequential positives and her recognition of these inform her
assessment of herself for which she is grateful. She has dated several men
since she was burned and has not isolated herself, though she did go
through a period of very trying times when she frequently, while in public
places, experienced acute anxiety attacks. These attacks were so acute
that she would have to immediately leave and get home. In spite of these,
and through therapy, she was able to cope with the changes brought
about by her burn. She dated and, while she was uncomfortable, she
persisted. Finding someone who allowed her to feel "unburned," she
ultimately realized that there was little else in the relationship and it was
terminated. She learned from that experience that it was possible to be
very comfortable in the presence of men and that, if it happened once, it

could happen again. This was similar to discoveries made by both Eric and Mike, experiences reported by other survivors as well.

Darleen Greenberg: Vehicle Accident

D: Did you have a man in your life when you were burned?

No. It was a very tragic situation. I had broken up with the guy shortly before the accident. And he didn't come to see me after the accident either. And I didn't really think about it because I was so drugged. And one day a mutual friend of ours came in and said, "I guess you're wondering why Wally hasn't been in to see you." I said, "Okay, why?" And she said that two days after my accident he had been in a very bad accident. He was swimming from a rope over a river and he fell in and broke his neck and he's been paralyzed ever since. So that was really something. So I don't know what it would have been like if I had a boyfriend at the time.

But again, I'll tell you, this has a lot to do with who you are going into the burn rather than who you are coming out of it because, regarding men and my sexuality, other than say a year or a year and a half when I was still going through cosmetic surgery. Even with me, I never really missed a beat. I have never had trouble meeting friends [men or women] before I was burned or after. I'm sure more men would be attracted to me without the scars, but that hasn't been a major void in my life either. I would guess that the percentage of men that I'm losing out to are,...you know, sort of weeds out the bad ones I guess, or the ones who aren't up to what I want out of a man. At this point in my life, I want a man of substance.

Obviously, the man of my dreams hasn't manifested himself yet or I'd be married. But I've had some lovely men in my life. I'm dating a guy right now who, I mean [he's] one of the men that women complain don't exist. He's a great guy. He pursued me for a long time before I said, let's give it a shot. The problems I have with men in relationships have not been due to my scars.

D: Were any men troubled by your scars?

I had one, early on, about ten years ago. In fact, he's still a good friend. My scars did trouble him a lot. But it was interesting it troubled him for he had scars of his own. He had a big scar across his face. He's a very good looking man but he was always so self-conscious about those scars on his face and that's why I think my scars bothered him.

When I was still in the hospital, one of the guys I had gone to high school with had come in to see me. He was a real attractive guy. He had been in an industrial accident and he had been burned pretty bad. So he had some scars on his face and a few on his arms. So he came to see me and everything was real nice. And I remember watching this guy and I thought to myself, "You know, this guy is incredibly attractive and sexy." The scars are very apparent, so what had hit my brain, it said your sexuality, what makes you attractive, has nothing or very little to do with your physical appearance. Men have always found me very sexually attractive. And that's something that comes from the inside, it's not something that comes from the outside.

I would say that it [being scarred] has made it 25 percent harder for me to meet people and you've got to meet someone before you start a relationship! So that's a serious problem. On the other hand, it has made me fifty to one hundred times more sensitive so that once I make a contact, I can sustain a conversation; I see past the superficial. There isn't a person out there, and I don't care if they have scars on their faces or not, that doesn't feel almost as if they did. You know, if they have a pimple or they are overweight or whatever. They're walking around with the same kind of stuff on their shoulders and it's weighty. I was always very outgoing and bold, but I think that was a coverup for insecurities. Today I am very outgoing and very bold, but I really feel it.

For Darleen, the fact that she has visible scars is not treated as a reason for having problems with men. There was never the suggestion that she feels she has any more difficulties with men than she believes other, nonscarred women might have. Indeed, she has not gone without intimate, affectionate relationships with men and such relationships have not been unique or singular. While her scars are not especially pronounced nor are they massive, her facial scars are apparent. Many people may not have any idea that she was burned, but I believe it would be impossible for people to not see that she is scarred.

Darleen's interpretation of the effect of her scars relative to her desirability to men contrasts distinctly with Ellen. Ellen feels devastated by her scars. She has felt, and continues to feel, that no one could love her or, perhaps, even like her because she is facially scarred. Yet, Ellen's scars are now less pronounced, because of surgery several years ago, than are Darleen's. Ellen attributes many of her self-identified failures to the fact that she was burned and is scarred. There are important background differences between Ellen and Darleen. Ellen was burned as a child. Growing up with scars, she experienced painful tauntings by other children who called her "scar face" and she has always deeply felt that her parents did not accept her or love her and, at least in part, this was attributed to the burn. There were also other obvious differences between both women. In general, it seemed from listening to Ellen that her whole life was emotionally impoverished. Her father and mother continuously denied the reality of the burn and its consequences. Her father was depicted as cold, uncaring, and aloof while her mother was portrayed as also uncaring and quite blind to what took place in the family.

There was also in Ellen's childhood the experience of sexual abuse by her brother, the memory of which had been repressed for many years. Again, with this significant issue, Ellen's parents reportedly remained oblivious to Ellen's repeated statements that it had occurred. As with the consequence of the burn, they again denied that the abuse could have happened, and in so doing, constituted further evidence for Ellen that neither of them really cared about her. In contrast, Darleen depicted her childhood as being relatively normal and her relationship with her parents as being loving. For Darleen, the burn was an accident, very unfortunate and consequential to be sure, but she has been able to overcome the effects of the burn. It is not construed as a monumental disaster which has destroyed her life. For Darleen, there have been significant relationships with men, while for Ellen there has only been one relationship and it was described as being platonic and short lived. For Ellen, there is substantial evidence in her life that the results of the burn continue to be life shattering, for Darleen there is no such evidence.

In considering the possibility that some conceivable relationships with men have been lost because of her scars, Darleen does what many survivors do when coping with others who are insensitive, intrusive or offensive: she interprets their identities as less than desirable or credible and as therefore being suspect. In Darleen's case, there are not specific examples which she recalls of rejection, but in visualizing such occasions, she makes an interpretation which, as a generic type, is very common to the survivors I interviewed. She defines such others as not being suitable; they are men who are deficient and therefore unacceptable as partners.

In the final sections from Darleen's interview, she states that had she originally recognized that she would be scarred, she would not have wanted to live. Appearance was very important, so much so that an appendectomy scar was bothersome. Yet now, in reexamining her life, she finds that this has not been the case. She provides some grounds for the conservative approach which surgeons take in discussing long-term appearance with hospitalized patients...had she known that scars would remain, she would not have wanted to live. At least, that is how she retrospectively interprets what happened. She goes on to compare her experience, by example, to that of a friend whose severely disabled infant child died. The death of a child is surely one of the most significant losses a parent can experience. Yet, what Darleen suggested is that even in this most profound loss, significance and meaning can be discovered. That fact does not eliminate the bitter, agonizing, nauseating feelings of emptiness and loss experienced, but it does, perhaps, lessen and ameliorate such feelings with the passage of time. In mutually going through this horrible experience, in facing bitter darkness and deep anguish, her friends found love for each other, as well as for the child that they had not before experienced. They discovered, in this deeply profound loss, positive meanings and values not previously anticipated, allowing them to transcend the anguish of the present and thereby grow. Darleen has been able to do much the same with her life. She has moved well past a preoccupation with appearance. She feels herself as now being more sensitive to others and she feels more assertive and forceful. She now sees these changes as assets whereas, previously, she saw them as defenses against her own feelings of inadequacy.

Jeff Asmore: Residential Fire

In recounting his experiences, both before and after he was burned, it seemed that the only person with whom Jeff had established and maintained a loving, intimate relationship was his mother. He claimed to hate the rest of his family, not only for what was done to him after he left the hospital, but for real or imagined wrongs committed before he was burned.

In the previous material on Jeff, his difficulty in adjusting to his new life, in which he was cared for by a despised sister, was painfully clear. When he was finally taken to California by a second sister, he was initially relieved, but any hope soon turned to further anguish and bitterness. His sister was involved in using and selling drugs and her husband was described by Jeff as exceptionally mean and jealous. Subsequently, Jeff was placed in special schools and in a foster home. He typically started out feeling good about such changes, but every situation ultimately became defined by Jeff as one in which others wanted to care for him only to get his disability and welfare payments. He went through a series of homes and schools, finally ending up on the street.

While attending a special school for disabled teenagers, Jeff met a female student who was interested in him. He liked her initially but she also was soon discredited. The theme of being used by others, others who initially appear as kind and benevolent but who become malevolent, is common throughout Jeff's account. He is forever being abused and used by others, he is forever disappointed, finding himself in marginal situations from which any permanent extrication seems impossible. He sees intimate relationships as places to be manipulated, used, and abused by others. At best, to Jeff, love seems to involve getting what you can from the other person. There is no sense of sharing commitment or enduring relationship, though that seems clearly to be what Jeff seeks. He needed someone to care for him and to care about him, but all of his relationships failed to form what he so desperately sought. His sense of isolation and emotional pain comes across all to well when he discusses how much he feared being alone.

D: Have you had any relationships with girls or women?

There was one girl, in high school, the special high school.

D: How did you meet her, did she approach you?

Not at first. How it happened was that my lips were really chapped, really bad and sore. This girl, she passed a note to me and said, "The reason why your lips are chapped is because you need to be kissed by a girl and I know who the girl is." And all this time there was a girl that was interested in me, but I didn't even think anyone would be attracted to me. And she was. And we finally got together. And I came to find out she was the school slut. She messes around with a lot of guys. But it was a handicapped school. But she was different and she was pregnant. And she tried to say it was I that got her pregnant. But when she started showing a little too soon, then I knew it wasn't mine.

D: Was she attractive to you?

She was beautiful. She became the school queen in a competition between the grades. I was really happy with her. But when she came up and said I made her pregnant, that turned me off for a long time. To go down so easily...I know a lot of women. They take men and they trap them into marriage. And usually they don't work out, but sometimes they do. But that's the way a woman gets a man through saying they're pregnant.

D: She wasn't repulsed by your scars?

No, it didn't bother her a bit. But a lot of people were. Just very few people weren't, like the guy who picked me up on the street, Mark Gibson. I think back on that day...he had a convertible. [I needed a ride] and he picked me up. Nobody else would stop or offered to help me that day. Of all the people that passed me that day that could have seen how tired I was. And it was obvious I was lost, I didn't know where I was going.

D: Did you meet any other girls?

A few, not many,...just a few.

D: And did you meet them in school?

No. Me and some guys that I ran into, we went out and we were bowling and there was a girl and we picked her up. So, it was just something that happened. We ended up with venereal disease, all of us, except that I didn't have anyone else to give it to. They had girlfriends and they gave it to them. So I was okay, but they weren't. That affected me a lot. I never had problems with the guys catching VD, only with the women. And three times with women I've caught VD.

D: These were women who met you and wanted to go to bed with you?

Twice I got them on my own and it was just something that happened, nothing great. It was just something that happened.

D: Before you got picked up by the guy in the convertible, had you ever had sex with a man?

Yeah. I was outside my sister's apartment and I had a top from Frederick's of Hollywood and I had a pair of white pants on. I was barefoot. And this guy in a van came up and I could hear my sister and her husband fighting inside. And so he asked me, and I knew it was a line. He asked me if I wanted to go for a ride and I said, "Sure, why not?" And so I took off with him and we stopped at a parking lot. And all that time he thought I was a girl.3 When I told him that I wasn't a girl he asks if I had a sex change operation. I said, "No, I didn't." And he goes, "Well, you look like a girl." I go, "Thanks, but I'm not so if you don't want me just tell me so and take me back home." So he goes, "Don't you want to go for a ride?" So I said, "Sure, let's go anywhere." So we ended up at his place. And I sort of got scared a little bit. But I really wasn't all that scared and, well, that was the first time.

Implicit in the game like interaction between Jeff and the other man was the possibility and the recognition that the encounter was to be sexual. When Jeff says "if you don't want me," the question seems to beg a sexual purpose. This interaction is interesting because what isn't said directly nevertheless informs what is said and indeed, informs the outcome.

D: Did many people think you were a female?

> Yeah. One time my sister had dressed me up in her clothes and had taken pictures. And I had put on a little makeup, just a little. And I was seeing a social worker and she got me an appointment with Dr. Rader, a psychiatrist. And I told my sister that even the tenants in the building thought I was a girl. This guy there, he wanted to fool around with me even after he knew that I wasn't a girl. But I wasn't interested in him.

D: Was he gay?

> No, he was married. People are fascinated when it comes to something different. It's like with Prince or Michael Jackson. When people see what they look like, they can't believe they're men. And people, they like something different. It takes time to get used to it, but once they do, they can enjoy it and see if something good comes from it.

D: Did you care what type of relationships you had, whether they were with men or women?

> At the time it didn't matter. I was alone. I didn't have anyone. And just to have some kind of communication and relationship with anyone was okay with me. But I didn't want it to be just anyone. I wanted it to be somebody. And I wanted something out of it.

D: You just wanted someone to be close to?

> I wanted somebody to care about me.

D: There are a lot of problems with your appearance, but some people didn't care about the scars?

> Very few didn't care. But when this guy with the convertible...when I met him, he didn't care. When I first started wearing make-up in high school, a lot of people there resented it. Even the staff, they thought something was wrong.

D: How did you use it?

> I would cover my whole face with makeup to cover the scars. I would wear eye liner, make eyebrows, mascara, but I never wore lipstick. That was too much. But they saw it differently. They saw it as if I was trying to be a female, but I wasn't. I just wanted to hide

the scars. In that way they rejected me and the attention I got from other people, which when you get some good responses, you usually go with the good. That's what I did.

D: And the good responses were?

When this guy saw me, when he was in the convertible. I've always loved convertibles so I went with him.

D: Did you think you looked like a woman?

Yeah. I still do. If I didn't have the mustache[4] (penciled on) and if I did have....And I bought designer jeans, skintight and everything. I can go out and can be a woman for a lot of men out there which don't care if you're a guy or not. And they'll be fascinated because when it comes to makeup, if you use it, you can do all sorts of things.

D: He was a pimp? He had several other males working for him?

A lot. Yeah, William, the pimp...when I first met him I wouldn't even get in [his car] because he was black. We had our conversation and I said, "Well, you know, you can't trust anyone." So he goes, "You can trust me." And I got in with him. And we went driving around and we talked and he asked me what kind of things did I like. I said, "I like music, I like to dance, I like tight clothes, I like makeup and I have a pet tarantula," which most people usually don't have.

I was fascinating. And he asked about the accident, how it happened and what I'd been through. I told him everything and he wanted to touch me, touch my arm and see what it felt like. And he was fascinated with the way I felt. It's just something different; it's not the same old thing as most people. In most people they want something different and something unusual.

D: When did you get out of prostitution?

It was when I moved that I stopped. It was when the guy from France wanted me to go back to France with him. I wanted to, but I just couldn't take that chance because it's too far and I wouldn't know anyone.

Throughout Jeff's extensive account, issues of abuse, social isolation, depersonalization, and alienation frequently emerged. Jeff appears as one who, naked and alone, has been cast into exile in a hostile world. A statement by Rollo May elegantly fits:

> He moves about in a state of homelessness, vagueness, and haze as though he had no direct sense connection with his world but were in a foreign country where he does not know the language,...[he] is always doomed to wander in quiet despair, incommunicado, homeless, and a stranger. (May 1958, 57)

The sense of alienation from himself, as well as from others, and the feeling of being alone without connection to others, is especially acute throughout Jeff's account. He objectifies himself in clothing and identity props, becoming a woman for those who want him to be a woman. His sexual identification and how he sexually portrays himself to others are ambiguous. Seeking others and emotional connection, he becomes engaged in instrumental relationships, trading sex for some sense of companionship. He has become a thing to be manipulated and used. There is a fundamental rift between what he would like to experience, a caring relationship where he is accepted as a person, and what he finds with others. In significant measure, he creates his own treatment. Damaged at an early age, perhaps long before he was burned, he has not learned to love, for he seems to be one who was not loved. Having not been loved, it is difficult to love or establish close, caring relationships. The authenticity of human existence occurs through care or concern, and it is through care that one's relationships with others is structured (Heidegger 1962, 148-168). It is within the structure of care that authentic being-with-another emerges. With Jeff, there is no sense of being-with-another; instead, there is the clear portrait of one whose existence with others is shallow and utilitarian. Upon reflection, the world Jeff knows seems to him to be hostile and bitter, so he is hostile and bitter. No matter how much he longs to find acceptance and relation, he is truncated. In echoing Binswanger, Sadler states:

> But longing that finds only lack sours into hatred, envy, and a general disparagement of the whole of life. The lack of love puts a seal of desecration and profanation upon the whole world. (Sadler 1969, 306)

The sense of depersonalization and instrumentality, that Jeff treats himself as an object to be manipulated for the desires of others, through dress, hair style or color, or mannerisms, suggest the relationship of *I-It* following Buber (Sadler 1969, 96-102). With Jeff it is carried even further, to *It-It* relationships in which the "I" is lost to reification. Others do not relate to Jeff as a person, they too relate to him as a manipulatable thing. If some do try to relate to him more honestly, he closes off, defending what is private and what remains from his past. He can't get close to others and he cannot allow others to approach him. For Jeff, the situation is extreme. There is nothing else; there is no communion with anyone; there is no dialogue; there is no honesty. He painfully seeks much more, but he miserably fails.

Issues involving intimacy and sexuality can be vexing and intransigent for burn survivors, and for many survivors of other forms of consequential physical as well as psychological trauma. Divorce frequently follows burn injury. This is true for adult survivors, and it also seems to be the case, where children are burned, that parents frequently divorce. There are frequently many unresolved issues in both types of situations; guilt and blame are common problems, and these are issues which often erode what had been long standing relationships.

Even relationships which seemed solid prior to the burn incident can end in hostile recrimination and divorce. In relationships which were difficult prior to the burn incident, the parties may initially pull together. There may be shared feelings of closeness and empathy in a relationship where there had often been frustration, anger, and distance. The injured partner may desperately need to be close, he or she may feel in critical need of emotional support from the other partner, and the partner may be willing to ignore previous problems, at least temporarily. Unfortunately, in many of the cases I've seen, the support, concern, empathy, and affection, born of sudden trauma, doesn't last. The injury, with all the attendant demands placed on both the survivor and his or her partner, places greater stress on a relationship which is already too fragile. Disfigurement, scarring, and disability take a further toll on the relationship in magnifying feelings which were damaged prior to the accident. Some relationships may be strengthened by the ordeal, most, over time, seem to be weakened as the lives of the survivor and significant other return to "normal." Old issues and conflicts resurface, and what had been a hopeful accord soon fails.

Survivors often feel, initially at least, that in having scars, they will never be loved again. If married or coupled the survivor fears losing the love and support of the other. If single, the survivor fears that he or she will never find someone who will accept him or her. The person who has only small scars, easily hidden under clothing, may express greater concerns than does the survivor who has massive scars. With massive scars, the survivor has virtually no choice in being noticed, but those with few scars, or scars that are hidden beneath clothing, can generally pass as "normal" until special circumstances arise where what was hidden will be revealed. So strong is the fear of being detected and rejected, that some survivors have reported shunning situations in which their scars might be seen. For example, those who previously loved going to the beach may no longer do so, or they may go swimming only where others are not likely to see them. Dress styles may also be altered to conceal that which could otherwise be seen. Only long sleeve shirts may be worn, even in hot weather. The survivor may wear high, buttoned collars to hide scars on the neck. In the case of men, with facial scarring, beards may be used as camouflage.

Most unfortunately, some single survivors will not attempt to establish any relationships where physical contact might be an expected or desired outcome. Some, who had dated extensively prior to being injured, may shun contact for a long time. It is clear, however, that many survivors do attempt to establish normal relationships after a period of time, often prolonged. Adjustment, involving the normalization of the survivor's life, is often slow and difficult. How others respond to the survivor is crucial in his or her adjustment. Social acceptance, and the support of family, friends, and others cannot be underestimated in a world that too frequently judges people, at least initially, on appearance alone. The entire area of intimacy and sexuality needs to be better addressed by survivors and medical support staff prior to the survivor's release from the hospital. This problem is not unique to burn survivors. Finally, it must be stressed that the population from which I drew my cases was small. In fact, if there is bias in the sample, I suspect it is clearly biased toward those who have adjusted quite well to their injuries. For an unknown number of burn survivors, there is not full normalization of their lives. Some people survive their physical injuries only to psychologically die to life. Their postburn lives remain truncated by scars which are both visible and invisible. The invisible scars may be those from which escape is most difficult.

6

The Crucible and the Forge:
Reconstructions of Self

In reality, however, every ego, so far from being a unity is in
the highest degree a manifold world, a constellated heaven, a
chaos of forms, of states and stages, of inheritances and
potentialities. It appears to be a necessity as imperative as
eating and breathing for everyone to be forced to regard this
chaos as a unity and to speak of his ego as though it were a
one-fold and clearly detached and fixed phenomenon....As a
body everyone is single, as a soul never. Man is not by any
means of fixed and enduring form. He is much more an
experiment and transition.
                              Hermann Hesse
                              Steppenwolf

In considering burns, fire represents potential annihilation, pain, and
suffering. More broadly, and throughout recorded history, as well as in the
myths, legends and stories of diverse and time-different cultures, fire has
been a primary symbol denoting such divergent processes as destruction,
transformation and change, creativity, love and procreation, and purification. The terror of hell, portrayed by Dante in *The Divine Comedy*, is one
of souls perpetually suffering the torturous fires of damnation, fires for
which there are no quenching waters.

Water quenches fire, fire transforms water, and each has been used to
represent purification and cleansing, two processes of significant ritual and
religious importance to both preliterate and contemporary humanity. Fire
and water, as two of the original primordial elements which were thought
to be derived from the four "humors" or "principles" (hot, cold, moist, and
dry) are opposites, each being the antithesis of the other. Within the
crucible of the forge, steel is deformed, softened, and melted. Through

annealing, involving intense heat, steel becomes transformed and hardened. Through the application of heat and cooling, the sword of the Samurai, of Charlemagne and the medieval Crusaders were tempered and then honed. As a metaphor, the processing of steel through the crucible and the forge suggests the personal journeys of many survivors who have appeared in this study. In looking back at themselves, many discover transformation and change made possible through the crucible and the forge of searing heat, suffering, and tears, resulting in the discovery of new meanings for self, and the forging of new identities.

For virtually all the survivors who were interviewed, there was minimally one lesson from the fire, chemicals, or scalding liquids that seared each of them: they left the hospital knowing that they survived something they never imagined they could have survived. They withstood pain and suffering they could not have imagined in their most frightening nightmares. Had they truly understood the intense, interminable pain they would endure, several believed that, given a choice, they would have chosen death. Several would have preferred death had they known that they would be permanently disfigured and this included some who are only moderately disfigured. Living as they did, each survivor invariably had to make some sense out of what happened to his or her life. Each had to grapple with what the burn meant and continues to mean. All of the survivors, except those who were burned as young children,[1] minimally discovered that they were stronger than they thought they were. All of these people were surprised by their endurance. To each, that endurance represented strength and fortitude which none had anticipated.

For most survivors, the meanings of the burn are multiple, involving some positive discoveries as well as the feeling that much was lost to the burn. For some survivors, including a few who are significantly disfigured, the meanings defined for the burn are mostly positive. The construction of meaning is eminently problematic. Survivors were challenged in many diverse ways by their injuries and not the least of such challenges involved making sense out of a catastrophic and tragic injury and coming to terms with what the whole event meant. The discovery of meaning is ongoing. It is a process that does not necessarily end when the person leaves the hospital, looks in a mirror, or finally returns to work. While some appear to make early closure on the burn, for most survivors the task of coping with the results of the injury, which entails discovering meanings not only for the burn but also for the self in relation to the burn, is an unfolding process which will continue for years.

Our lives are in continuous flux and transformation, and at each stage of noticing change, we reinterpret who we are. We continuously discover who we are; we continuously reinvent ourselves as new roles are entered and as old roles are abandoned, as we meet new friends and see old friends depart from our lives, as we change jobs, get married, have children, get divorced, become ill, recover. On and on, our lives are characterized by change and transformation. We are continuously being socialized and resocialized. At each juncture, we seek to understand where we came from and where we are going.

In searching for the meaning of the present, we examine our pasts. Over time, we most probably feel ourselves to be the same persons we were yesterday, or ten years ago even though we know we have changed. The objective permanence of self is a myth we create in order to anchor ourselves and to give our lives the feeling of continuity and stability. The feeling that we are the same now as we were previously—yesterday or twenty years ago—is not a myth. It is a belief born of memory, habit. and routine, a subjective feeling more than a demonstrable fact, and as belief or self-myth, it seems important to our subjective sense of well-being in the world. Most of the time, we take our identities quite for granted. Unless questions are raised or problems arise, we have no need to question who we are. In crisis situations, such as burns, serious accidents, or life-threatening illness, significant questions about self and identity are commonly raised. For some, there are no big mysteries; they cope, recover, and go on with lives that are very similar to their preburn lives. This is not to suggest that there is not change, perhaps significant change, but they do not see themselves as essentially new people.   For others, however, there seems to be almost a complete reconceptualization of self and the feeling that they have undergone radical and global change, not just in appearance, abilities, or interests, but in the general way they understand themselves, others, and the world. Paradoxically, at the very moment of seeing themselves as invariably different, they can still feel that "I'm me, the same Robert I've always been, inside."

In the confrontation with, and recognition of, overwhelming change of great moment, the survivor will maintain a subjective feeling that "I'm the same me" even while acknowledging change and transformation. The subjective sense of continuity and permanence, even in the face of substantial evidence of discontinuity and change, was maintained by several survivors even while they were fully cognizant of transformation in their lives. The subjective feeling or sense of permanence that survivors and others maintain[2] in the face of threat, rather than the actual permanence of the self, as if it were an object of transituational stability, is of consequence. We all require histories that make sense to us, the burn survivor no less than the person who has never been injured or seriously ill. Part of each life is devoted to making sense out of change and finding continuity and permanence in the flux and metamorphosis common to all human lives. Perhaps now, much more than in the times of our ancestors, the creation of our personal sense of permanence is more difficult to achieve than it was just fifty or one hundred years ago. We live in a time of rapid social, technological, and personal change, all of which can be very disquieting and, indeed, threatening to identity and self. For most of us, change comes more slowly than it does for those who face catastrophic events. Yet, all of us seek to integrate the discontinuities in our lives, producing a uniform history which makes sense and which gives us order in our lives.

In large measure, how the survivor defines the meanings of the burn and, therefore, how he or she constructs the social reality of the injury, is an accomplishment which is contingent, in part, on the definitions made by others, particularly by significant others. The attributions, definitions and interpretations made by others are of consequence throughout the survivor's course of hospitalization and recovery, and they continue to be of importance as the survivor grapples with the consequences of the injury as he or she reconstructs a normalized or disabled life.[3] At many turns, the survivor finds quandaries and dilemmas that require solutions. Many routine, taken-for-granted typifications about self and world no longer fit or make sense. For what was lost, new meanings, be they enabling or disabling, must be sought.

Eric Mathews: Vehicle Accident

Prior to being burned, Eric's life consisted of going to classes in college, working part time, and frequently partying. He had a drinking problem and he was using marijuana. His biggest problem was with alcohol. He had been jailed several times as a minor for being "under the influence." His father also had a long-term problem with drinking and, for years, this had caused embarrassment for Eric. Family problems often revolved around his father's drinking. Eric resented what his father's drinking had done to both him and his family, yet Eric was following in his father's footsteps.

> I was the youngest of four children. My dad had a drinking problem which caused conflict in the family, which was part of the things I wasn't ready to accept. We never talked about it, never discussed it. It didn't exist. We had our own lives outside the family and I would exclude everything from coming into the home. I wouldn't consider bringing anybody over.

> And then the embarrassment that would come from that. So a lot of those factors, which were reasons for me to be out [drinking], another good excuse for me to say, "Well, at least I'm not as bad as he was."

Q: Did you see a relationship there?

No. At that time, he was a good excuse. For me, I think it was an excuse, "Well, even if I do, I'm not as bad as him. Look how much he does." One of the catch-phrases afterwards, when I was thinking about it, was "Well, I had what?...twenty years to go catch up to be as bad as he was." And that was kind of the path I was taking. And so [before the burn] the alcohol and the drugs and whatever else was a means of getting away. I didn't want to be in control. I wanted to be out of control. I was good at turning away emotional pain which hurt, was a matter to be avoided, to be ignored. *And then at the time of the burn, it set me down and I had nowhere to run, but to look inside* [my emphasis]. When I looked inside I had some pretty big skeletons, things I didn't want to admit about myself. Again, "Why me?" might be a result of not accepting responsibility. Why did I do these other things to other people? I had no answers, but it was time for me to look and evaluate myself, what I've done, and then try to make amends for that, just to be sorry for the things I did to people.

Q: So you were forced to look at yourself?

Exactly, and there was nowhere to run. I had to sit down, I was like, "Well, regardless of what he did, or anybody else did, what am I?" And that's pretty much the thing I had to get to. You're looking at the world. How can the world be happy when I'm in so much pain?

Q: Before you were burned, did you realize you were in pain?

That's part of the problem. It was covered over by activities and drinking and having fun. Yeah...and that manifested in trying to *show* [his emphasis] how happy I was: Look at what a good time I'm having, see? So that was pretty much a result of it. *My identity of who I was, I was no longer. So then it was a complete search* [my emphasis].

In other parts of the interview, Eric stated that before he was burned, he never looked forward to where he was going, at least, not seriously. He had always looked back, but even then, he never confronted the serious questions that could have been raised. After he left the hospital, he recognized that he was in a "bad situation," and he also knew that he didn't want to stay there. So he had to search for answers, he had to search for and take responsibility for his future. He finally had to confront the situation he was in:

You're thinking that people don't get over the "Why me?", they're not willing to look at what's going on right now. There's a lot that happens with the acceptance of, "This is who I am, this is the situation that I am in." Most of the problems, people can't identify that. They're in their illusionary world of, "This is how I want to be," and not looking at how it is.

To take responsibility for what his life was going to be, he was forced to recognize his concrete situation, a task that many people, not just burn survivors, find difficult to achieve. Finding out exactly where he was, and who he was (each of which is relative and open to further elaboration and interpretation), is an achievement made over a period of time, through intense introspection, meditation, and therapy, and through periods of doubt, depression, and despair. Of significance is the fact that the latter experiences, while temporarily painful and probably disabling, were seen by Eric as leading toward his transformation and metamorphosis.

Q: This can be very crushing, being forced to examine these issues.

If this is how it is, that I chose this, then I can choose something else. People have the ability to direct and control their lives. If they have felt that they've always been out of control and "it's the world's fault for me doing this, it's God's fault, it's my parents' fault for me doing this," they never accept the fact that, well, they had a part in their life. In fact, they had the main part of choosing some of these things.

Q: Do you feel you have more control now than you had before?

I would say that before, I wanted to be out of control. Because I couldn't control how my parents acted; I couldn't control what they did to me or what other people did to me, how teachers acted toward me, or so I thought. Therefore, I felt like I did not have the control in my life as much as now, because I wasn't willing to accept the pain that goes with it. Afterwards, I had no way but to accept it: "Hey man, this is a painful situation."

Paradoxically, through the loss of all normal control over his life, Eric gained a sense of control over himself. To gain all, he gave up all. This statement, and the underlying attitude it represents, is remarkably close to an idea expressed by D'Annunzio as quoted by Bachelard in the *Psychoanalysis of Fire*: "After having gained all through skill, through love or through violence you must give up all, you must annihilate yourself." Bachelard is somewhat less extreme: "To lose everything [is] to gain everything" (Bachelard 1964, 17). Similar to this is the Taoist notion that to be filled, as by wisdom, you must empty yourself of all. Nor is it significantly different from Husserl's concept of phenomenological reduction, though the purpose of reduction, as a practice, is to better articulate the basic structures of the prescientifically existing world. The idea expressed by D'Annunzio and Bachelard becomes not simply poetic expression, but also a metaphor which describes discoveries made by survivors such as Eric, Maria, and others in their everyday lives as they search for and find meanings for their burn experiences. Also found in Eric's account, and in his own terms, is a theme that is central to an existential ethics: the need for the person to be free, which he is fundamentally speaking about, entails choices and choices require the acceptance of personal responsibility for the choices that are made. Without responsibility, freedom cannot be realized. Furthermore, there is no possibility of being fully authentic. The person who evades responsibility, who lives in the moment, who lives in lies and deception, will never realize his or her full possibilities with another. Genuine and deep love becomes unavailable, and full disclosure of one person to another, which is required if love is to flourish, is impossible without trust. Trust is impossible in a relationship where neither self nor other is responsible.

The meaning of Eric's present was not founded only in the present, but was constituted in reference to his past and future. Eric took what others might consider to be failures and treated them as further challenges. He also treated as challenges statements by surgeons or therapists that it would be at least a year, maybe two, before he could walk. When he was told that he would never play soccer again, he did not become overwhelmed by depression and resignation. This too, became another hurdle to overcome; he was insistent to himself that he could play soccer as he had prior to being burned. Indeed, he felt that a pessimistic prognosis forced him to move forward.

> Then they said these things, and it was like they were slapping me in the face, like "I challenge you." And for me it was like, "Well, I'll show you."And that helped carry me through.

Responsibility was not initially seized by Eric. It took time before he realized that he was "giving his power and responsibility to the doctors." Eric originally felt that it was the doctor's responsibility to heal him while he could remain passive. He was blaming his caretakers for not healing him fast enough. Blame for them turned into a question: "Well, what am I doing about this?" A corollary question became not "What happened to me?" but instead, "Where do I want to go from here?" He came to realize that the surgeons, physical and occupational therapists, and nurses could only do so much and that even the healing of his physical body was contingent on what he did. He began to take responsibility for what was happening to his body. This recognition did not come easily. It was a discovery that involved acute and prolonged anguish and suffering, deep doubts about himself, and fears about his future. It must be said that he was devastated by his injuries. It was three years before he could return to college, but he was determined that his life would not end just because he had been horribly injured. It should not be thought that he was free from depression, for he wasn't, but depression was a necessary stage through which he passed. He did not sink into it and remain as if he had been entrapped in a tar pit; others have.

Many burn survivors have found answers to some of their questions, and mutual support, in self-help burn recovery groups. Others have found that the groups offer little useful support. Three or four survivors specifically found the groups to be little more than "bitch and cry" sessions for survivors whom they felt preferred to complain rather than getting on with their lives. Most of the others found the groups to be very worthwhile. Eric found the groups to be useful to him, not because he was significantly helped by the experiences of others, but because he could help others:

> I didn't want to go to bitch sessions and hear people complain; I had enough problems to deal with myself and then I figured, if I'm so bad, if I'm so awesome, I'll go help somebody else. And just being there, and seeing people with 20 percent, 10 percent, 4 percent burns. See, by this time I was out playing soccer and doing good, they felt embarrassed and go, "Well, I've got no right to feel this bad anymore." That paid for the point where I felt I gave the doctors my power.

In being badly burned, Eric felt that he was born again. This was mentioned by several survivors and it has been stated by other survivors I've met. It is even suggested in the title of Alan Jeffry Breslau's book, *The Time Of My Death,* a personal account about recovering from massive burns sustained in a plane crash. To symbolically die, through gross and terrifying change, and then to survive, is to experience rebirth. Rebirth is not just a metaphor for postburn experience. It is more than this; it is a way of conceptualizing experience and self, for themselves and for others. Several survivors pointedly explained themselves as having been reborn through fire. Somewhat like the mythological phoenix, several survivors conceptualized their experience as being singularly momentous and pivotal, as when Eric says,

> I felt that I was born again; I was reborn through the fire. I had the awareness, the personality of someone who's lived through twenty years, but the body was someone new. What happened before, those twenty years, really didn't apply to the body I had. So I had to retrain it; I had to learn how to stand, how to walk, how to feed myself. And so I saw the similarity of myself with my niece [a young child]. And she taught me a lot, from watching how babies get hurt: they let it out, then they move on. So her resilience was a lesson to me. And they keep trying, keep doing it; keep growing...[it] was a

tremendous effect on me. And so I took on the same, with the eyes of a child. I needed to keep all the childlike qualities of being happy, of being able to laugh...So that made me happy and helped heal me.

Eric's young niece, with whom he lived after he left the burn center, became a model for his growth. Indeed, he attributes his healing, in part, to her. She provided a schematic plan for him to follow, in his own way, a schema or model involving trial, error, and continued persistence in spite of failures and setbacks. Her tasks were very different from his, yet she served, reflexively, as a basis against which he could interpret and visualize his own necessary work. This is another way that others, including even a young child, are implicated in the construction of self, in a world where selves are inherently open to change. Here, Eric chose to open himself to his possibilities, possibilities that he would create.

Q: It sounds like you always had hope through this.

Like I said, my ignorance in the first part, I didn't know how serious it was. The feeling is also spiritual, which I can't overemphasize. It was an inner knowing. Nobody else had to see anything [his near death experience], but I knew it. It was the beginning words, "It's all right, this was meant to be. You will make it through this." Certain things came through which I didn't believe or hear [before he was burned]; I didn't have the ear for it before, to hear certain things. When I was in there, there's an expression. There are two tracks on the beach. That's when the person dies. He looks back, and God's showing him, "Look along the beach. There's two sets of footprints. In certain spots, you'll see only one set of footprints." And the person says to God, "See, I told you. You left me there. You left me, abandoned me." And God says to the person, "No. That's when you stopped believing, and I had to carry you." To nobody else, but to me, I understood that. That rang true, that felt true. And although I probably didn't show it outwardly, I was crying because of the emotional release and how much it touched me at the core. I knew that God was with me, and I knew He would be there. You are going to be tested beyond your strength. So why did this happen to me? Because I was strong enough to make it through.

Surviving his injuries provided the documentary evidence of strength and this, in turn, is interpreted as being a gift from God, a gift anticipated from the beginning when, in the first seconds of the accident, Eric was given an ultimate choice: to live or die. Survival was not extraneous, it was not random, and it wasn't circumstantial. It was chosen in an act of faith and belief when he was still in his burning VW.

Q: Were these discoveries made in therapy?

> The first one, the part on the beach, that happened before. But those were silent things that clicked in. It was the reverse effect. Where before I was physically strong and emotionally, I'd say, I was really at a weak point because I couldn't face any of the pain I had [in his pre-accident life]. Afterwards, going through the pain of that first year, physically I was low and emotionally I became strong. I became just as strong emotionally as I was, formerly, physically. It was with that knowledge that I was going to build the physical, because of my physical and emotional strength.

In speaking of his intimate experiences with women, Eric had specifically emphasized that these were caring, loving experiences. I therefore asked if his previous experiences had been caring and I found that he had redefined the meaning of love and personal relationships:

> They were, as much as it was possible for me at the time. Because I wasn't able to feel...men were there to be strong and to think but not feel—that's a woman's job. When I allowed myself to feel the pain [emotional pain] and the love, there was an awareness of how much people did love me, which was a strength. I would be okay, I was loved. A lot of people think that they're not loved before, and then if they're burned, they're screwed two ways. Because now, they are not being looked at in the physical body. Where mine was the difference. I wouldn't accept any love because I didn't want the pain. Now, I got both: I knew there was pain and I felt it, but the love was stronger. And I knew it was going to be okay.

Also, he has had opportunities to have more intimate experiences, but these were offers from women he did not select:

> I have a different approach to it, too. I'm not in a desperate search, hoping that someone will take this poor soul. But I know that's how some people would look at it, and think, like I did before, "I'm so ugly, if anybody would want me, I'd take it." It's different for me. I am a whole person. I am sufficient to be who I am. The intimacy will be someone who also, I feel, is a person who is solid, who is a whole person, who is making that choice from a position of strength, not of weakness. I see a lot of relationships where they want the other person to fill their void. I've felt that which is from God and knowing his presence,...I'm satisfied in knowing that I'm a unique creation with abilities and I'm not alone. And that's a big thing. A lot of people are surrounded by parties, but they're always lonely. Inside,

I'm satisfied. So my choice of another partner will be based on love, not desperation.

Q: Were you lonely before the fire?

I'd say, yeah. I had a lot of intimate relationships that, although they were from my desire for love,...but it was empty, an empty love.

Q: Your relationships are deeper now?

Yeah. Even the nonphysical ones, because I know who I am, and I have no desire to use anyone else. Like before, the alcohol. Where I drink now, my desire is to be in control. Before, it was to drink to be hammered until I threw up, and then drink some more until you can't see. Well now, that's not the case. I don't have to drink. And I don't have that desire to use alcohol as an excuse or as a pain killer.

Q: So for you the burn was not all negative?

Well...I'm sure I would not say, "I would like it to happen again." Looking back on it, that's how I look at it: I don't want it to happen again. But looking back on some of the things I encountered and that I chose to deal with,...yeah, I had tremendous lessons that I learned. And from that, I found myself. And now I'm developing myself. I found out there's a lot to myself, which was a lot more than physical. I have love, and I build that ability to love and be loved. I know who I am and I know I'm special. But before, I didn't even want to know me because I was hurting. And now that I accept that I'm not perfect, I have flaws and I've done things that are really ugly,...Once I recognized that, I said, "From this day forward, I won't do anything that I know is going to hurt other people or try not to." My personality is the same,... which is happy. I joke a lot. But there's another side of me that I didn't let people see a lot.

There are numerous and cogent themes in Eric's material, many of which are beyond what can be covered here. His material describes how he interprets himself as well as others. It shows how he constructs knowledge about himself in the present through his interpretation of the past, and it shows, essentially, how he reconstructs self and reality. I would like to examine only a few themes here, allowing the rest of the themes to speak for themselves through Eric's material.

When Eric recounts how he evaded responsibility in his former life, when he ran from situations where he would have to look at himself, I am reminded of Sartre's conception of "bad failth" and Heidegger's *das Man* (the One). The life of "the One," who is always everyone and always no one in particular, is characterized inauthentically by locating his or her meaning in the world of things, idle talk and calculation. The self of *das Man* is the social self, there is little else of any substance. *Das Man* parallels Goffman's portrayal of the self, as the self of external appearance and of reflections born of mirrors, smoke and fictions. It is the inauthentic self, reified as any other object in the world. Such, frequently, is the self of everyday, secondary relations. Heidegger's conception of the person who flees before realizing his or her deepest possibility, which for Heidegger is the possibility of being impossible, or death, sketches the One as living in the moment. His or her life is fallen and inauthentic; it is routine, shallow, and predictably absorbed in the everyday world, quite unreflectively. Where reflection exists, it is calculating and absorbed in things rather than deeper significance. It is a life filled with waking, eating, going to work, and seeking pleasure, not much more. There is little thought of any weight, and talk is mere prattle. Talk and activities are carried forth to cover the frightening specter of emptiness, an idea initially sketched by Sören Kierkegaard. A similar image of the contemporary, "postmodern" person is found in Marcuse's description of the *one dimensional man*, in Marcell's conception of *mass-man*, and in the writings of Karl Jaspers when he speaks about communication and intersubjective relations. These writers depict the alienated person as one who finds the totality of his or her being in external relationships of the most pedestrian type. The value and meaning of self is found in possessions and things rather than in self and other.

Eric's reflexive conception of himself suggests just such a shallow, unreflective self, which is totally absorbed in the world of objects and shallow relationships. He is afraid of facing himself. He fears his possibilities, possibilities that would be too distressing and painful to acknowledge. So what does he do? He lives for the present, burying his concerns in alcohol, drugs, and partying, in anything that can fill his emptiness, anything that can fill time so that he does not confront haunting silence. In particular, Jaspers and Berdyaev stress the importance of solitude and silence as the *dis*-covering grounds for the revelation of authentic being. This theme is very beautifully expressed by Clark Moustakas in his personal account, *Loneliness*. It is in loneliness that silence and solitude become available; and it is through the experience of loneliness, where one steps back from the world of everyday life, that one finds new meanings and new possibilities for self:

> Loneliness is a condition of existence which leads to deeper perception, greater awareness and sensitivity, and insights into one's own being. New images, symbols and ideas spring from the lonely path....Out of pain or loss, the bitter ecstacy of brief knowing and having, comes the glory of a single moment and the creation of a song for joy. The individual's loneliness is an experience in growing

which leads to differentiation of self. The person's identity comes into relief as he breathes his own spirit into everything he touches, as he relates significantly and openly with the universe. (Moustakas 1961, 50)

To be authentic is to experience ontological anxiety, for in the shattering of the outward trappings of the self, which is absorbed in everyday life, and which finds its meaning in things and in routine, the person is thrown back on his or her own devices in order to find meaning and significance. No longer can the person blame others for all his or her failures. Eric discovers that he is responsible for his life. Such a discovery can be terrifying and anomic. The meanings that normally legitimate society and which have been used to legitimate the person's life, may be seen as shallow, fictional constructions, as shams that bitterly taunt. In recognizing legitimating meanings as fictive, though artful social constructions, the person confronts chaos (Berger and Luckmann 1966, 102-103). No longer do such meanings represent wisdom from ancestors, deities, tradition, or friends; the person recognizes that he or she must ultimately rely upon himself or herself. There is in this recognition, ontological anxiety and this is anxiety which cannot be localized in anything, neither in objects nor in concrete, specific experience. It is the anxiety whose source is nothing in the everyday world; it is the ontological anxiety of being-in-the-world as such. It is that anxiety which is fundamental to human existence and which is therefore grounded in nothing but human existence. Nothing turns out be more than merely the absence of things and common objects that provide routine moorings and anchorage points for self, for it is much more profound than this: it is the confrontation with *nothingness* (das Nichtige in Heidegger's usage) or non-being itself as the primordial threat to existence. Yet that threat is basic and fundamental to the very nature and structure of human existence:

It is the world itself which gives anxiety to my existence. Real anxiety [ontological anxiety] makes me feel estranged, alienated from the everyday world to the point that my world "collapses." Though anxiety makes me terrified, it also liberates me from my daily cares by making them appear trivial. Anxiety makes the world "stand still," and in the stillness the voice of conscience may be heard.

The subjective feeling of discovering the ground of existence, the ground of which itself is nothing, is homelessness—it is the feeling of alienation and not being at home in the world. Ontological anxiety is so overpowering that it "cuts off awareness of the past and future, nearly obliterating foresight. In existential terms we might say that anxiety shatters existential temporality, which includes one's cognitive being unto his own truth" (Tiryakian 1962, 113).

Before he was burned, Eric didn't recognize anxiety. There was neither time or silence in which he could face himself. He was too busy defending himself against recognizing the seething darkness of his soul, his defenses being numerous activities including drinking and drugs. His everyday mode of being-in-the-world was thus insensitive to his deeper possibilities. It can be remembered that Eric described his past life as characterized primarily by his recognition of the past. He had little insight into the future except for the immediate future of activities, parties and otherwise escaping from the pain of his life. In ignoring his future and the roots of his present, he could not realize his authentic possibilities of being complete and whole. The paradox was that his life had to be nearly destroyed for him to realize his possibilities. The retrospective feeling of alienation, of being uprooted, is captured in Eric's account of himself above, as well as elsewhere in this study, and similar versions will be found in the accounts by Maria, Paul, and other burn survivors.

Nothing said above concerning the subject's recognition that he or she is the creator of meaning within his or her life should be taken as suggesting that others are not of consequence in this process, for they are. As stated previously, the meaning of one's life is available, in significant measure, through one's relations with others. While Heidegger has been criticized for casting Dasein (human being-in-the-world) in an isolated light, he did recognize that human-being was a being-with (Mitsein) and, more specifically, it is a being-with-others (Mitdasein) (Tiryakian 1962, 127). Heidegger's problem was that in acknowledging the importance of others, he then seems to go on and bypass this important theme. Other writers, such as Sartre, Buber, Berdyaev, and Jaspers, have done much to articulate the importance of the Other to self. The significance of one's life and world is contingent on the relationships formed with others: my being is inextricably linked to the being of other persons. Others, especially those who are significant, are of paramount importance to the survivor's life and to the unfolding meaning which the survivor finds for his or her life. It is apparent that others were of consequence to Eric as he sought new meanings for his life and as he sought to normalize himself. His relationships with his sister, friends, niece, and lovers were of immense significance in allowing him to see that he was worthwhile, that he could be loved, and that he was loved. In spite of setbacks, he could continue trying, on and on. It was not as an isolated, unconnected individual that these discoveries were made.

The suggestion that one is responsible for his or her life does not suggest full or complete autonomy over one's life. The person is always constrained by situations over which full control, and even understanding, is not possible. It is within situations that possibilities are realized, but some possibilities always remain obscure and hidden, unavailable from the position the person occupies within the situation. The person, according to Jaspers, is related to the world through his or her existence in finite spatial-temporal situations. The situation always exists within a horizon of possibilities, the full extent and dimensions of which can never be fully articulated or uncovered. The situation extends beyond the present; it may involve many others and remain beyond direct control. Eric could not exert control over his accident; he could not, while the accident was occurring, stop what was happening any more than Burk Lassering could stop his hands and feet from burning once he was in the burning tunnel. In many situations there is a point of no return regardless of what we do. We are constrained by events and processes over which we cannot exert control. Eric cannot stop others from staring at his scarred face; Maria and Paul cannot stop others from treating them as if, because of their scars, they are retarded. What can be controlled is how they respond to and interpret such challenges. Survivors can become absorbed in anger, seeking verbal retribution, or they can go on with their lives, assigning such others to the category of the uninformed, stupid, foolish, or whatever else suffices.

In the absorption with the world, Heidegger's inauthentic man evades recognition of his or her own final possibility: death. Within the domain of everyday life, death is hidden behind continuous activities, talk, and funerary practices, which serve to camouflage and conceal the vivid, cutting presence of death. Eric was forced to confront and deal with his own possible death. And, while he may not have initially realized how close he was to death, he later understood how marginal his life had become. Having no place to run, he had to begin confronting these issues. Having been confronted with the possibility of his own nonexistence, as the ultimate threat to self, he could then confront less-overwhelming challenges and threats.

When Eric describes his former life, the person he describes appears both deaf and blind. This discovery is made from the perspective of one who has confronted the possibility of his own annihilation. It is the discovery of one who has been in the special situation that Jaspers referred to as a limit or boundary situation. In the limit situation, the person finds that activities of the day and objects of the world provide no anchor and no solid reference from which bearings can be taken. Eric retrospectively finds that he evaded responsibility, and this suggests to him that his life is seriously wanting. In the present, where he discovers his previous life to have been shallow, there is no suggestion that, within the perspective of his former life, he had any knowledge of that very same shallowness which he now finds as requiring remedy. From his perspective, it is only in living through the crisis which was imposed by being catastrophically injured that he can finally see how impoverished his former life had been. The veil of self-deception is retrospectively lifted, the cataracts are excised from his eyes, and he can finally see.

The blindness of his past can be characterized as "selective inattention" (Sadler 1969, 279). In finally seeing what his former life was, through biographical reconstruction, he can judge his current life. In his former life, he depicts himself as being both deaf and blind. His former deafness and blindness was double: in living his former life and in fleeing from what he feared, he not only depicts himself as unseeing and unhearing that which he ran from, but he was also blind about his blindness. That problems existed was not even intimated until he had passed through crisis. In the present, he finds that he is not who he was.

In his present life he discovers a new ability to love and to care. Love and care were unavailable to him before because he feared the pain of loving. In his former life he says he couldn't feel; it is as if he was anesthetized by activities, alcohol and drugs. Anxiety is a threat to love and relationships. His previous life represented an attempt to evade anxiety. A paradox here is that in confronting anxiety, and here I refer not to ontological anxiety, but to the anxiety which stems from concrete threats to one's security (Sadler 1969, 272), and in recognizing his emptiness, he is able to transcend that which gave rise to his emptiness and his fears. He is thereby able to love. In being anxious, or in the attempt to avoid anxiety, the person is defensive. In being defensive, the person's life is truncated and closed off to complete relationships. Love requires openness and the person who feels threatened and vulnerable fears being open to mutual encounter (Sadler 1969, 236). By acknowledging that which was dreaded, and which obscured important opportunities, he was able to achieve what he sought: the possibility of realizing authentic relationships. No longer might he need take just anyone who was available, for now he could trust himself to find someone who wanted him from a position of strength rather than weakness. He is no longer "needy." He has choices and options not previously available. In need, one takes what one can get and often ends up resenting what was chosen.

For Eric, such a choice, which is constrained rather than free, is no longer warrantable. In discussing others who are lonely while surrounded by parties and people, he suggests his own former feelings of being alone, and isolated while surrounded by others. His past loving was depicted as being empty; he was empty. His intimate relationships represented an "empty love," but again, at the time, this emptiness was not recognized. In his past life he didn't even realize he was in pain; it was too well hidden. It was only in retrospect, through reviewing his life, that he came to understand just how much pain he was in, that he found authentic relations with others, through love, was unavailable. It was in retrospect, through his understanding of his present, that he found himself open to loving relationships. The former pain of his past life is discovered against the backdrop of his very acute pain, both physical and emotional, which resulted from being burned. In losing much, he discovered that he gained much.

Eric's statements, which provide a biographical account of himself, also depict the historical nature of the self. His self-description is sensible as an historical document. Knowledge of self is historicized. He makes sense of his present by reference to his past. The self is therefore seen, as stated previously, as temporally achieved, as being embedded in time. And again, as his life evolves, the meanings which he attributes to himself in his unfolding present or his reconstructed past, may change significantly from what he provides here. The process of biographical construction goes on, paralleling the evolutionary process of his unfolding life. Along the way, in going through other changes, he will reinterpret his life. In the future he may become an eminent therapist, working with others whose lives have been shattered by sudden catastrophe or illness. Perhaps one day he will find that his life's meaning was possible only through his traumatization. In doing so, his injuries, which motivated his personal search, will be seen as informing the lives of future others.

While these statements have been made about Eric, in the accounts provided by other survivors, such as Maria and Ralph, similar themes are also found. Eric was not the only survivor who reevaluated his entire life after he was burned. Other survivors also found their lives radically changed and, not infrequently, some of what changed was for the better.

Maria and Ralph Porter: Residential Fires

It was almost a year before Maria got out of the hospital. She had gone from the burn center, where she spent over seven months, to Riverview, a rehabilitation hospital where she spent approximately four months. When she got out of the hospital, she had two prosthetic "hooks" instead of hands. She had a child, but no husband or boyfriend. It was a very different world, immensely changed, because she had changed. It was at the rehabilitation center where she started coming out of deep depression, depression which had enveloped her even before she had seen her face and realized that she would always be badly scarred. When she saw her face she stopped eating and talking. At Riverview she started eating and she found that she could learn to care for herself in spite of what appeared to her as a monumental disability and impossible situation: the loss of both hands.

Maria had generally construed herself as being rather independent. Others had often told her that she was independent and that was one of the complaints made by her former boyfriend. Maria is from Guatemala while he was from Mexico. He resented the fact that she wanted to work and have some life outside the home, and he especially resented any suggestion that Maria should go to college, something that she wanted to do but that she really didn't seriously consider. Maria felt, in many ways, that their relationship was not working and might be over even before she was burned. Though he continued to visit her, and there were promises of marriage, Maria felt certain that marriage would never happen. For her, it seemed like he was just trying to reassure her. No concrete actions were taken toward marriage and he seemed uninterested in anything except talking.

Maria had often had to take care of herself and her brothers and sisters. More than once her mother packed up and returned to Guatemala for extended periods of time. Relatives helped out, but Maria often felt forced to stay home from school to take care of her siblings and she resented this, for she liked and did well academically when she was able to attend classes. She dropped out of school in the eleventh grade. It wasn't that Maria felt that her mother did not love her children, but rather, that her mother was tormented by the death of Maria's father some years before. The death of Maria's father, and her mother's inability to adjust to it, served to explain her mother's changed conduct when the remaining family moved to the United States.

Q: So being burned, that helped you decide that you wanted to continue with your education?

> **Maria:** I wanted an education and I wanted to be able to take care of myself and help other people,...feel helpful. And self-sufficient. I was able to feel helpful and self-sufficient even before I thought of going back to school. Not before I thought of it, but before I went back.

Somewhat obliquely, Maria compared herself to Tina, another young woman whom she had met at Riverview while Tina was hospitalized. Maria was working as a volunteer in the surgical/burns service. Tina had been badly burned in a vehicle accident and she had moderate facial scars. Tina had been described by her mother as a very wild kid; but after she was burned, Tina would hardly ever leave her home. If she went out it was mostly at night and, when she did go out during the day, she always wore a large brimmed hat and oversized sunglasses.

> **Maria:** She had this idea that she was going to someday look as good as she did. She said that she didn't want to do anything until all her surgeries were finished. She's like thirty now. They called Trisha and me [Trisha and Maria are often called by staff to assist other survivors], and she was very aggressive, very defensive. I became her friend, but she was aggressive with me too. She knew I was taking psychology. She kind of felt like, "Well, what do you have to compare me to?" She sat there and I said, "We're all in the same boat; I'm no different than you are. They said you needed to talk to someone. I don't know if you want to talk." She got more open.

In speaking about her work with other burn survivors like Tina, Maria stated that many of them don't see any options or opportunities. She also stated that a lot of the people she has talked to were not doing very well before they were burned and they were doing worse after their accidents. Very importantly, however, Maria and Ralph stated that some people seemed to do much better after they were burned and this included themselves.

Ralph: A lot of people who weren't doing very good before the fire do better after the fire.

Maria: I feel a lot better with my life now. My sister says our lives changed a lot, my whole family's lives, my life and her life. Especially hers, because she was with me and she went through it all the way. Our lives really changed.

Q: For the better?

Maria: For the better. We're not as empty as we were before. Is it worth it, the price we had to pay to learn all these things? If I had a choice of going back to the way I was before, and being as empty, of not knowing what to do and feeling a sense of not belonging anywhere, I wouldn't go back. If I had the choice of going back and just being the same way, I think I'd rather be this way.

Ralph: I would say the same thing.

Maria: I feel much more content with my life; I can make decisions that really benefit me and I can learn from my mistakes. Before, it felt like every mistake just feels so bad. Instead of learning, it would just make it worse.

Q: What have you found from this?

Maria: I think strength and wisdom. You can see things so differently. I never thought it was this way, or never realized it. Now I can truly care about someone and be glad about it. Before the fire we [she and her sister] valued physical beauty and things like a nice car, having material things. We valued that a lot. Now, we can still appreciate them, but that's not our primary thing anymore. We value other things. We can really talk to people and understand people and even my mother...before the fire, we still had so much anger towards her. Now, it came so easy to understand that she was a widowed woman with all these kids. It's easy to understand those things now.

Q: You said before that you used to feel empty and lost?

Maria: I felt empty, like there's nothing in there, like lost,...not belonging anywhere, like I had to be from one place to another, never feeling like I belonged there. Now I feel like I can really belong anywhere I feel happy, and I can find a place where I can be happy.

Q: At group meetings, Kevin and Mat have said if they could go back to physically being as they were, they would do so, but only if they could still know what they have learned. How about you?

Ralph: I wouldn't want to go back. I think this was one of the best things that happened in my life, that I got the most out of anything that ever happened in my life.

Q: Have you ever thought about where you might be if you weren't burned, Ralph?

Ralph: I'd be in the same place. I'd be hanging out with the same people and doing the same stuff. I seriously don't think I would have gone far from there. That'd be about it. I did a lot of drugs then, and party was my basic goal for the day. I didn't have any long-term goals.

Q: So one of the things the burn did was to give you...

Ralph: A more serious look at life, what could be, what I could do. That I can make something with it besides just hanging out. It still came slow.

Q: Did you ever go back to your previous life-style?

Ralph: No, not so much. I smoked a lot of weed since I was little, and I always did that, but not like I did before the fire. I always, since the fire had enough *in me* [my emphasis]. It felt so good to be alive, and to walk. All new things. Like I said before, it's just like being a baby again. I didn't even remember what hand I did things with; I knew I was right-handed, but to experience it all over again felt so good. It kept me so high naturally. I felt so good. I would get depressed at times and it would go for a day or a couple of hours, and then I would say, "stop," and start doing things. I started seeing a counselor and setting things up for school, and that's when I started dating Maria. I started going to church again; I almost went on a [Mormon] mission. Then Maria came and wrecked my life!

Q: Maria, were you very religious?

Maria: No, my family is not very religious. I was never very religious. When I was in the hospital, I got letters from all over the states [several newspapers carried stories about her], and some people who were very religious would send me letters and say, "I want you to know that God is this and God is that." It never meant anything to me, I would skip those letters. I had this priest who would visit patients on Sunday mornings. He would come and say, "Do you repent your sins?" and I would say, "No. I don't have any sins. I don't think I did something so bad that this had to happen to me. I don't think I have sinned." He would get so upset. He would say, "You're going to pray so many Hail Mary's." He knew I was Catholic. Priest are different. I met another priest, and he was so sweet. He never came in and started asking me about my sins. He baptized little Maria and he brought his whole thing to the hospital. We had the baptism right there. I believe in God. I think someone must have put us here, and that someone can't be so cruel to put us here and then do this to us. Whoever made us, made us vulnerable. How do we know if we don't experience?

Maria and Ralph were not, by far, the only survivors who found important personal lessons written in the aftermath of the flames that seared their bodies, but they were the only survivors to say that, if they had to do it over again, they would, if that was the only way they could change. This is a rather remarkable statement. Certainly, it is not one I expected to ever hear from survivors, especially not from someone as badly burned as Maria or Ralph. It is certainly not that they don't recognize negative experiences for as their interview shows previously, they have suffered greatly because of their injuries. There is no denial of reality here, there is acceptance and, accepting who they are, they run with their possibilities. In doing so, they have constructed lives that they describe as being distinctly different and more enriching than were their former lives. Some may see their reports as being self-deceptions born of rationalization; I do not see it this way at all. What I see is a genuine transformation in the reflexive meaning of self for both Maria and Ralph, a transformation in basic elements of their respective individual identities and their shared identities. While much was taken from them, they were both able to find significance and values to replace that which was destroyed. In their reconceptualization of themselves, they found their former lives to be lacking and empty. There was a clear transformation and it was of such magnitude and importance that they would not wish to return to their former lives.

Susan Bayer: Vehicle Fire

Though Susan is not one of the survivors I felt was having overwhelming problems in coping, she sees her burn experience primarily in a negative light. She developed breast cancer after she was burned and this was attributed to her burn injuries. She has been plagued by serious, debilitating medical problems and she has viewed these as stemming from the burn. At the same time, she did not retreat from normal family life. She has struggled to rebuild a normal life in spite of continuing medical problems and disabilities.

One of the problems Susan encountered was a generalized fear of such normal things like riding in elevators or being near dogs. These are fears that she had not experienced before she was burned. While in the hospital, she experienced repeating, terrifying nightmares in which she relived the fire. These consisted of images of entrapment and fire, much like the actual situation she faced when she was burned. She would wake up screaming and sweaty, terrorized by feelings of impending death. When I interviewed her, seven years after she was burned, she still felt anxious and afraid of some ordinary things in normal life but she felt that she was coping relatively well. That she recognized her fears as illogical and groundless made no difference, they persisted as disruptions of her life. Through therapy, she was slowly able to resolve at least the most bothersome terrors she faced, all part of her reaction to overwhelming trauma.

Even after she physically recovered from her burns, her life was still overshadowed by physical illness. After she recovered from her burns, her life seemed to be absorbed in illnesses, illnesses that were not, for some time, recognized or legitimated by her physicians.

> I didn't realize it would take so long for me to feel well again. It took years. Physically and emotionally. Especially physically. I really felt sick for a long time. Even after my child was born, I felt sick, and she was born about two years after that.

Q: And you feel this was related to the burn?

> Yes. It's been so long. It's been seven years and I've been sick almost the whole time. I would say that I have felt really sick for at least six of those seven years.

Q: How were you sick?

> It's hard to explain. At first depressed, I didn't have any energy. I would try to do things, but I couldn't. I kept going to my psychiatrist and saying, "What's wrong with me, why am I not getting better?" I thought it was emotional. Every MD I went to told me it was

emotional. Then I finally found out I had hypoglycemia, quite a ways down. And I know that directly related to the accident.

Q: And you had breast cancer. How did you find you had breast cancer?

Two years ago, I found the lump in November, two and a half years ago. And again, I had a doctor that didn't listen to me, and just watched my lump for eight months. But I was beginning to feel better. I was feeling real good. I wasn't particularly concerned about the lump because I was feeling good. That was four years after the accident and it was when I started feeling like I was normal.

Q: Did you have a mastectomy?

Yes. A mastectomy is an inconvenience. I think I went through the emotional trauma about disfigurement with the burns because I really did feel that I was disfigured after the burns. I don't like it, but I would have another one if I found I had a lump in my other breast. What bothers me is disease. Since the surgery, they have found nothing.

Q: Was there any connection for you between the burn and the cancer?

Instantly. Mainly because it was on the right side and that is where the burns are the worst. And because I had all those years of not feeling good, I just made an immediate connection. At the time I was diagnosed, I did not know there were other cancers in my family. So I was the only person that I knew of in thirty four people who had cancer, the only one that was burned. Because I felt so awful for so many years and because of the hypoglycemia being connected with the burns, I just really think that the trauma of the burns just messed up my system, so that it didn't respond properly. It wasn't just the lump, all my lymph nodes were involved.

Q: How has it been more recently?

I've gotten into sports, it's kind of a "I'm going to show them," whoever "them" is. Just that I'm going to do it. I'm just kind of proving something to myself. I ride a tandem bike with my husband and we ride thirty to forty miles.

Q: What has all this done to your family?

It's been hard, really hard on my husband and my daughter. I have her seeing a counselor now. She seems to have a fear of authority

figures and she has a real fear of injury. She can fall out of her chair
and not hurt herself, but just the fall will make her hysterical. She is
terrified of being injured. She worries about cancer,...she doesn't
understand the disease. She asked me one time if she was going to
grow up and have the same disease as mommy has.

After being burned and having both cancer and hypoglycemia, Susan
resented advice and unsolicited opinions from others about what was
wrong with her or what she should do, a theme frequently echoed by
other survivors.

I find it hard talking to some people because I find it very offensive
when people start advising me when they haven't been there. As a
matter of fact, I usually cut them off. These are acquaintances. Well,
one is a close friend of my husband's. His mother had bad arthritis.
But what he did was to compare the cancer to arthritis. And that was
at a point where we thought I was going to die. And somehow that
is a real offensive comparison because she might be crippled, but she
is living. I wasn't crippled, but I had a very good chance of dying.
And I found this comparison intolerable. My mother does this. She is
the type of person who claims she's never been sick a day in her life.
And when I was on chemotherapy, and I was getting really sick, she
would say, "Well, you are just going to have to decide that you are
just not going to be sick this time." And John would just walk out of
the room. I told her that I wished I could just decide that I wasn't
going to be sick because I certainly would.

And some people feel free to lecture you. I got so mad at Jobst
[manufacturer of pressure garments for burns], and this young sales
girl. I think she thought she was encouraging me, she dug out
pictures of some really severely burned people, and the results they
got from wearing Jobsts. Then she gave me a lecture on how lucky I
was that I wasn't that badly burned. And I knew those people were
worse off than I was, but I really resented her telling me that.
Because what I was going through was really awful and the hideous
deformities are just too frightening to think of. But I was feeling so
badly that I didn't think she had the right to belittle the injury that I
sustained. And yet she thought she was doing me a big favor.

Susan has compared herself to her grandmother, a woman who was
burned and who subsequently died of cancer. Others in her family also
saw Susan's development of cancer as being related to her burn accident.

Like some people I know, it can trigger things like diabetes. My
grandmother was burned and this is probably one reason I was so

frightened by the cancer. She was diabetic and she went into a coma and fell on her heater and was badly burned. She lived for a number of years after that but she never really healed up properly, and then she got cancer and died. So the similarity of what happened to her and the sequence of what happened to me were very hard to deal with too.

For Susan, the meaning of the burn has been continuing illness and disability. It is seven years after her burn and she is only now feeling that she has recovered from problems that she sees as stemming from her injury. There is still the possibility that the cancer could return, even though all recent tests have shown no continuing problem. Since she connects the cancer to the burn, the burn continues to be interpreted as open, in the sense that it continues to overshadow and threaten her life. The meaning of the present, whether she is well or not, will be determined by the future course of her life.

She finds, in her family evidence, that her illnesses have caused problems for both her daughter and her husband. Her husband blames himself for not realizing that the lump in her breast was cancerous. He, like Susan, relied on a physician who continued to dismiss the lump as unimportant. But her husband had specialist medical knowledge as a oral surgeon and pathologist; this has made it more difficult to place blame only on the apparent ignorance or indifference of Susan's physician.

Her daughter, who is five years old, has emotional problems that Susan also connects to her own illnesses. The child is terrorized by fears of illnesses and she asked if she too would get cancer. For most of the child's life, she has known only a sick mother who, because of her illness, could often not provide the nurturing support that Susan felt her daughter required.

Susan felt that she was defined by physicians as deviant and as unreliable, her symptoms being dismissed by physicians when it was realized by them that Susan was under the care of a psychiatrist for her burns. Even producing what she thought were "good symptoms," she was not treated as having serious or "real" problems. Her recognition of good symptoms suggests her interpretation, seen here as social knowledge-at-hand, of what medical practitioners look for in assessing patients. It suggests how she typifies medical assessment as a practical enterprise in which she must give, or verbally produce, an account of herself that would place her, for the physician, in the category of a legitimate patient with real problems. The symptoms which she verbalizes must be treatable by the physician as clues that point to a real underlying problem. Instead, the reported symptoms were seen, not as clues or markers for real physical problems, but were instead seen as markers denoting psychiatric problems. Rather than being accorded normal patient status, her "good symptoms" were apparently overshadowed by her identity as a person who needed psychiatric help. The evidence for discounting her as a real, treatable patient was provided by the mere fact that she was in therapy. Being in therapy was grounds for dismissing her, in toto, as a legitimate patient. For the physician, she was essentially deviant in terms of her presentation to him as someone claiming a legitimate patient status. This is another example of how one imputed identity marker can serve more globally as the basis for others to impute a discrepant *master status* to the person.

It is apparent also that Susan, at least partially, defines herself in terms of illnesses and possible illnesses. Her world is imbued, since her burn, with a foreboding threat which stems not only from her own subsequent medical history, but also from her interpretation and knowledge of her family's medical history. Within her family's history she has found information which she utilized in forming her own definitions of self, what might be metaphorically called her "medical self." Regardless of what label is applied, she sees herself as vulnerable. She describes herself as "paranoid" and, like many others who are labeled as paranoids, there is in her life the evidence of real events that allow her to constitute her world as threatening and dangerous. There was nothing in her interview to suggest that she was unusually concerned about health and illness prior to her accident. Her concerns about health evolved after she was burned and she began exhibiting various symptoms of illness. As time went on she found that she did have very real and significant medical problems. As this happened, she increasingly defined herself in medical-illness terms. Her current behavior, where she has become rather athletic, an interest she did not previously have, is informed by her interest in health and her fear of becoming seriously ill again. This interest is also constituted in reference to her construction of her family's medical history.

Ann Saunders: Scalding Oil Injury

Many survivors found religious beliefs to be important in helping them accept their injuries, their scarring, and disfigurement. Ann also found religion to be of importance as she rebuilt her life. After she was burned and returned home, she began having acute anxiety attacks. Through therapy she traced the attacks back to her recognition that she would ultimately never look the same as she once had. She felt that she had lost control over her life and herself. For Ann, the world no longer seemed quite as safe as it had before she was injured. There were voids in her life and religion helped fill the emptiness she experienced.

> When I was burned, I was not going to church on a regular basis. Yet I still felt a need to have that spiritual void filled. When I was burned, I had an immediate feeling that the Lord was with me. Nothing ecstatic or bizarre, nothing like that, but a sense of God consciousness.

Again, when I was in the hospital those first few days, I was very comfortable, felt at peace, wasn't afraid I was going to die and I thought, maybe the Lord had his hand in this, in letting me know that I was under his care and I was going to be all right. And, being burned, and the experiences immediately after, I think helped to intensify whatever search I had been undertaking to find some spiritual comfort.

Actually, it put into focus a lot of questions. I never questioned it, "Why me?" I just said, "Okay, here we go, big adventure." That's a kind of off handed attitude, but part of what faith is, is to accept things that you can't hang onto tangibly. Okay, I will accept this without having it picked apart or explained to me. Aside from having the spiritual void filled, in doing so, I had a lot of things that came out when I was burned, solved. I don't have the problems I used to have with my dad, how I used to react in emergency situations, get upset, freaked out like my mom. You lay around in the hospital, maybe on the brink of death, you start thinking of things like that. It has a lot to do with how I feel about myself now. And people would ask me, "Weren't you depressed, or want to commit suicide?" And my attitude was, at the time, there must be some reason for this. I can work it out. It can be something good, or bad. And it might just as well be something good.

Ann describes herself as not being especially religious when she was burned, yet she also recognizes that there was a spiritual void in her life. In being burned, her spiritual search was intensified as she sought comfort and understanding for what had happened to her. While she did not consider herself to be especially religious, she felt the presence of God and knew, or felt, that she would be all right. The fact that she was burned did not result in any immediate, intense conversion. She does not depict herself as the repenting sinner who is confronting death. For her, religion was personal and it was not until several years after her injury that she began attending church.

There was, for Susan, no great mystery about why she was burned. It happened. Unlike Sharon and Paul West, there was no questioning of God, though many of the answers to other questions and issues in Ann's life were answered through her religious beliefs. Religion was not a causative theme in Ann's burn experience yet her religious beliefs obviously provided a context within which she could understand what happened to her; what happened must have had a reason, good or bad, and she had chosen to look at the good. Her injury has caused her to reexamine her life, and to be concerned with issues which would not have arisen had she not been burned. There has obviously been emotional pain and frustration, but she has been able to move on and rebuild a normal life.

Kevin Davis: Chemical Burn

After he left the hospital, Kevin became involved in drugs. He began using marijuana as well as cocaine. Previously, he had used marijuana only infrequently, but he had not used other drugs. He also developed a problem with alcohol after he came home from the hospital. He attributed part of the cause for his changed conduct to his feeling that he no longer occupied the position of status that he had held in his family as provider. He could not immediately return to work. Indeed, he was on disability assistance for five years and he is just now preparing to return to work. Until he was burned, he had for years been the wage earner in his family. He supported his elderly mother and two brothers, who couldn't or didn't work. Coming from a black ghetto, he had achieved a good job as a meat cutter. In fact, when he was first working, right after he finished high school, he actually found it rather "deviant" to have a normal job. Having a job, and earning money, made him different from many of his friends. He was earning more money in a week than some of his friends earned in a month. He subsequently married and bought a house, something which set him apart from many of the young men with whom he had attended school. He was later divorced, but he continued to help support his two children and his mother and brothers. When his support was lost, it affected several lives. Disability payments were not the same as his earnings had been, and things were at times difficult, not so much because of lost money, but because of his personal losses.

Kevin was one of the survivors who said that those close to him, such as his girlfriend, were also "burned" by his injury. Problems in his family, and the eventual loss of his girlfriend, were also seen by Kevin as contributing to his problems.

> You see, I feel every member of my family is burned, because they never get back the person they lost, too. Like Kelly's ego was in my face too. You know, the handsome guy that she met, that she can be next to, that can stand next to her and make her look good. Now, here's this ugly guy, predominantly ugly guy, plus I had an attitude, that by using drugs, I was ugly too. All that plays on her, because she had the heartaches, all the pain, all the loneliness, and she seen it all even though she didn't feel the pain that I was feeling. She felt the pain she was feeling, that she could think of in her head. Understand what I mean? Like you see a little kid with a broken arm, you can feel the pain that kid had.

Q: Did you and Kelly ever talk about this?

> Way back a long time ago she said she just ain't ready, 'cause I wanted her to go to therapy with me—"the doctor can help both of

us. Maybe you need to deal with some of these crazy things that's going through your head." And she said, "No." But I knew something was wrong there. I know that she was burned too.

It took Kevin quite some time to stop using drugs and alcohol, especially alcohol. What stopped him was the recognition that he had no more savings. Also, he realized that his brothers, who had little money, were using him to get what they wanted. I've known Kevin for several years and I realized that for quite a while he wasn't attending the burns group, but I didn't realize he had a drug problem. He is a very kind person, and he has always seemed warm and open, but he finally decided that being this way caused part of his problem in that his brothers took advantage of what he could provide for them. He finally entered a substance abuse treatment program and then joined AA. With this, he was able to stop using both drugs and alcohol.

Q: Do you think you've gotten past a lot of your pain, have you been able to let some of it go?

I was always giving. So I often didn't think of me, even when I was hurt. That's why this accident is sort of a blessing. Because it pulled everything in for me, to look at me and reevaluate things, looking how inside out things can come out the other way. Understand what I'm saying. Which I never would have had the opportunity to focus in on me. Because I was always out. Everything was always going out. I didn't really care about me. That's why I started doing drugs, I didn't care about me. Like I say, it's a whole new other world. Plus, I haven't lived that yet. All I know is today, and it's working. Now how I got all this knowledge is through talking to people. God gave me...surround me with good people that I can learn from. And it has been a learning process these five years. Or my whole life has been a pretty good learning experience. 'Cause of things that went down. Everything just worked out. Like I say, I count it as a blessing.

Q: Did you ever get really mad that this happened?

Well, yeah. I still stop every so often and figure, "God, why did I have to get this face, that goes through these changes?" But I never get an answer. Things just happen.

As Kevin prepares to return to work, his outlook is very positive. Like others noted above, Kevin is able to find positive meanings, even blessings, in the fact that he was burned. Again, like the others, he does not discount the fact that there were very significant and painful losses, not the least of which was the loss of one eye. Certainly, Kevin became very depressed about the loss of his eye and the fact that he would be disfigured. He would never look the same as he did before he was burned by chemicals, but he was not, ultimately, overwhelmed by his injuries. He was able to transcend his losses and move toward the future. He finds in the injury, much as did Eric, that he had to stop and evaluate his life and where he was going. Being burned forced him to consider issues which were never salient previously. One of the things he found in himself was emptiness. He tried filling what was lost with drugs and drinking but he eventually realized that this conduct just led to additional losses. He found himself within a new world that others helped him understand. His girlfriend left him, but, they continue to see each other and remain friends. He will return to work as a meat cutter but he realizes that should he not go back to that work, which he enjoys, he is capable of doing something else.

Implications

This study has examined catastrophic burn injury from the standpoint of the personal, subjective world of the survivor who must reconstruct his or her everyday life. More broadly, while specifically concerned with burn injury, this study relates also to how people reconstruct self, meaning, and their lives after they have undergone dramatic change. Essentially, this study is about the rebirth of self. The metaphor of rebirth is especially appropriate. Not only did several survivors describe their recovery as representing their rebirth, but they also described being burned as suggesting their deaths. The process of birth is painful, but from the pain comes new life and, for many survivors, new lives rose from the destruction wrought by their injuries. Certainly, this was not stated by all the survivors. The lives of some, especially those with less severe injuries, have gone on much like their preinjury lives. All survivors did recognize change, for some the changes were moderate while for others the changes were truly consequential.

Drawing on research with burn survivors, I have attempted to suggest some of the ways in which shattered lives are refashioned and reconstructed. Reconstruction has been shown to be inherently intersubjective. This is to say that the "rebirth" of self, meaning, and identity is contingent not only on the actions, definitions, beliefs, and feelings that the survivor constitutes or brings forth, rather, such "rebirthing work" very frequently can be seen as implicating the actions, projects, definitions, and feelings of other people with whom the survivor interacts over time. Friends, family members, therapists, other survivors, and even those who are met on the street or in public places are all involved, to greater or lesser degrees, in weaving the emerging identity and self of the survivor, regardless of

whether the survivor seems to make a "positive" or "negative" adjustment to his or her injuries.

The ongoing task of refashioning self, meaning, and life has been
shown then to be inherently contingent. More than this, it is a process
that is evolutional, open, and potentially never complete just as the self can
be understood as ultimately never finished. The fact that the person
confronts new situations and new others as his or her life unfolds, displays
the inherent openness of self, as well as the time-contingent nature of self.
Temporality, and the survivor's reference to time as he or she reconstructs
identity, personal world, and self is an invariant property of the emerging
process of reconstruction.

Following Heidegger, Jaspers and other existential philosophers, the
human is viewed as the special being who must decide who and what he
or she is to be. This choice is embedded in the very structure of human
existence and freedom: it is informed by the person's basic concern for his
or her existence. Thus, he or she must decide what it means to exist; he or
she must decide how life is to be lived. This is not just the task for
philosophers. In everyday life, thought may hardly be given to such
issues, yet we make choices day in and day out that determine the
character of our lives. Wisely or unwisely, for good, evil, or indifference,
we cannot do otherwise. The need to decide, to choose, and to take
responsibility for ourselves is a constraint imposed on us by existential
freedom. The choices made may be poor, we may cause harm to others, or
to ourselves. We may make choices which are shallow; we may affairm
ourselves in a succession of instants of pleasure, as explified by Eric in his
preburn life. Doing so, we may lose ourselves for eternity (Tiryakian 1962,
86-87).

Choices may, of course, be constrained; crucial decisions are frequently constrained. Often our options are very limited, or we may find
ourselves ensnarled in vexing dilemmas from which disentanglement seems
impossible. We are constrained and compelled by the actions and inac-
tions of others, and there are limits to what each life may accomplish. Yet,
given all the problems one may face, even for those who encounter the
gravest of challenges, the human has a seemingly unique ability of self-
extrication and recovery. Others are critical to that process.

The survivors I interviewed who experienced ongoing problems in
coping with life were all people who had little, if any, social support. Two
of them, Ellen and Jeff, were described here, two others were not. All of
them were burned as children; all grew up with lives that were tormented,
at least in part, by being scarred. Of the four, three significantly appeared
to come from homes where little affection for the survivor, as a child, was
demonstrated. Indeed, in the cases of Ellen and Jeff, there were clear
indications that both had been abused. Ellen reported sexual abuse, Jeff
reported physical abuse, and both painted a picture of their respective
childhoods as seriously lacking in warmth and affection. Sorting out the

influence of the burn on their subsequent development is difficult. It is nevertheless clear that both of them see the burn and its results as their major problem.

Of the two others, both of whom were males with minor to moderate facial disfigurement, one reported a very distant and indifferent relationship with his parents, while the other reported a loving and supportive family. The former survivor, like Ellen, stated that his family could *never* talk about his injury. He could never discuss his feelings and, if he tried to tell about being teased, he was ridiculed for paying any attention to others. At twenty years old he was so concerned about his family knowing that I was interviewing him that we had to secretly meet away from his home. That he was in therapy for six months was also hidden from his parents. He described a home much like Ellen's. The father was portrayed as cold, stern, and dominating, while the mother was depicted as emotionally ineffectual. Interestingly, but coincidentally, both fathers had military careers. That all of the survivors who reported significant problems were burned as children is, I feel, also coincidental.

Finally, the fact that all of the survivors discussed in this study still maintained hope is crucial, I believe, in understanding who they are. Even for those who have the most difficulties, like Ellen and Jeff, there is still the hope and anticipation that their lives will get better. There is the anticipation that somehow they will be able to move on, and in so doing find acceptance. Acceptance is twofold; it represents self-acceptance, and acceptance by others. Each is intrinsically linked. But even without yet finding such acceptance, there is not a deep sense of paralyzing hopelessness for any of the survivors. Jeff comes the closest to being overwhelmed by hopelessness and, while he has periodically appeared suicidal, these episodes seem to be momentary rather than continuous. It is in unrelenting hopelessness, where the person's life is self-construed as embittered and destitute, where the person's biographical history is experienced by self as a history of continuous failures and disappointments, that we expect to see suicide not as periodic ideation, but as a culminated act. Hope, even when exceptionally tenuous, seems to insulate one from a final act of self-imposed destruction. And while this seems to be a most ordinary observation, I would suggest that we need to better understand the dichotomous nature of hope and hopelessness as major themes in the lives of trauma survivors.

There are several implications that arise from the survivor's accounts about their postinjury lives. It must be noted that all of the following comments are based on interviews with a very limited and selective number of survivors. However, it is also true that I've encountered similar concerns from a larger group of survivors, such as those met at conferences and in recovery groups. The six issues, that follow, while not universal by any means, are representative of relatively common concerns for burn survivors:

1. The medical staff must develop strategies for more inclusively working with the families of burn patients.

Too frequently, family members feel that they are ignored and that staff members have too little time to explain what is really going on. Communication problems may result, not only from staff reluctance, based on time or other constraints to more fully discuss details of the case, but also because the survivor or family members fear asking direct questions. Further, family members often haven't a clue about what to ask. Family members report frequently feeling that the staff doesn't have the time or the patience to answer questions, but upon questioning, it also appears that family members, when asked if they have questions, may be mute due to their own fears about raising difficult and painful issues which they do not want to face. Clinical social workers with training in trauma and burn care are especially valuable, but physicians also must understand the importance of openly communicating with the family. Families and friends need to know that their support is crucial to the recovery of the survivor. Love, understanding, and continuing assurance, which is genuine is very important to the survivor. This should not be underestimated as an import- ant aspect of the survivor's total care.

2. School, community, and work related reentry programs should be considered a necessary adjunct to existing care.

Many survivors appear to leave the hospital quite unprepared for experiences in the outside world. Some had preparation, but many did not, and survivors often felt ill prepared for taking their initial steps outside hospital walls. Even with significant preparation, the tasks associated with returning to life will be arduous, painful and difficult. If nothing else, a medical staff member, preferably a clinical social worker or therapist, should discuss the more prominent postdischarge issues that both the survivor and his or her family will face. Recovery groups can be very valuable as well. Survivors often feel alone long after they are back at home and with others again. They frequently feel lost. They feel no one understands what they have gone through, and they may feel that their experiences are truly unique. In recovery groups, survivors discover that they are not alone, others have been there before them, and that others do understand what the journey through hell was about. For survivor children, recovery groups and summer camps provide similar support. This type of assistance, for adults and children, is very important for many survivors.

3. Survivor concerns about sexuality should be directly addressed by the medical, nursing, and therapy staff.

Sexuality is a crucial subject and a concern for most survivors. To ignore the survivor's concerns about intimacy and sex is to do the survivor a true injustice. If staff members are unprepared to frankly deal with such topics or are themselves uninformed about how being burned might affect survivors, then staff needs to undertake further training and sensitization. Medical staff should not wait for the survivor to ask questions, for many will not do so. Staff needs to open the subject. If the survivor is uncomfortable or uninterested, he or she will let will know they can ask when ready to do so.

4. No facially injured survivor should be allowed to leave the hospital before fully seeing himself or herself.

This should be a planned action with appropriate support. It seems terribly cruel to leave the survivor to his or her own devices in this matter, especially where facial disfigurement exists. That several survivors reported this problem seemed amazing. Only a few survivors reported any real psychological support from clinicians. In the area where the research was conducted, only one hospital out of four offered routine psychiatric evaluations of all burn patients. Assistance wasn't mandated, but it was available. Some patients will not want help, some will resist, but many, I believe, will be significantly aided by at least brief crisis intervention. Others may require more assistance, and it should be readily available.

5. Further research, focusing on those whose lives are shattered, and where recovery seems remote or impossible, must be conducted.

There are reasonably large numbers of survivors who don't do very well after they physically recover, yet we know little about their lives. They are a hard group to reach. Many may not want to cooperate, but they need to be understood if we seek to reduce their numbers. Recovery groups are one way to get them involved, as are follow-up clinic visits, but it is recognized that this may be more difficult than it sounds.

6. Research needs to be conducted on human behavior in fire and burn situations if we are to better prevent injuries and death.

Accidents don't just happen. Fires and burn injury situations are not random events over which victims typically have no control. There are certainly situations where the victim doesn't have control, such as a plane crash or vehicle accident with postcrash fire. Many injuries and deaths occur in this manner, but most others are preventable. Even in the situation of a plane or vehicle accident, while the victim may not be able to prevent the accident, the use of different materials and construction technologies could dramatically reduce postcrash fires. This has been demonstrated with both planes and cars. The technology to reduce fires, in many situations, exists now, it is just not utilized. A considerable body of research presently exists on fire and burn injury, and some of that research has informed prevention efforts by fire departments and other concerned organizations. More attention needs to be devoted to fire and burn reduction, and, as with crime, we need to understand that the costs of failing to act, are too high for both those who are victimized, and for society. Communities must become involved. Fire is a social problem like crime, poverty, disease, and homelessness.   Often, they are all interwoven.

Appendix

Survivor Profiles

1.
Name	Ann Saunders
Age	29
Age When Burned	24
Type of Burn	Scalding Oil
Extent of Burn	30% Mixed 2nd and 3rd degree
Areas Burned	Face, Neck, Cest, Arms, Hands
Visible Scarring	Face, Neck, Arms, Hands
Facial Scars	Minor Disfigurement
Work Status	Human Factors Specialist
Education	University Degree
Marital Status	Single
Ethnicity	Caucasian

Ann was burned when she and friends entered a Mexican restaurant through the rear door, a door frequently used by patrons to enter from the rear parking lot. In passing a stove, Ann slipped and fell, apparently on grease or oil on the floor. Putting her hand out to catch herself, she hit a pan of hot oil which spilled over her. She was transported to a nearby hospital's emergency room, and then transferred to a burn center.

2.
Name	Burk Lassering
Age	30
Age When Burned	29
Type of Burn	Flame
Extent of Burn	15%, mostly 3rd degree
Areas Burned	Both Hands, Both Feet
Facial Scars	None
Work Status	On Disability
Education	Some College
Marital Status	Single
Ethnicity	Caucasian

Burk was burned as a stuntman when he tried running through a long, burning tunnel constructed of light wood framing, chicken wire and hay. The temperature in the tunnel was thought to be approximately 1,800-2,000 degrees F. His carefully selected clothing was not suppose to burn, but both his gloves and his boots did burn, badly burning both his hands and feet. He sees this as a setback to his career and he recognizes that it could end his career, but he doesn't feel it will in any way ruin him.

3. Name   Darleen Greenberg
    Age   35
    Age When Burned   19
    Type of Burn   Flame/Vehicle Accident
    Extent of Burn   35%, mixed 2nd and 3rd degree
    Areas Burned   Face, Arms, Hands, Back, Chest
    Visible Scarring   Face, Arms(limited), Hands
    Facial Scars   Moderate/Partial
    Work Status   Self-Employed Writer
    Education   College Graduate
    Marital Status   Single
    Ethnicity   Caucasian

Darleen was burned in a vehicle accident while on vacation from college. She
and friends were traveling from central California to the coast when their ve-
hiclewas rear-ended. The gas tank ruptured and the fuel immediately ignited.
She was in the back. She was knocked unconscious and only escaped
because other motorists, including Forest Service rangers, who saw the
accident right after it occurred, were able to pull her out.

4. Name   Ellen Rensberg
    Age   35
    Age When Burned   3
    Type of Burn   Flame/Flammable Liquid
    Extent of Burn   25%, mixed 2nd and 3rd degree
    Areas Burned   Face (one side, partial), Arms
                                      Chest, Hands
    Facial Scars   Minimal but noticeable
    Work Status   Unemployed
    Education   Some college
    Marital Status   Single
    Ethnicity   Caucasian

Ellen recalls going out to play and, as she went around the corner of the apartment building, being hit with aburning liquid. The fiery liquid may have been
thrown at her or merely away from the two boys who were apparently playing with fire.Regardless, she was burned.Her scarring,on her face, is visible
but not especially pronounced. She said that her scars are now much less
obvious now than they were ten years ago or when she was a child. She w a s
never able to talk about the burn to her family and she feels that she a
significant emotional problems caused by the burn. As a twelve-year-old girl,
she was forced into having sex with a brother. This was forgotten for many
years until, one day i group therapy at a psychiatric facility, she recalled being
raped by her brother. She has divorced herself from a family which she
experiences as being unloving, and she is attempting to rebuild herself and
her life.

5.   Name   Eric Mathews
     Age   27
     Age When Burned   20
     Type of Burn   Flame/Gasoline, Vehicle Accident
     Extent of Burn   95%, mostly 3rd degree
     Areas Burned   Virtually his entire body
     Facial Scars   Very Extensive Disfigurement
     Work Status   College Student
     Education   Near completion of BS
     Marital Status   Single
     Ethnicity   Caucasian

While in his second year of college, Erik was catastropically burned when his VW bus hit a highway divider, went out of control, and rolled over. The gas tank ruptured, engulfing the rear of the van in fire. The front doors of the van were jammed closed and the only escape route was through the fire that was spreading to the front of the bus. Before he got out of the bus, Eric had what he defines as a near-death experience. He openly discussed this exper i e n c e yet it seemed that he felt potentially discredited by admitting the experience. His description was virtually classical relative to the research by Moody, Sabom, and others. He sees the burn as having significantly altered the course of his life; in many ways this has been for the better.

6.   Name   Jeff Asmore
     Age   22
     Age When Burned   12
     Type of Burn   Flame/Gasoline, Residential Fire
     Extent of Burn   85%, mostly 3rd degree
     Areas Burned   Face, Head, Neck, Chest, Back,
                                       Arms, Hands, Legs
     Facial Scars   Very Extensive Disfigurement
     Work Status   Unemployed
     Education   Some HS
     Marital Status   Single
     Ethnicity   Caucasian

Among the survivors interviewed in this study, Jeff stands out as having the most difficulty with "normal living." He has contemplated suicide several times and he reports asking doctors to put him to sleepbecause of his feeling that he can no longer tolerate the pain caused by his injury. He believes that his stepfather, who is now deceased, intentionally causedthe fire in which one brother and his mother died. He claims to despise or hate all of his surviving siblings; and he feels that his two sisters, who cared for him after his release from the hospital, were only interested in him because of the state payments to care for him. Though obviously intelligent, he seems to lack any significant insight into how he continues to ruin his own life. He has had several jobs but he either quits, claiming that others tease and ridicule him until he is forced to quit, or he is fired. He has had several problems with the pollice, mostly involving behaviors that were thought by the police or others to represent self-endangerment.

7.
Name	Jim Gonzales
Age	29
Age When Burned	28
Type of Burn	Gasoline Fire/Vehicle Accident
Extent of Burn	54%, mostly 3rd degree
Areas Burned	Face, Neck, Arms, Hands, Chest
	Legs (amputation of left leg)
Facial Scars	Minimal
Work Status	On Disability. plans to return
	to work
Education	HS Graduate
Marital Status	Married
Spouse	Kathy
Ethnicity	Hispanic

Jim was burned when the motorcycle upon which he and his best friend were riding was hit by a van that turned directly in front of them. The gasoline tank on the cycle ruptured and both men where burned. Jim was the least burned but, because of burns to his left leg as well as the fact that it had a compound fracture, his leg required amputation. His best friend died shortly after the accident and Jim still vividly recalls the horror of seeing his friend lying in the street engulfed in burning gasoline. He is haunted by that vision. He mourns his friend's death and is still filled with guilt that he could do nothing to save him.

8.
Name	Kevin Davis
Age	36
Age When Burned	32
Type of Burn	Caustic Chemical
Extent of Burn	15%, mixed 2nd and 3rd degree
Areas Burned	Face and Neck
Facial Scars	Moderate around mouth, eyes,
	and forehead (one eye was destroyed)
Work Status	On Disability, Preparing to
	return to work
Education	HS Graduate
Marital Status	Divorced
Ethnicity	African American

Kevin had worked as a butcher for several years at a large grocery store in a poorer section of a large city. He supported his mother and two brothers, having the only steady income in his family. He enjoyed his work and he was proud of the life he had been able to build for his family, which also included two sons from a previous marriage. He was burned when a chemical reaction resulted from pouring lye into a clogged drain at the market. The chemicals splashed into his face, blinding him. He eventually lost one eye and his remaining eye never regained full vision. He is now preparing to go back to work and though he has lost a great deal, including "the old Kevin," he also feels he has significantly benefited from his burn experience.

9.	Name	Maria Porter
	Age	27
	Age When Burned	19
	Type of Burn	Flame/Residential Fire
	Extent of Burn	90%, mostly 3rd degree
	Areas Burned	Face, Head, Neck, Chest, Back, Arms, Hands, Legs and Feet (amputation of both hands and forearms)
	Facial Scars	Very Extensive Disfigurement
	Work Status	College Student
	Education	HS Equivalency
	Marital Status	Married
	Spouse	Ralph
	Ethnicity	Hispanic

Maria was seven months pregnant when she was very critically burned in an apartment fire. She and her Sister were sleeping in a second-story bedroom when they were awakened by smoke and the noise created by the fire. They were unable to go down the stairs and their only other escape route was through a window. The convinced each other that they had to jump. The sister went first, Maria was to follow but when it was time to jump she couldn't, she was afraid that the fall would kill her child. The room was becoming very smoky and she recalls feeling the intense heat from the rapidly spreading fire. She recalls nothing else. Terribly burned, she was rescued by fire fighters. Her child, named Maria, survived.

10.	Name	Mike Lawson
	Age	20
	Age When Burned	16
	Type of Burn	Flame/Gasoline, Motorcycle Accident
	Extent of Burn	80%, mostly 3rd degree
	Areas Burned	Face and Head, Neck, Chest, Back, Arms, Legs, Feet
	Facial Scars	Extensive
	Work Status	On Disability
	Education	Some College
	Marital Status	Single
	Ethnicity	Caucasian

Mike was burned when his motorcycle hit a truck which turned left in front of his path. He and his motorcycle skidded under the truck where he was pinned in a pool of burning gasoline, the plastic gas tank on the cycle having ruptured during the collision. He recalls people yelling at him to get out of the fire; because of the intensity of the fire they were unable to directly help him. He knew he would die if he didn't escape and he was able to crawl out from underthe truck. He stumbled and fell, his left leg was badly fractured with bone protruding and a large wound. Now, several years after the accident, he still faces the possible amputation of the leg due to recurring infections.

11. | Name | Paul Guiterez |
     | --- | --- |
     | Age | 29 |
     | Age When Burned | 26 |
     | Type of Burn | Flame/Structure Fire |
     | Extent of Burn | 45%, mixed 2nd and 3rd degree |
     | Areas Burned | Face, Chest, Back, Hands |
     | Facial Scars | Minimal |
     | Work Status | Fire Fighter/Paramedic |
     | Education | HS Graduate |
     | Marital Status | Married |
     | Ethnicity | Hispanic |

Paul was burned in a fire department training accident. He was sent into a training building where a fire had been set in pallets of wood; this was one of his first live experiences with fire as a trainee. The pallets were piled with hay that had been impregnated with jet fuel which was then ignited. He w a s burned when he became separated from other fire personnel. He became disoriented and lost his charged hose line so he couldn't find his way out of the training building. He became unconscious and was rescued by other fire fighters. His burns were from steam and heat, not flames.

12. | Name: | Peter Shrader |
     | --- | --- |
     | Age: | 32 |
     | Age When Burned | 30 |
     | Type of Burn | Flame/Vehicle Accident |
     | Extent of Burn | 40% mixed, 2nd and 3rd degree |
     | Areas Burned | Face, Arms, Chest, Neck, Back |
     | Visible Scarring | Neck, Arms, Hands |
     | Facial Scars | No Disfigurement |
     | Work Status | Not working at interview time; plans to return to work |
     | Education | HS Graduate |
     | Marital Status | Married |
     | Spouse | Lynn |
     | Ethnicity | Caucasian |

Pete was burned in a Nissan pickup truck when an engine fire occurred while he was driving. He was unaware of the fire until it spread into the vehicle through what he described as a cardboard fire wall. He drove off the freeway, over a curb, and into a dirt and grass covered field as the cab filled with smoke and fire. He knew he would live once he got out of the truck. Another motorists helped him get away from the fire, and fire fighters stationed just across the freeway, saw the accident and reached him almost imediately. Even so, he suffered severe burns.

13. | Name | Ralph Porter |
|---|---|
| Age | 25 |
| Age When Burned | 16 |
| Type of Burn | Flame/Gasoline/Residential Fire |
| Extent of Burn | 80%, mostly 3rd degree |
| Areas Burned | Face, Head, Heck, Chest, Back, Arms, Hands, Legs |
| Facial Scars | Moderate on one side |
| Work Status | LVN/Nurses Assistant |
| Education | HS Graduate |
| Marital Status | Married |
| Spouse | Maria |
| Ethnicity | Caucasian |

Ralph was sleeping in his living room on the couch when an assailant threw a fire bomb through the window early in the morning. The bomb was meant for his brother who had been involved with a married woman who lived in the area. It was believed that the jilted girlfriend was the arsonist. Though arrested, the woman was not convicted of the crime. Ralph met Maria when he was undergoing reconstructive surgery at a regional rehabilitation hospital.

14. | Name | Sara Jensen |
|---|---|
| Age | 68 |
| Age When Burned | 66 |
| Type of Burn | Heat from a Brush Fire |
| Extent of Burn | 60% mixed 2nd and 3rd degree |
| Areas Burned | Legs, Chest, Back, Arms, Hands Neck, Face |
| Visible Scarring | Arms, Hands, Neck |
| Facial Scars | None |
| Work Status | Homemaker |
| Education | Some College |
| Marital Status | Married |
| Spouse | Walt |
| Ethnicity | Caucasian |

Sara was burned in a brush fire that occurred in densely populated area of southern California. The fire was set, according to witnesses, by a male and female who stopped along a winding highway and ignited heavy brush. The fire killed three people. Sara was the most critically injured of several people who were burned in the fire, which destroyed over twenty expensive homes. Her burns were from intense, convected heat that came up the hill and over her house as the fire was cresting just below her home. She had gone into the

backyard to try to protect her house with a garden hose. She managed to
escape the flames, run out of her yard, and get to a corner where arriving fire
fighters found her at the curb trying to put gutter water on her burned feet and
legs. Walt, Sara's husband, sustained very minor burns and was not hospitalized. Critically injured, Sara spent several months in a burn center.
Considering her age and injuries, she has recovered very well.

15. Name   Sharon West
    Age   27
    Age When Burned   24
    Type of Burn   Flame/Alcoholic Beverage
    Extent of Burn   25%, mixed 2nd and 3rd degree
    Areas Burned   Face, Chest, Arms, Hands
    Facial Scars   Minimal
    Work Status   Homemaker
    Education   College Degree
    Marital Status   MarriedSpousePaul
    Ethnicity   Caucasian

While having drinks and dinner with friends at a favorite local restaurant,
Sharon was seriously burned when an unintended flash fire resulted from a
a waiter serving a flaming drink, an unusual though not unknown cause of
burns (the injuries usually happen to the server). Sharon's blouse ignited.
She attempted to run, but was tackled by patrons who quickly extinguished
her burning clothing. In a few seconds her chest was deeply burned and
what was to have been a pleasant evening out, away from family concerns, turned into an experience of terror which lasted for many months.
While she and her husband have good medical insurance, the fact that they
must pay 20% of a $500,000 medical bill has threatened their middle-class
life. The restaurant's insurance carrier offered them a $200,000 settlement,
ifthey would settle all claims, the day after Sharon was injured. Since her
husband refused the offer of the insurance company, the attitude of the carrier
has been to ignore any requests for even temporary assistance until the case
goes to court.

16. Name   Susan Bayer
    Age   34
    Age When Burned   27
    Type of Burn   Flame/Gasoline, Vehicle Fire
    Extent of Burn   43%, mixed 2nd and 3rd degree
    Areas Burned   Face, Chest, Back, Arms, Hands
                                  Legs
    Facial Scars   None
    Work Status   Homemaker
    Education   College Degree
    Marital Status   Married
    Ethnicity   Caucasian

The burn incident involved a fuel leak and fire in a Porsche 911, a car well known for fuel fires. Susan was a passenger in the car. The fire resulted when the car was started in a very narrow garage. She had to run through the flames to get out of the garage; in attempting to flee, she slid in the burning gasoline and fell into the fire. She was immediately pulled out of the fire by her brother-in-law. She subsequently developed other serious medical problems, including breast cancer, which she attributed to being burned.

17.	Name	Trisha Carson
	Age	37
	Age When Burned	33
	Type of Burn	Flame/Gasoline, Vehicle Accident
	Extent of Burn	40%, mostly 3rd degree
	Areas Burned	Face, Head, Chest, Back, Arms and Hands. Loss of several fingers.
	Facial Scars	Extensive
	Work Status	Teacher/Social Worker
	Education	College Graduate
	Marital Status	Single
	Ethnicity	Caucasian

Trisha was burned in a Nissan 240 Z, which was rear-endedwhile stopped a ttraffic signal. Her boyfriend was able to get out of the car with only minor burns but she was trapped in the front, thrown partially under the dashboard. Police arrived almost instantly, as the accident was across the street from a police station; however, because of the fire, she was not immediately seen. Fortunately, a passerby thought he saw someone still in the car. She was rescued before the car became fully engulfed in fire.

Postscript On Some Survivors

Eric completed college, earning B.A. and M.A. degrees in psychology. He is currently working on his doctorate. He married a woman he had known in high school, after he met her at a conference. He plans to become a psychotherapist after he finishes his education.

Kevin and his girlfriend, who had separated, got back together and were married. They now have a young son and Kevin seems very happy.

Trisha has continued working with burn survivors and the survivors of other types of physical trauma, especially trauma that causes disfigurement. She subsequently married and is doing very well.

Maria and Ralph had two more children, and both are doing well. Maria continues to help other burn survivors

Approximately two years after our interview, Susan died from cancer.

Notes

Introduction

1. The idea of the burn as punishment or retribution was suggested in interviews with two survivors and one sibling of a third survivor. One survivor suggested that, perhaps, he was being punished for all the wrongs in his life while another survivor more tacitly found a parallel between his injuries and those of a fellow student, a girl, whom he had previously shunned because of her scars. The sister of a third survivor attributed her brother's burns to her immediately previous conduct of cultivating, selling, and using marijuana: his burn was her payback.

2. The Hindu rite of suttee (meaning the good, pure, virtuous wife)—the immolation of the wife of a man who has died—is no longer practiced; but a horrifying parallel practice has developed among segments of the married poor in India. One of the ways in which an unwanted wife is removed from the family is by killing the wife by burning. Kerosene is widely used in open fires for cooking, accidents are common, and this fact is used to the devious advantage of murderous families, the members of which may conspire to plot the "accident." Some of the victims have survived and a number of cases such as these have been reported in the international burn literature. While most of the women are murdered, some are systematically pushed and hounded into suicide by burning by husbands and the marital family. If the woman doesn't comply, her children's lives may be threatened until she finally immolates herself. In a segment on Sixty Minutes (CBS, 24 January 1993), it was stated that during 1991, there were five thousand such deaths reported in India. This figure is probably very low compared to actual deaths caused by intentional burning, for it was also noted that the police, judges, and physicians often conspire to cover up such crimes, especially where the marital families can pay to cover up the crimes. Payments may be made to keep corrupt officials quiet, and it is not only poor women who are at risk. While it is most common among the poor, similar murders have also been reported within middle class and wealthy families. All women are at risk in India.

This practice raises a question concerning the extent to which, in various cultures and in subpopulations in the United States, fire is used as a weapon for injury or death. I am not aware of studies examining this question, except in the case of child abuse, though there are limited anecdotal reports that some ethnic groups use fire as a weapon more commonly than do others. At the Burn Foundation, and at burn centers, we periodically see children who were intentionally burned by their parents or caretakers, often by the use of scalding liquids, or hot objects, less frequently by setting the child on fire. The majority of these children are poor, and are from ethnic minorities; however, abuse by burning also occurs in white families, and not all families are in the lower socioeconomic classes (Deitch and Staats 1982). Parents may tell investigators that they really didn't *intend* to seriously injure the child (sometimes infants), but that they were only "punishing" the child, or trying to teach the child a lesson. There are many excuses but in all cases, such conduct remains well beyond comprehension.

3. This statement sounds as if meanings are responsible agents, in some way causing some state of affairs for the survivor. Agency is not attributed to meanings in any sense. The survivor, often assisted by others, constitutes the meanings he or she discovers. What is discovered is created and interpreted, often as meanings or explanatory attributions that are widely available within the culture as recipe knowledge the specificity of which is occasioned by a particular interpretive situation. In locating and constituting such meanings, the subject apprehends the meanings as being objective, "out there," and separate from his or her artful work of interpreting, producing, and applying meanings. In the act of apprehending, meanings are objectified and externalized. They can also be internalized in situations of self-attribution, or where the person constructs meanings for self. The relationship between subject and meaning is circular and dialectical.

4. Suffice it to say that I have doubts about the veracity of Castanada's works, which over time became more suspect. His first three books remain, however, provocative. Even if Castanada fabricated his books without any actual field research, they have pedagogic importance in that they illuminate phenomenological insights into the social construction of meaning and reality.

5. Douglas (1971) has criticized the positivistic methods of sociology specifically and, more generally, his comments also apply to much of psychological theorizing. Positivism is exemplified by quantification, which essentially seeks to elucidate mechanism and cause. This is true whether "social forces," "personality traits," or "personality" dispositions, drives, or needs are discussed. In each case, the underlying philosophical foundation for positing a mechanistic version of the person, and reifying "society" or "social forces" into causative agents, stems from the use and acceptance of a Cartesian paradigm which is typically taken for granted by the researcher or theorist.

Descartes (I think, therefore I am), who was also instrumental in introducing a dualistic subject/object split (mind/body) into philosophical thought, believed that scientific procedures can "provide us with absolute truth about the world. This truth was absolute in that it did not vary with persons, situations, time or place: its absoluteness was expressed by the invariant system of Cartesian coordinates" (Douglas 1971). The attempt was to eliminate subjectivity from truth. Further, this resulted in eliminating virtually all theorizing about the situated, meaning-endowing nature of human praxis in the everyday world of lived experience. Indeed, there was a complete indifference to the issues of meaning and experience as humanly constructed. While this philosophical belief provided the natural and physical sciences with a useful foundation, it greatly obfuscated the attempt to understand people as they create and live their lives.

In the attempt to be scientific, that is, to legitimate themselves, practitioners in the social sciences, with but a few exceptions, have artfully adopted the methodologies of the natural sciences. Methods and language used to study and articulate the natural/physical world of inanimate objects were used to study people. Quantification, questionnaires, instruments, and contrived laboratory studies became the hallmark of the social sciences. It was believed that if people could be treated as things, objective data could be reached and truth would be achieved. No matter that most of the studies were modeled after animal studies, treating people much like laboratory animals; no matter that studies were highly contrived and artificial (like measuring cognitive dissonance, attitudes, levels of induced anxiety, measuring social forces and vectors, etc.), it sounded scientific so it must be scientific. After all, the use of such methods, and language that sounded scientific has resulted in big research bucks for many investigators.

In sociology, such methods were an inherent part of sampling populations, building questionnaires and the attempt to demonstrate "social facts" as something worth looking at on one hand, and as separate from what such decontextualized "facts" actually meant to respondents, on the other hand. In psychology, the practice of science, or scientism, was expressed by a deep and fundamental belief that a presuppositionless, objective methodology could be created. This led to the search for stable personality traits, dispositions, drives and needs which, when uncovered by the well funded researcher, could tell us all we needed to know about humans. It would not matter what people said (as long as they correctly answered the questions which would confirm the research protocol), thought or felt. All subjectivity was ignored, as were feelings, thoughts, and ideas that didn't nicely fit the protocols. Indeed, the psychologist or social psychologist whose research interest included feelings, was virtually viewed as heretical.

A major conceptual shift has developed over the past twenty to thirty years as exemplified recently by constructionism in psychology, and by ethnomethodology and the existential sociologies in sociology. Within the emergent paradigm, objectivity itself is considered invariantly problematic. There is a sensitivity to human subjectivity and consciousness, to the long-ignored topic of feelings, and to the artful practices through which everyday life, and human lives, are created, maintained, and altered.

6. According to Krahé, the first attack on trait theory in personality research is attributed to Hartshorne and May in 1928 in their study of personality consistency in children (Krahé 1992, 16). The debate was on, but muted. On one side were those who believed in traits, dispositions, and trans-situational consistency. On the other side were those who proposed a situational model, and who felt personality could best be understood as arising out of situational contingencies. Still, traits and dispositions remained the stable of personality theory until much more recently when, according to Krahé, Theodore Mischell's 1968 attack on trait models provoked a crisis in personality research (Krahé 1992, 11). The crisis continues. Indeed, Krahé herself has attempted to produce some synthesis between the conflictual positions, but she seems to fail to understand the broad criticism of personality models outside the narrow domain of traditional psychology. Much of the situationist work she refers to remains enmeshed in the problems of postivism as noted above. For example, while she is concerned with interaction and situations, she seems also dedicated to experimental studies as the best way to uncover objective truth. Her use of "interaction" and "situation" remains narrow, ignoring research in allied fields. In fact, it appears that while her use of language has been updated, the result is dressing up old personality concepts in language borrowed from sociology and psychological construnctionism, without having insight into the theoretical foundation from which such terms have been borrowed.

Burkitt has retained the term personality but, writing from an interactionist and constructionist perspective, he has used personality much differently than it is used in psychology (Burkitt 1991). Burkitt sees personality in Meadian terms when he states that,

> For Mead, the self only develops as part of objective social activity and can therefore be studied as a social object... that is, an object to others w h ic h is invested with meaning and, thus, takes on a new dimension in the course of its existence. In human terms, this new dimension is the personality. Society and personality do not represent separate systems which 'interpenetrate' each other, as Parsons thought, but instead, for Mead, they evolve from the very beginning in tandem with each other. (Burkitt 1991, 45)

Burkitt provides an excellent introduction to Mead and an insightful analysis of the philosophical issues beset positivism.

7. Fire injury and burn injury are related though not necessarily synonymous events. All fire injuries are not burn injuries and not all burns involve fire as the agent of injury. For example, a fire injury can involve smoke inhalation without external or internal thermal injury and burns can result from several agents, such as scalds, electrocution, radiation, contact with hot objects (e.g., an exhaust manifold), molten substance contact or immersion, and contact with chemicals. Most of the available data on burns caused by agents other than fire come from local or regional burn centers.

8. The reader who is interested in this area is directed to materials available from the National Fire Protection Association (NFPA), especially to regular reports furnished in *Fire Journal.* Also suggested are the journals *Fire Engineering, Firehouse, Fire Technology,* and *Fire.* There are scant but growing data available about human behavior in fires. The NFPA, the Department of Commerce, Fire Research Laboratory, and the United States Fire Administration, as well as similar agencies in the United States and abroad, conduct post-fire investigations of major life loss incidents but it has only been more recently, perhaps over the past twenty years, that detailed attention to human conduct in fires has been of significant interest. The private research organization TriData Corporation, in Arlington, Virginia, has also conducted extensive inquiries regarding fire prevention and education. All of these efforts remain rather esoteric. The American public generally remains unaware of the very tragic personal and social costs of fire and burn injury and fire loss.

Chapter 1

1. Intentionality is derived from the work of Edmund Husserl; it is a widely used concept in existential and phenomenological sociology and psychology. See, for example, Rollo May's *Intentionality: The Heart Of Human Will.* Intentionality refers to the pretheoretical grasping of an object by consciousness or to the subject's ability to turn towards and illuminate or constitute an object through

consciousness. Subject and object are thus inextricably linked rather than being split and separate.

2. Abraham Maslow uses the term peak experience as a descriptor to designate unique, highly affective/cognitive experiences, which, in effect, throw the self into relief against the everyday world of routine life. Such situations are not necessarily critical or crisis-related. As in crisis situations, the self may be radically redefined with new meanings discovered for reflexively defining who and what one "really is." Such an experience may be seen by the subject as a crucial turning point in his or her life, an incident or moment of great importance, change or insight.

Chapter 2

1. There are several reasons for the surgeon to be conservative in assessing the patient. This is especially so during the first hours and days of a serious or critical burn. A conservative or cautious approach represents pragmatic concerns by the surgeon and medical staff relative to the patient's care. Immediate or early definitive assessment of the patient can be very difficult or problematic since the appearance of the burn provides inadequate clues to its depth. What appears as a second-degree burn shortly after injury may, in several hours or a few days, actually be a third-degree burn. The initial appearance of the injury will change over time. Indeed, the depth of the injury may take several days, or weeks, to determine (Solem 1982, 12). Burns can also "convert" to deeper burns due, for example, to wound infection. If the patient has been initially stabilized and assessed at a local emergency room, prior to arrival at the burn center, burn center staff may be very reluctant in accepting definitions/classifications made at the ER. ER staff may have little experience with large burns and, not infrequently, their assessments often are judged as faulty by burn center staff. Early assessment made at the ER or by paramedics, at best, serves as a loose or provisional guide for burn center staff as they begin definitive care. Further, and importantly, in the first hours of care problems with major organ systems may not be in evidence. After a few days, compromise of these systems may critically threaten the patient's life. That such problems would arise can be anticipated, but still remain indeterminate early on. Therefore, for the surgeon, there is also a "wait and see" attitude.

The exact nature of the injury, in establishing what the surgeon would consider an accurate assessment, is therefore constituted within an open temporal horizon within which physiological changes in the patient's condition can be anticipated, measured, and accounted for. "Wait and see" is in no way a unique feature of burn assessment, nor indeed of medical assessment. Discovering what something means in the here-and-now frequently relies upon a prospective reference to a presumed but not yet visible course of events. As a methodological practice, it is seen in the arcane work of police detectives, fire cause and arson investigators (Stouffer 1970, 1971), and scientists; it is also seen in the most mundane problem solving within everyday life, for it is a routine but little noticed methodology employed in everyday reasoning.

For the physician, looking at what are taken as properties of the person, the person's injury or an illness (symptoms, specifics of injury), the constituted properties serve as clues to what is now happening. But in recognizing such properties as clues to what is actually going on, the clues are understood as having a meaning which is potentially changeable through time, even if the present meaning of a specific clue is seen *now* as having an absolute meaning. What this shows is how, as an accomplishment of practical reasoning, phenomena such as bodily symptoms are constituted by a witness, in this case a physician, in order to make a broader judgement. All of this is taken-for-granted, and the process of reasoning and typifying utilized is not unique to this situation, but rather, the process is very general.

Another reason for making a conservative diagnosis involves the practical handling of distraught families. It is easier to prepare families for bad news early on than to have to explain later why and how a hopeful situation turned bad. In conducting extensive research in emergency rooms, I noted that physicians will be very cautious in explaining the patient's condition to family members. The physician wants to avoid providing grounds for false hope, especially in situations that appear bleak. Family members may frequently take anything that sounds less that totally hopeless, and use that information (sometimes supplied by what the physician doesn't say), as grounds to create hope, to create the temporary belief that all may turn out all right.

2. It can be argued that there is an experiential difference between that which is taken to be one's personal world as contrasted to the world one knows indirectly, through the media, reports by others, and so on. In common everyday life, people find themselves in both worlds. The two intersect, in terms of my constructions, definitions, involvements, and concerns. The contrast and difference is experienced in terms of distance and proximity, relative to space, time, affect, and personal concern or project-at-hand. The world as such is that which I read about or see on the news, it is a world of others which I can know only indirectly. It is Beirut, hostages held somewhere, the dissolution of the Soviet State, chaos and death in Bosnia and someone from Fresno who just won thirty million dollars in the California lottery. When these distant events come closer to me, they become part of my personal world. If I work in the defense industry, the dissolution of the Soviet State and its threat may mean job loss for me so that even a globally distant event comes to bear directly upon my life. If I have just returned from a trip to Europe and I now learn that two heavily armed Hesbolah terrorists were arrested at Frankfurt/Main Airport, just after I departed from there, a very distant event clearly could have had a substantial effect on my life. As I become aware of the particulars in Frankfurt, I see my personal world as expanding, perhaps terrifyingly so, to include unknown others with whom I have no normal connection but whose projects and intentions inextricably penetrate my personal world. What is at one moment close and personal may in the next moment take on very different proportions. What is now distant may suddenly come to occupy my attention, and so on.

3. That the world is familiar and treated as routine in no sense suggests that one is satisfied or comfortable with one's world or life. It means only that, in general, one takes his or her world for granted.

4. There is no suggestion as to how "stubborn," as an imputed behavioral attribute, is constituted by either Lynn or Pete. Nothing said by Lynn tells us specifically what conduct is stubborn but what is clear is that in referencing such an attribute, an explanation is derived suggesting how Pete survived. Being stubborn also, in part, constitutes for Lynn an identity definition for Pete. The identity may be highly situational and transitory or it may be more generalized and trans-situational. What is seen is Lynn's production of an interpretation and how she constructs "knowledge" as a practical theorist within a real world of pragmatic concern.

5. A especially interesting examination of "waking up" is provided by Dr. Oliver Sacks in *Awakenings*. Concerned with his experimental use of L-DOPA with Parkinson's patients, his work examines the deep human tragedy and hope that he found with patients who lived a most marginal existence.

Chapter 3

1. This theme has been elucidated differently by Mead and it is also found in the works of Alfred Schutz, Martin Heidegger, Maurice Natanson, and Rollo May. For example, Heidegger is concerned not with self but with the foundation of human existence-in-the-world, Dasein. Dasein means *Being-There*, clearly stating the concrete and situated character of human existence. Heidegger and all those cited place particular emphasis on the open, plastic, temporal, as well as situated nature of human existence.

2. Rejecting an essentialist conception of the self and person, Harré notes that the person is, significantly, a sociocultural artefact:

> A person is not a natural object, but a cultural artefact. A person is a being who has learned a theory, in terms of which his or her experience is ordered. I believe that persons are characterized neither by their having a characteristic [i.e. determined] kind of experience nor by some specific genetic endowment. They can be identified neither phenomenologically nor biologically, but only by the character of their beliefs. (Harré 1983, 20)

Harré goes on to note that whatever we believe about the structure and nature of personal being has its foundation "in a socially sustained and collectively imposed cluster of theories" (Harré 1983, 21). Part of the theories, or beliefs, we each hold are theories and beliefs about ourselves. But these are not merely extraneous theories and beliefs that can be discarded at will. To a large measure, they constitute our deepest sense of selfhood.

It is crucial to note that what Harré suggests, with which I concur, in no sense implies the sociocultural determinism of the person except in a weak or loose sense. The thrust of this study is to suggest that what the person is or becomes, is significantly determined by the person, influenced by the actions of significant others. There are always choices, often constrained to be sure, but we decide, daily, what we are to be, and what we are to become. While we are shaped by historical, social and cultural realities, we play a very direct role in determining the nature of our lives, and this fact can be seen in the stories of survivors who appear in this study.

3. For example, possessions such as home, car and one's worldly toys, mementos of one's life and the lives of those who have been treasured can all be part of the self. Survivors of disasters, who have lost their homes, often find the greatest grief, baring the deaths of loved ones or pets, in the loss of small treasures like mementos and photographs, perhaps art work they have created or other objects of special significance. These objects constitute, in part, not only the person's interests but very frequently, they constitute significant sectors of the person's history. An object is a memento because it evokes the past, through it, memories are constituted, and stories are told and passed on to children, and friends. Such objects provide moorings for the self, seen and often unnoticed but nevertheless important (Radley 1990).

4. There are several interesting sociological as well as psychological studies that examine the nature of threat to personal and social identity. The works of Erving Goffman are frequently concerned with these issues though Goffman was mostly concerned with social identity and his interest never penetrated to deeper levels of self. In a different manner, Milton Rokeach, in *The Three Christs of Ypislanti,* was directly concerned with identity and how threats to identity are obviated. His book remains a classic study in belief, identity, and delusion.

5. It should be obvious throughout this study that I treat with caution all quantitative research. Virtually all the research on the social or psychological results of burns are quantitative. Such research gives us no idea about the concrete lives and experiences of survivors, and we are left with no understanding of what being seriously burned and disfigured means to the survivor. The importance of the quantitative data is that it can sensitize us to the problems and issues confronting survivors.

6. This is not a criticism of Goffman, it is merely an observation. Goffman took his task to be the unmasking of everyday social dramas, and that he did astutely. He never denied that there were deeper levels of the self, reaching below surface interaction and staged displays. Interest in the deeper meanings of self simply was not in his domain of inquiry.

7. Kim was very badly burned in a murder-suicide act committed by his father who had become despondent over his life since coming to the United States from Asia. Mr. Lin ignited a container of gasoline in his car as he and his children drove down a freeway. Witnesses reported seeing the car full of children suddenly

explode in flames as it continued to travel down the freeway before crashing along the side. Police and others were able to pull Kim, his sister Tia, and one other child from the rear of the car. The father and other child died in the car while the third child died a few days later. A gifted child, Tia remains one of the most disfigured children I've encountered during the past eighteen years of work with the Burn Foundation. I had wanted to interview Kim, but because of serious speech difficulties resulting from his burns, I was unable to do so.

Chapter 5

1. Memoric reconstruction of the self is not only cognitive, involving the use of language, but is frequently emotional as well. It is important to understand that language cannot be narrowly defined as only verbal. The deaf, for example, can develop complex signed languages, which can be exceptionally descriptive and explicit. Memoric reconstruction also involves what Susan Langer has referred to as "presentational" levels. Presentational meanings are those that are prelinguistically created in terms of images to which words are not attached, such as "body language" cues, which people may only indirectly attend to as tacit background features of an interactive scene.

2. The sexual revolution of the late 1960s through the present has challenged many traditional ideas and values concerning the roles of men and women, and the importance of marriage and the traditionally structured family. This is most evident in the United States. Long-held beliefs that, in order to be happy and to have a good life, one must be married are no longer widely accepted without question. The fact that many people are remaining single, or that many postpone marriage, has necessitated a reevaluation of many traditional concepts. Current economic concerns have only exasperated the situation. A cottage industry has been created to cater to the "new singles," involving everything from advise-giving pop psychological soothsayers to the producers of single-serving frozen meals. Regardless of this, marriage (albeit, often multiple serial marriages) remains a dominant though battered institution.

3. Two psychotherapists independently said that Jeff periodically looked more like a female than a male because of the way he dressed. He sometimes would appear wearing partially green, purple, or yellow dyed hair and the clothing he chose made it difficult, from a distance, to determine his sex. When I first saw him, his hair was colored but thereafter, his hair was not dyed.

4. This was painted or penciled on, looking quite strange. Jeff is severely disfigured and there is probably little he can do, without additional reconstructive surgeries, to normalize his physical appearance. While his attempt, in wearing penciled eyebrows and moustache, may have been to normalize his appearance, he seems to have achieved the opposite results. He has accentuated his odd appearance, knowingly or not. His message seems to be, "OK, if I am going to look like a freak and be treated like one, I will really look bizarre."

Jeff distantly reminds me of a legendary patient at the Lakeview Rehabilitation Center about whose exploits I was told. This patient had attempted suicide by self-immolation and had, in drenching himself with gasoline, almost succeeded. He was extensively burned and grossly disfigured. Reportedly, while recovering, this man got tremendous delight out of the fact that he could scare visitors. He would hide off the main corridor and, as people passed, jump out at them. He told therapists that he was glad he survived because he could now scare people just by looking at them. Defined as psychotic, he was eventually placed in a state hospital. Jeff's conduct is far less unusual but there is in his conduct and dress a sense of dramatic staging. I had wanted to learn more about his life but he abruptly terminated our interview when we started getting into sexuality.

Chapter 6

1. In my research, the only survivors who defined themselves as having significant long-term problems, happened to be burned as children. This finding is circumstantial and reflects, I believe, the small number of people I interviewed. Nothing specific about childhood burns should be inferred from this finding. The Burn Foundation sponsors a special summer camp for child burn survivors. While some of these children have deep psychosocial problems, often only partially resulting from their injuries, many of the kids, as they get older, do reasonably well in coping with their disfigurement. Some do exceptionally well.

2. In the *Three Christs of Ypislanti,* Milton Rokeach found that relatively re-gressed schizophrenics, when confronted with severe threats to their artfully created identities, utilized numerous coping strategies for maintaining their respective, challenged identities. This demonstrated how stable the personal sense of identity can be even when seriously challenged. I am reminded also of John Lofland's study, *Doomsday Cult,* which dealt with the maintenance of discrepant beliefs that were challenged by everyday reality. Rather than being threatened by contradictory evidence, discrepant beliefs, for *true believers,* were strengthened. Contradictory evidence served to reaffirm beliefs which, from the position of a nonbeliever, would discredit basic beliefs.

While many survivors felt terrorized and inherently threatened, and felt that sectors of their worlds were in some ways collapsing, over time none experienced the terror that they were unreal or that they were dissolving as some schizophrenics report. The survivors remained very real, agonizingly so, as did the world, only the world was no longer familiar and safe.

3. "Disabled" is used very broadly, and does not necessarily refer to physical disabilities that result from the injury. It also includes the survivor's finding that his or her life has been truncated by the injury, as in the case of Ellen, Jeff and others.

4. The rehabilitation center where Maria worked as a volunteer treats a large number of welfare patients. Many of these are minority group members who have come to the hospital with histories of violence and drug abuse. It is common to

find people with criminal records and long-term gang involvement. Many of the patients had been burned in accidents where drugs or alcohol had been used and some were burned as a result of assaults. Although I interviewed several patients at Riverview, none were included here.

Bibliography

Andreski, Stanislav. (1972) *Social Science As Sorcery*. New York: St. Martin's Press.

Bachelard, Gaston. (1964) *Psychoanalysis of Fire*. Boston: Beacon.

Baker, Nancy. (1984) *The Beauty Trap*. New York: Franklin Watts.

Becker, Howard S. (1963) *Outsiders*. New York: The Free Press.

Berdyaev, Nicolas. (1951) *Dream And Reality*. New York: Macmillan.

Berger, Peter L. (1969) *The Sacred Canopy, Elements of a Sociological Theory Of Religion.* New york: Doubleday-Anchor.

Berger, Peter and Hansfried Kellner. (1970) "Marriage and the Construction of Reality." In *Recent Sociology 2*, edited by Hans Peter Dreitzel. New York: Macmillan.

Berger, Peter, and Thomas Luckmann. (1967) *The Social Construction of Reality*. Garden City: Doubleday-Anchor.

Bernstein, Norman R. (1976) *Emotional Care of the Facially Burned and Disfigured*. Boston: Little, Brown and Company

Bernstein, Norman R. and Martin C. Robson. (1983) *Comprehensive Approaches To The Burned Person*. New Hyde Park, NY: Medical Examination Publishing Co.

Bernstein, Norman, Alan Jeffry Breslau and Jean Graham. (1988) *Coping Strategies For Burn Survivors And Their Families*. New York: Praeger.

Bertaux, Daniel. (1981) "From the Life History Approach to the Transformation of Sociological Practice." In *Biography And Society*, edited by Daniel Bertaux. Beverly Hills: Sage.

Billig, Michael, Susan Condor et al. (1988) *Ideological Dilemmas*. Newbury Park: Sage.

Binswanger, Ludwig. (1963) *Being-In-The-World*. New York: Basic Books.

Bowden, Leona M. et al. (1980) "Self-Esteem of Severely Burned Patients." *Archieves of Physical Medicine & Rehabilitation, 61*

Breakwell, Glynis M. (1983) *Threatened Identities*. New York: John Wiley & Sons.

Breslau, Alan Jeffry. (1977) *The Time of My Death*. New York: E. P. Dutton.

Bringold, Diane. (1979) *Life Instead*. Ventura: Howard.

Brittan, Arthur. (1983) *Meanings And Situations*. London: Routledge

Brody, Gary S., and Mark Johnson. (1979) "Severe Burns." Burn Rehabilitation Service, Rancho Los Amigos Medical Center, Downey, CA.

Brodzak, Wanda and Herbert Thornhill (1985) "Burns: Causes And Risk Factors." *Archives of Physical and Rehabilitative Medicine,* 66 (11).

Buber, Martin. (1958) *I and Thou*. New York: Charles Scribner's Sons.

Bunch, R. H. (1981) "Complications In Burn Injuries." In *Care Of The Burn Patient,* edited by Mary M. Wagner. Littleton, MA: PSG Publishers.

Burkitt, Ian. (1991) *Social Selves*. Newbury Park: Sage.

Charmaz, Kathy. (1980) "The Social Construction of Self-Pity in the Chronically Ill." *Studies in Symbolic Interaction* 3:123-145

Cicourel, Aaron. (1972) "Deliquency and the Attribution of Responsibility." In *Theoretical Perspectives On Deviance*, edited by Jack D. Douglas. New York: Basic Books.

Clarke, A. Murray and H. L. Martin. (1978) "The Effects Of Previous Thermal Injury On Adolescents." *Burns Including Thermal Injury* 5(1)

Cohen, Elie M.D. (1953) *Human Behavior In The Concentration Camps*. New York: Grosset & Dunlap.

Cooper-Frapes, Cynthia. (1984) "Denial: Implications of a Pilot Study on Activity Levels Related to Sexual Competence in Burned Adults." *The American Journal of Occupational Therapy,* 38(8).

Coulter, Jeff. (1979) *The Social Construction of the Mind*. New York: Macmillan

Davidson Terrence, Leona Bowden and Irving Feller. (1981) "Social Support and Post-Burn Adjustment." *Archives of Physical Medicine & Rehabilitation,* 62

Davis, Fred. (1967) "Deviance Disavowal: The Management of Strained Interaction by the Visibly Handicapped." In *Symbolic Interaction*, edited by Jerome G. Mannis and Bernard N. Meltzer. Chicago: Allyn & Bacon.

Deitch, E. A., and M. Staats. (1982) "Child Abuse By Burning." *Burn Care And Rehabilitation,* 3(2).

Denzin, Norman. (1987) *The Alcoholic Self.* Newbury Park: Sage.

Dimik, A. R. (1982) "Pathophysiology." In *Comprehensive Rehabilitation of Burns,* edited by Steven Fisher and P. A. Helm. Baltimore: Williams & Wilkins.

Douglas, Jack D. (1982) *The Sociology of Deviance.* Boston: Little, Brown & Company.

Douglas, Jack D. (1971) "The Theory of Objectivity in Sociology." A paper presented at the American Sociological Asociation Meeting, Denver, CO.

Douglas, Jack D. (1970a) *Deviance And Respectability.* New York: Basic Books.

Douglas, Jack D. (1970b) *Understanding Everyday Life.* Chicago: Aldine.

Douglas, Jack D. (1967) *The Social Meanings Of Suicide.* Princeton: Princeton University Press

Erikson, Kai T. (1966) *Wayward Puritans.* New York: John Wiley & Sons

Feller, Irving and S. Flanders. (1979) "Baseline Data on the Mortality of Burn Patients." *Quarterly Review of Burns,* 7(4)

Ferrarotti, Franco. (1981) "On The Autonomy Of The Biographical Method." In *Biography And Society*, edited by Daniel Bertaux. Beverly Hills: Sage.

Fiedler, Leslie (1978) *Freaks: Myths And Images Of The Secrete Self.* New York: Simon & Schuster.

Fontana, Andrea. (1984) "Existential Sociology And The Self." In *The Existential Self In Society*, edited by Joseph Kotarba and Andrea Fontana. Chicago: University of Chicago Press.

Frankel, Viktor (1963) *Man's Search For Meaning.* New York: Washington Square Press.

Garfinkel, Harold. (1981) "The Work of a Discovering Science Construed with Materials from the Optically Discovered Pulsar." *Philosophy And Social Science,* 11:131-158.

Garfinkel, Harold (1967) *Studies In Ethnomethodology.* Englewood Cliffs: Prentice Hall.

Gergen, Kenneth. (1971) *The Concept of Self.* New York: Holt, Rinehart and Winston

Gergen, Kenneth, and Mary Gergen. (1983) "Narratives Of The Self." In *Studies In Social Identity*, edited by Karl Scheibe. New York: Praeger Scientific.

Gergen, Kenneth and Mary Gergen. (1985a) *Social Psychology*. New York: Springer-Verlag

Gergen, Kenneth. (1985b) "Social Constructionist Inquiry: Context and Implications" In *The Social Construction of the Person,* edited by Kenneth Gergen and Keith Davis. New York: Springer-Verlag

Gergen, Kenneth. (1987) "Toward Self As Relationships." In *Self And Identity*, edited by Krysia Yardley and Terry Honess. New York: John Wiley & Sons.

Goffman, Erving. (1961) *Asylums*. Garden City: Doubleday Anchor.

Grabau, Richard E. (1967) "Communication Through Transcendence." In *Existential Philosophers: Kierkeggard To Merleau-Ponty*, edited by George Schrader. New York: McGraw-Hill.

Gurwitsch, Aron (1970) "Problems of the Life World." In *Phenomenology And Social Reality*, edited by Maurice Natanson. The Hague: Martinus Nijhoff.

Hamburg, David A., and Beatrix Hamburg et al. (1953) "Adaptative Problems And Mechanisms in Severely Burned Patients." *Psychiatry,* 16(1)

Hankis, Agness. (1981) "Ontologies Of The Self: On the Mythological Rearranging of One's Life-History." In *Biography And Society*, edited by Daniel Bertaux. Beverly Hills: Sage.

Hanus, Steven, Norman Bernstein, and Kathlene Knapp. (1981) "Immigrants Into Society." In *Clinical Pediatrics*, 20(1)

Harré, Rom and Paul Secord. (1973) *The Explanation of Human Behavior.* Totowa, NJ: Littlefield, Adams & Co.

Harré, Rom. (1976) *Social Being.* Totowa, NJ: Littlefield, Adams & Co.

Harré, Rom. (1984) *Personal Being.* Cambridge: Harvard University Press

Harré, Rom, David Clarke and Nicola De Carlo. (1985) *Motives And Mechanisms.* London: Methuen

Harré, Rom (1986) *The Social Construction of Emotion.* Oxford: Basil Blackwell

Harré, Rom. (1987) "The Social Construction of Selves." In *Self And Identity*, edited by Krysia Yardley and Terry Honess. New York: John Wiley & Sons.

Harries, Karsten. (1967) "The Search For Meaning." In *Existential Philosophers: Kierkegaard To Merleau Ponty*, edited by George Schrader. New York: McGraw-Hill.

Heidegger, Martin. (1964) *Being and Time*. New York: Harper & Row.

Jaspers, Karl. (1956) *Philosophy*, Vol. 2. Chicago: University of Chicago Press.

Jones, Edward, Albert Farina, Robert Scott et al. (1984) *Social Stigma: The Psychology Of Marked Relationships*. New York: Freeman.
Kogon, Eugene (1958) *The Theory And Practice Of Hell*. New York: Berkley.

Kohli, Martin. (1981) "Biography: Account, Text, Method." In *Biography And Society*, edited by Daniel Bertaux. Beverly Hills: Sage.

Kotarba, Joseph. (1979) "Existential Sociology and the Self." In *Theoretical Perspectives In Sociology*, edited by Scott G. McCall. New York: St. Martin's Press

Krahé, Barbara. (1992) *Personality And Social Psychology*. Newbury Park: Sage.

Kubler-Ross, Elizabeth. (1969) *On Death And Dying*. New York: Macmillan.

Kudson-Cooper, Mary S. (1981) "Adjustment To Visible Stigma: The Case Of The Severely Burned." *Social Science & Medicine,* 15B.

Landy, David, and Harold Sigall. (1974) "Beauty Is Talent." *Jounnal of Personality and Social Psychology,* 29(3)

Langer, Susan K. (1951) *Philosophy In A New Key*. New York: New American Library.

Larson, Catherine, and Jeffery Saffel et. al (1992) "Lifestyle Adjustments in Elderly Patients After Burn Injury." *Burn Care And Rehabilitation,* 13(1).

Lee, Dorthey. (1959) *Freedom and Culture*. New York: Prentice-Hall.

Lester, Marilyn. (1984) "Self: Sociological Portraits." In *The Existential Self In Society*, edited by Joseph A. Kotarba and Andrea Fontana. Chicago: University of Chicago Press.

Lilliston, Barbara A. (1985) "Psychosocial Responses to Traumatic Physical Disability" *Social Work in Healty Care,* 10(4):1-13

Lofland, John. (1966) *Doomsday Cult*. Englewood Cliffs: Prentice Hall.

Luckmann, Benita. (1970) "The Small Life-Worlds of Modern Man." *Social Research,* 37(4): 580-596.

Luckmann, Thomas. (1973) "Philosophy, Science and Everyday Life."
In *Phenomenology and the Social Sciences*, edited by Maurice Natanson.
Evanston: Northwester University Press

Lynch, James. (1977) *The Broken Heart.*. New York: Basic Books.

Macgreggor, Frances Cook. (1953) *Facial Deformities And Plastic Surgery.*
Springfield: Charles Thomas.

McAndrew, Craig and Robert B. Edgerton. (1969) *Drunken Comportment.*
Chicago: Aldine.

McHugh, Peter. (1968) *Defining The Situation.* New York: Bobbs-Merrill.

Malt, U. (1980) "The Long Term Psychosocial Follow-Up Studies of Burned
Adults: Review of the Literature." *Burns Including Thermal Injury,* 6(3).

Mannon, James M. (1985) *Caring For The Burned.* Springfield: Charles Thomas.

Marcell, Gabriel. (1950-1951) *The Mystery of Being.* (2 vol.) London: Harvill.

Marcell, Gabriel. (1965) *Being and Having.* New York: Harper & Row.

Mead, George H. (1934) *Mind, Self & Society.* Chicago: University of Chicago
Press.

Mead, George H. (1956) *On Social Psychology.* Chicago: University of Chicago
Press

Mead, George H. (1959) *The Philosophy Of The Present.* La Salle: Open Court.

Merleau-Ponty, Maurice. (1962) *Phenomenology Of Perception.* London:
Routledge & Kegan Paul.

Millman, Marcia. (1980) *Such A Pretty Face.* New York: Berkley.

Mills, C. Wright. (1967) "Situated Actions and Vocabularies of Motives." In
Symbolic Interactionism, edited by Jerome Mannis and Bernard Meltzer.
Boston: Allyn & Bacon.

Mischel, Theodore. (1977) *The Self: Psychological and Philosophical Issues.*
Oxford: Basil Blackwell.

Molinaro, John R. (1978) "The Social Fate of Children Disfigured by Burns."
American Journal Of Psychiatry, 38(8)

Moustakas, Clark E. (1961) *Loneliness.* New York: Prentice-Hall.

Natanson, Maurice. (1970) *The Journeying Self.* Reading, MA: Addison-Wesley

Noyes, Russel and N. J. Andreasen. (1971) "The Psychological Reaction to Severe Burns." *Psychosomatics*, 12(6).

Pollner, Melvin, and Don Zimmerman. (1970) "The Everyday World As Social Phenomenon." In *Understanding Everyday Life*, edited by Jack D. Douglas. Chicago: Aldine.

Praiss, Israel and Irving Feller. (1980) "The Planning And Organization of a Regionalized Burn Care System." *Medical Care,* 28(2).

Pruzinsky, Thomas, and Linda Rice et al. (1992) "Psychometric Assessment of Psychologic Factors Influencing Adult Burn Rehabilitation." *Burn Care And Rehabilitation,* 13(1).
Psathas, George. (1980) "Approaches To The Study Of The World Of Everyday Life." *Human Studies,* 3: 3-17.

Psathas, George. (1973) *Phemenological Sociology.* New York: John Wiley & Sons.

Radley, Alan. (1990) "Artefacts, Memory and a Sense of the Past." In *Collective Remembering*, edited by David Middleton and Derek Edwards. London: Sage.

Rogers, Mary F. (1983) *Sociology, Ethnomethodology, and Experience .* Cambridge: Cambridge University Press

Rokeach, Milton. (1964) *The Three Christs of Ypislanti.* New York: Vintage.

Sacks, Oliver M.D. (1989) *Seeing Voices.* Berkeley: University of California Press.

Sacks, Oliver M.D. (1985) *The Man Who Mistook His Wife For A Hat .* New York: Harper & Row.

Sacks, Oliver M.D. (1983) *Awakenings.* New York: Dutton

Sadler, William (1969) *Existence And Love.* New York: Charles Scribner's Sons

Sarbin, Theodore R. and Karl E.Scheibe. (1983) *Studies In Social Identity.* New York: Praeger

Sarbin, Theodore R. (1986) *Narative Psychology.* New York: Praeger/Greenwood

Sarbin, Theodore R., and John I. Kitsuse (1994) *Constructing The Social.* Thousand Oaks: Sage.

Schaenman, Philip S. (1982) *International Concepts In Fire Protection.* Arlington, VA: TriData Corporation.

Schaenman, Philip S., and Edward Seits. (1985) *International Concepts In Fire Protection.* Arlington, VA: TriData Corporation.

Scheff, Thomas. (1966) *Being Mentally Ill.* Chicago: Aldine

Scheff, Thomas. (1969) "The Societal Reaction to Deviance." In *Deviant Behavior And Social Process,* edited by William Rushing. Chicago: University of Chicago Press.

Scheibe, Karl L. (1985) "Historical Perspectives On The Presented Self." In *The Self And Social Life,* edited by Barry Schlenker. New York: McGraw-Hill.

Schilder, Paul. (1950) *The Image & Appearance Of The Human Body.* New York: John Wiley & Sons.

Schlenker, Barry. (1980) *Impression Management.* Monterey: Brooks/Cole.

Schlenker, Barry, ed. (1985) *The Self And Social Life.* New York: McGraw Hill

Schneidman, Edwin S. (1974) *Deaths of Man.* Baltimore: Penguin Books.

Schutz, Alfred. (1967) *The Phenomenology of the Social World.* Evanston: Northwestern University Press.

Schutz, Alfred. (1964) "The Homecomer." In Alfred Schutz, *The Collected Papers* Vol. 2, edited by Arvid Brodersen. The Hague: Martinus Nijhoff.

Schutz, Alfred. (1964) "The Stranger." In Alfred Schutz, *The Collected Papers* , Vol. 2, edited by Arvid Brodersen. The Hague: Martinus Nijhoff.

Schutz, Alfred. (1963, 1967) *The Collected Papers.* Vol. 1 and 3. The Hague: Martinus Nijhoff.

Schutz, Alfred, and Thomas Luckmann. (1973) "The Everyday Life-World and the Natural Attitude." In *The Structures of the Life World.* Evanston: Northwestern University Press.

Scott, Robert A. (1972) "A Proposed Framework for Analyzing Deviance as a Property of Social Order." In *Theoretical Perspectives On Devinace,* edited by Robert A. Scott and Jack D. Douglas. New York: Basic Books.

Scott, Robert A. (1969) *The Making Of Blind Men.* New York: Russel Sage Foundation.

Secord, Paul F. (1982) *Explaining Human Behavior.* Beverly Hills: Sage

Shotter, John. (1983) *Social Accountability and Selfhood.* Oxford: Basil Blackwell

Shotter, John. (1993) *Conversational Realities.* Thousand Oaks, CA: Sage.

Slaiku, Karl A., and Steven Lawhead. (1987) *Up From The Ashes.* Grand Rapids: Zondervan.

Solem, Lynn D. (1982) "Classification." In *Comprehensive Rehabilitation of Burns,* edited by Steven Fisher and Phala Helm. Baltimore: William & Wilkins

Steiner, Hans and William Clark. (1977) "Psychiatric Complications of Burned Adults: A Classification." *The Journal Of Trauma,* 17(2)

Steiner, Jean-Francois. (1966) *Treblinka.* New York: Signet Book.

Stone, Gregory. (1962) "Appearance and the Self." In *Human Behavior And Social Process*, edited by Arnold M. Rose. Boston: Houghton Mifflin.

Stouffer, Dennis J. (1970a) "Visibility of Persons as Productive Features of Normal Police Environments." Unpublished paper, Department of Sociology, University of California, San Diego.

Stouffer, Dennis J. (1970b) "On The Availability of the Suspect as a Constitutional Feature Of Practical Police Work." Unpublished paper, Department of Sociology, University of California, San Diego.

Stouffer, Dennis J. (1971) "The Writing is on the Wall: The Search for Cause and Intent in Criminal Investigations of Suspected Arson." Unpublished paper, Department of Sociology, University of California, San Diego

Szasz, Thomas. (1961)*The Myth of Mental Illness.* New York: Delta

Szasz, Thomas. (1970) *The Manufacture Of Madness.* New York: Dell.

Tiryakian, Edward. (1962) *Sociologism And Existentialism.* Englewood Cliffs: Prentice Hall.

Tiryakian, Edward. (1973) "Sociology and Existential Phenomenology." In *Phenomenology and the Social Sciences*, edited by Maurice Natanson. Evanston: Northwestern University Press

Tolmach, Robin and Raquel Scheer. (1984) *Face Value: The Politics of Beauty.* Boston: Routledge & Kegan Paul.

Ton, Mary Ellen (1982) *The Flames Shall Not Consume You.* Elgin: David Cook.

Vogtsburger, Kenneth and Ross Taylor. (1984) "Psychosocial Factors In Burn Injury." *Texas Medicine,* 80(10)

Weigert, Andrew J (1983) *Social Psychology.* Notre Dame: University of Notre Dame

Worf, Benjamin Lee. (1956) *Language, Thought & Reality.* Cambridge: M.I.T. Press

Wright, Beatrice A. (1960) *Physical Disability: A Psychological Approach.* New York: Harper & Row.

Yalom, Irwin. (1980) *Existential Psychotherapy.* New York: Basic Books.

Young, Karen A. (1974) "Stigmatization of Burn Patients." *Association of Operating Room Nurses,* 20(5).

Index of Names

Allport, Gordon 107
Andreasen, N. J. 108
Andreski, Stanislav 9-10
Bachelard, Gaston 210
Baker, Nancy 115
Baldwin, James Mark 96
Becker, Howard 108
Berdyaev, Nicolas 216, 218
Berger, Peter, 18-20, 25-26, 29-30, 60, 98, 109, 189-200, 219
Bernstein, Norman R. 8, 11, 111, 114-115, 174, 180
Bertaux, Daniel 12-13
Billig, Michael 175
Binswanger, Ludwig 11, 204
Blummer, Herbert 100
Bowden, Leona 8, 108
Breakwell, Glynis 108
Breisach, Ernst 102
Breslau, Alan Jeffry 1, 143-144, 180, 214
Bringold, Diane 141-142
Brittan, Arthur 98, 100, 107
Brody, Gary S.14
Brodzak, Wanda 14-15
Buber, Martin
Bunch, R. H. 15
Burkitt, Ian 255-256 n. 6
Castenada, Carlos 5, 254 n. 4
Charmaz, Kathy 123
Christian, David 1
Cicourel, Aaron 9
Clark, William 8, 108
Clarke, Murray 108
Cohen, Elie 3
Cooley, Charles Horton 96, 105
Cooper-Frapes, Cynthia 108, 177
Coulter, Jeff 98
D'Annunzio 210-211
Dante 2, 207
Davidson, Terrence 8
Davis, Fred 108
Deitch, E. A. 14, 253 n. 2
Denzin, Norman 8, 12, 108
Descartes, René 254 n. 5

Dimik, A. R. 15
Don Quixote 3, 5, 7
Douglas, Jack D. 6, 8-10, 12, 109, 111, 254 n. 5
Edgerton, Robert 108
Erikson, K. T. 109
Feller, Irving 8, 14
Ferraoti, Franco 13
Fiedler, Leslie 115
Flanders, S. 14
Fontana, Andrea 8, 166
Frankel, Viktor 3
Fraser, Linda 177
Garfinkel, Harold 6, 9-10, 101
Gergen, Kenneth 8, 11, 96, 104
Gergen, Mary 11
Goffman, Erving 28, 100, 103-104, 108-109, 114, 260 n. 6
Grabau, Richard 24, 98
Graham, Jean 178
Gurwitsch, Aron 18, 20, 29
Hall, John 14-15
Hamburg, David 108
Handlin, D. 174-175
Hankiss, Agnes 105
Hanus, Steven 174
Harré, Rom 8, 103, 104, 259-260 n. 2
Heidegger, Martin 21, 48, 101, 204, 217-218, 210-220, 237, 259 n. 1
Heisenberg, Werner 9
Herries, Karsten 25
Hesse, Hermann 207
Husserl, Edmund 18, 20, 23-25, 212, 256-257 n. 1
James, William 11, 96, 98, 105
Jaspers, Karl 29, 218, 220, 237
Johnson, John 8
Johnson, Mark 14
Jones, Edward 110, 114
Jung, Carl 17, 114, 141
Kellner, Hansfried 187-188
Kierkegaard, Sören 216
Kitsuse, John I. 21

Index of Subjects

Accounts 8, 13, 34, 71, 104, 180-181, 222
Abandonment 157, 172
Adjustment 178, 237
Aero Mexico crash 45
Agency 253 n. 3
Alienation 118, 121, 157, 203, 219-220
Amputation 92
Anger 4
Anguish 17, 90, 126
Annihilation 2, 17, 207, 221
Anomie 219
Anonymity 135, 174
Anxiety 22, 195, 219-221, 254-255 n. 5
Appearance 126, 151, 174, 187, 189, 193, 198, 206, 209
Arson 14
Assessment 8, 12, 44, 73, 257-258 n. 1
Autonomy 86
Awakenings 106, 259 n. 5
Balance Theory 102
Beauty Trap, The 116
Beauty 107-108, 133
Being-in-the-World 25, 219-220
Beliefs 108
Biography 13, 21, 24, 32 55-56, 59, 71, 85, 104, 158, 181, 189, 222, 223
Body 21, 26, 31-33, 36, 40, 78-79, 90, 106-107, 113, 118, 138, 189, 212
Body Image 32
Boundary Situations 29-30, 221
Burn center 18
Burn death 14
Burn injury 14, 256 n. 7
Burn recovery groups 13, 113 152, 163, 214
Burn survivor 1, 5, 7, 8
Burn victim 5, 17, 22, 69
Cancer 228-230
Care 204
Cartesian paradigm 254 n. 5

Causality 6, 9
Cause 9
Clues 124, 134, 231, 257-258 n. 1
Coitus 178
Color Purple, The 116
Concern 204, 237
Consciousness 6, 19, 23, 25-26, 47, 59-60, 71, 77, 98-100, 256-257 n. 1
Constructionism, psychological 8
Continuity 209
Contractures 80, 149
Control 7, 61, 76, 137
Coopersmith Inventory 8
Core self 103
Crisis 6, 19, 30, 209. See also, Boundary Situations
Crucible 105-106, 207-208
Cues 106-107
Cultural recipes 27
"Devine Comedy" 207
das Nichtige 219
das Man 217-218
Dasein 21, 101, 220, 259 n. 1
Death 14, 17, 18 29, 37 40, 47-48, 51-52, 60, 79, 84, 218, 221
Debriedment 77
Delegitimation 189
Denial 47-48, 132-133, 227
Depersonalization 90, 202
Depression 22, 131, 134, 214, 236
Deviance 110-111
Deviant Identity 109, 111, 232
Disability 2, 109, 147, 155, 205, 231, 262 n. 3
Discourse, See Language
Disfigurement 2, 15, 95-96, 101, 108, 114, 131, 135, 138, 140, 143-144, 173-174, 179, 205, 208
Disorientation 56
Distance 45
Divorce 152, 209
Doomsday Cult 262 n. 2
Dreams 59-60, 133
Dressing changes 62, 86-87
Eating 7

Helping Organizations

Alisa Ann Ruch Burn Foundation
Stephanie Knizek, Executive Director
20944 Sherman Way
Canoga Park, CA 91303
(818) 883-7700 (800) 242-BURN
Public Education and Survivor Support

The Phoenix Society For Burn Survivors
Alan Jeffry Breslau, Executive Director
11 Rust Hill Rd.
Levittown, PA 19056
(215) 946-2876 (800) 888-BURN
Public Education and Survivor Support

Let's Face It
Betsy Wilson, Director
P. O. Box 711
Concord, MA 01742-0711
(508) 371-3186
Assistance for People with
Facial Differences

Faces
P. O. Box 11082
Chattanooga, TN 37401
(615) 266-1632
National Association for the
Craniofacially Handicapped

About the Author

Dr. Dennis J. Stouffer is employed by Hughes Aerospace and Electronics Company as an emergency planning and management specialist in El Segundo, California. He holds a holds a B.A. degree in Political Science and Sociology from the California State University at Long Beach. His graduate work was completed at the University of California, at Los Angeles and San Diego, and at the Union Institute in Cincinnati. He holds a Ph.D. in Sociology with specializations in Social Psychology, Medical Sociology, and Deviance. He also holds a professional certificate in Fire Protection Engineering from the University of California at Los Angeles Extension, and has extensive training in critical incident and crisis intervention. He has been concerned with fire protection, fire prevention and burn injury for most of his professional life, and since 1976, has served on the Board of Directors of the Alisa Ann Ruch Burn Foundation in Canoga Park, California. He has extensive research experience with fire and police departments, with paramedics, and with hospital emergency services. He is the author of several articles on fire safety and fire department operations, and he is a member of the L. A. County Psychological Association and American Red Cross Critical Incident Team in Los Angeles. He is married, and has two children.